The Kidney Sellers

The Kidney Sellers

A Journey of Discovery in Iran

Sigrid Fry-Revere

CAROLINA ACADEMIC PRESS

Durham, North Carolina

Library of Congress Cataloging-in-Publication Data

Fry-Revere, Sigrid, author.
  The kidney sellers : a journey of discovery in Iran / Sigrid Fry-Revere.
      p. ; cm.
  Includes bibliographical references and index.
  ISBN 978-1-61163-512-6 (alk. paper)
  I. Title.
  [DNLM: 1. Kidney Transplantation--ethics--Iran--Personal Narratives. 2.
Living Donors--ethics--Iran--Personal Narratives. 3. Tissue and Organ
Procurement--ethics--Iran--Personal Narratives. WJ 368]

  RD129.5
  174.2'97954--dc23

                              2013035401

              CAROLINA ACADEMIC PRESS
                    700 Kent Street
              Durham, North Carolina 27701
              Telephone (919) 489-7486
                  Fax (919) 493-5668
                   www.cap-press.com

         Printed in the United States of America

For Steve and Maurie
I wish they had lived to see the book they helped inspire.

All author royalties go to support the SOS,
Solving the Organ Shortage, project
www.ethical-solution.org/projects/sos

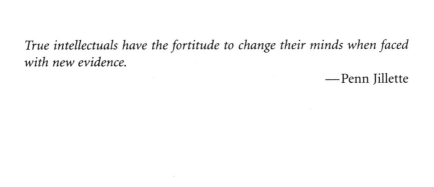

True intellectuals have the fortitude to change their minds when faced with new evidence.

—Penn Jillette

Contents

A Few Words about This Book

This book is nonfiction, based on true accounts and authentic research. From November 14, 2008, to January 1, 2009, I traveled to six different Iranian cities to explore the market for human organs. I interviewed hundreds of people, including physicians, nurses, the administrators who run and operate transplant and hemodialysis ("dialysis"* for short) units, clergy, government officials, the staff of the non-governmental organizations (NGOs) that arrange paid transplant matches, and of course the kidney sellers and recipients themselves. I collected over 100 hours of filmed interviews and over 200 transplant stories, primarily from those who had sold their kidneys or were in the process of arranging such a sale. Later, in August 2011, Simin Golestani (an intern at the Center for Ethical Solutions, which I run) traveled to Tehran to visit family and to do follow-up telephone interviews with the kidney sellers and recipients I had interviewed.

I could have written an academic monograph, but I was sure my material would interest more than just academics. I wanted readers to share in my journey of discovery and to experience the drama of the stories of the kidney sellers and recipients I'd met. To that end, I decided to write a nonfiction adventure with only a few vestiges of the original academic book I'd planned. I limited the number of footnotes to minimize interference with the flow of the narra-

---

* There are basically two types of dialysis used to keep end-stage renal disease patients alive: hemodialysis which usually cannot be done at home and peritoneal dialysis which usually is done at home. Throughout this book I use the word "dialysis" to refer to both types of dialysis interchangeably.

tive but kept some detailed analysis, references, and further-reading resources in a Notes section at the end of the book.

Another issue I faced when deciding on the format of this book was how to accurately portray the very personal stories of the people I'd met without violating their privacy or putting their safety at risk. What would happen if the Iranian government took issue with my book? Almost every kidney seller and recipient I interviewed signed a consent form allowing me to use their personal information, including their image, in the documentary film I was making or in a book should I decide to write one. Nonetheless, I want to take at least one important precaution to protect them while still staying true to their personal narratives—I've changed the names of all the donors and recipients described in this book, as well as the names of any medical or administrative personnel who hesitated about being recorded. All other details described are accurate and based on taped interviews or Dr. Bastani's and my notes. I have not used fictitious names for other Iranians or the Americans interviewed because they fully understood my project and participated willingly, if not enthusiastically, in talking to me about their lives.

A less significant problem I faced writing this book is that I had to decide how to translate certain Farsi/Persian terms integral to understanding my experience in Iran. I have tried to use phonetic versions of Farsi pronunciations where obvious English translations weren't available in a language dictionary. For example, "institution" or "association" doesn't adequately communicate the distinct nature of the non-governmental non-profits that arrange kidney sales in Iran, so I used the phonetic transcription of the term commonly used in Iran for such organizations and italicized it—"*Anjoman.*"

One word in particular caused me difficulty because its Farsi transliterations have potentially confusing associations in English. The Farsi word for "bread" is phonetically spelled "noon" or "nun." I decided not to use either but instead went with the Indian word "naan." Most English speakers are familiar with Indian flatbread, and the word "naan" will conjure up a more accurate image of what Iranian bread is like than "noon" or "nun."

I had yet a different problem when it came to choosing aliases for some of my Iranian interviewees. I didn't want to simply give everyone a Persian name. Instead I gave each person a name that reflected the cultural origin and spelling of their given names. For example, you might see both "Muhammad" (the typical Arabic transliteration) and "Mohammad" (the typical Farsi transliteration) or both "Sara" (a Farsi or Arabic version of the Biblical name "Sarah") and "Zahra" (a common Arabic name of different origin). You will also see Turkish and occasionally Western names and spellings of names. I understand that Iranian parents, like parents all over the world, don't necessarily give their children names that reflect their heritage, but this way at least the aliases I've chosen reflect the same degree of name diversity that existed among my interviewees.

Finally, the adventure I have to share is not only interesting because it took place in a far away country that Americans rarely visit, but also because the United States is struggling with a problem Iran seems to have solved.* This book provides both the data and the context for understanding the Iranian solution to its kidney shortage. I also provide valuable insights into the ethical complexities of living organ donation as understood by those who participate in Iran's kidney market. I do not claim to know how to solve the U.S. organ shortage, but I do know that there are notable lessons to be learned from Iran's more than 25 years of experience with legalized compensated kidney donation. I hope that sharing my discoveries will result in a better understanding of both the Iranian and U.S. systems of organ procurement. I also hope that this book can serve as a window into the lives of the remarkable people I met both in the United States and Iran. I could never have anticipated the things in store for me or the way they would move me.

---

* Other countries such as Singapore and Saudi Arabia have more recently begun compensating living donors but, as yet, neither has succeeded in eliminating its kidney shortage.

Prologue:
A Personal Journey

Haaj Khanoom, "one who has been on a pilgrimage." It was an expression of respect from a young man at the Vakil Bazaar in Shiraz, struggling to pass me with a wooden flatbed cart overflowing with cooking pots. He was right. I was on a pilgrimage—a pilgrimage not to Mecca or Jerusalem, but to Iran—in search of a solution to a serious medical ethics problem: How can we solve the U.S. organ shortage? How can we save the more than a hundred thousand Americans who need organs right now? Might Iran, of all places, hold clues to the solution?

In Iran scarcely a week, I was starting to feel comfortable—maybe a little too comfortable, given what would happen to me later that day at the Vakil Bazaar. But things hadn't started out that way. In the beginning, the thought of going to Iran seemed preposterous. An American woman doing research and filming without permits in one of the most repressive, anti-American regimes in the world? Although my fear of going to Iran was significant, my compulsion to find an answer to the organ shortage ran deeper. There was little anyone could do to dissuade me from traveling to find the truth about Iran. Were the rich exploiting the poor? Was the government forcing people to sell their kidneys? Were drug addicts selling their kidneys to support their habits, or worse, forcing relatives to do so? Were kidney sellers dying for lack of post-operative care? And were the desperately poor selling their kidneys only to find themselves in more debt than before?

In graduate school I studied the problem of organ allocation, but the topic isn't merely academic to me. Not long after completing my doctorate in philosophy (specializing in patient-care ethics), I experienced firsthand the fear of losing a loved one to kidney disease. My son Ian, at just 10 months old, was diagnosed with kidney cancer. Surgeons operated and removed his left kidney. They told me the functioning of his good kidney would need to be monitored closely and that Ian would probably need dialysis and a kidney transplant by the time he was a teenager. While my life has taken many turns since then—clinical ethics, food and drug law, health law, teaching, consulting, and writing on many different topics related to patient-care ethics—never has the intractable organ shortage been far from my mind.

In 2007 I began studying the merits of compensated organ donation* for the Cato Institute, where I was the director of bioethics studies. I set out to explore certain searching questions: Does prohibiting compensated organ donation violate a donor's right to self-determination and self-ownership? Would paying donors beyond reimbursement for transplant-related expenses cause exploitation, offend human dignity, or degrade the medical profession? And how does one weigh such countervailing concerns? To help explore these questions, I organized a Cato forum where leading experts** debated compensated organ donation. At the event, which was held on February 21, 2008, I was astounded to learn that each speaker had strong opinions on Iran and its system of legalized kidney sales, but none had ever been there.

When I researched the issue further, I realized no Westerner had ever gone to see what organ procurement was like in Iran. Numerous articles and reports had been written about the Iranian system, including the one I had edited for Dr. Hippen, but no one had done a comprehensive firsthand examination of the Iranian system of compensated kidney donation. No one had interviewed actual or potential kidney sellers. Iranians had conducted some regional studies that involved donor and recipient interviews, but no national studies, and no studies had been done by Westerners.

I left my job at Cato because—among other reasons—the Institute's administration didn't want me to continue researching Iran's kidney market. I suspect this was because it was politically risky to suggest that Iran might be doing

---

* See the Notes section at the end of this book for a discussion of the appropriateness of using "donation" terminology in situations where money is exchanged.

** The panel included four top authorities in the field: Dr. Francis Delmonico, professor of surgery at Harvard Medical School and former member of the board of trustees for the United Network for Organ Sharing (UNOS), a staunch critic of the Iranian system; Dr. Arthur Matas, professor of surgery and director of the renal transplant program at the University of Minnesota, known for his studies on altruistic donation and possible alternatives; Dr. Benjamin Hippen, clinical associate professor of transplant nephrology at the University of North Carolina at Chapel Hill School of Medicine, author of a recent paper on kidney selling in Iran; and Dr. Samuel Crowe, Ph.D., deputy director of The President's Council on Bioethics, known for his defense of professionalism in medicine.

something right—after all, President George W. Bush had called Iran a member of the Axis of Evil. I argued that I didn't know what I would find: For all I knew, Iran would be just as guilty of mishandling its organ shortage as it was of mishandling its relationship with some of its Middle East neighbors. But the Cato administration was adamant that it would hurt the Institute's reputation as a serious Washington player to even consider finding anything positive about Iran—regardless of the truth. Consequently, I created my own think tank, the Center for Ethical Solutions, and initiated the Solving the Organ Shortage (SOS) project. A team of scholars was formed to study the worldwide organ shortage. I wanted answers, and it looked more and more as if I would have to go to Iran to get them.

Dr. Delmonico, whom I'd met organizing the Cato event, mentioned that the next biannual Middle East Society for Organ Transplantation (MESOT) conference was scheduled to be held in Shiraz, Iran. I contacted MESOT organizers and was invited to join the conference as a speaker in November 2008. This left me little more than eight months to figure out how to get from attending a conference in Iran to researching the Iranian system of organ procurement.

I hardly knew where to begin, but like many things in life, a fortunate coincidence saved the day. My friend Alison Griffin, the daughter of the former head of NASA Michael D. Griffin, happened to remember an Iranian engineer who used to visit the house when she was a little girl. She contacted her father, who introduced me to Professor Assefi, who in turn passed on my note of inquiry about Iran to his physician daughter, Nassim. Before I knew it, I was getting emails from Iranian expats all over the United States and even Europe who were interested in hearing more about my research and eager to help arrange interviews and come along as translators.

Of those who contacted me, I decided Dr. Bahar Bastani would be the best choice to accompany me on my trip: Firstly, he was a nephrologist—a kidney specialist—who taught in the Department of Internal Medicine at St. Louis University. Secondly, he could set up a lecture tour of several major cities in Iran where he knew hospital staff would be interested in learning about recent developments in transplant medicine and perhaps even about transplant ethics in the United States. And best of all, he could arrange to have directors of the programs where we would speak cover our travel expenses from one city to the next. In exchange for our lectures, hospital administrators would also give us access to their transplant wards and clinics and would introduce us to the *Anjomans* (the non-profit organizations that arrange living donor matches— the "kidney brokers," so to speak). At all these locations we could interview actual kidney sellers, but the *Anjomans* had the added advantage of also providing us access to potential sellers who were at various pre-transplant stages of the donation process. Dr. Bastani's plan worked perfectly. Before we even left for the MESOT conference, he had us lined up to visit major university hospitals in six different cities, each for a week or more.

I returned from Iran with 211 firsthand accounts from kidney sellers, donors, recipients, and their families. Over a period of more than two years, American-Iranian volunteers (mostly U.S. college students) graciously helped translate over 100 hours of video that corresponded with my photos and Dr. Bastani's and my notes. After reviewing the material, I realized that there were no simple answers to what was going on in Iran or to solving the U.S. organ shortage. The truth lies in the stories of the people I met: the desperate, willing to help each other, but afraid because their lives, financial well-being, and health were at stake; and the courageous who set up a donor-compensation system in defiance of what the rest of the world was doing.

I learned that the Iranian system, unlike kidney markets in the rest of the world, has laws in place that protect the basic rights of compensated donors. For example, in Iran, kidney sellers are guaranteed at least a modicum of informed consent, and there are mechanisms in place to help ensure compensated donors are paid the money they are promised. As a result, selling a kidney in Iran is less risky and more socially acceptable, and there is a waiting list to donate, not a waiting list to receive a kidney as there is in other countries.

This book tells the stories of the Iranians I met, along with my story of discovery in a land where the government can be hostile toward foreigners and almost everyone is leery of an American with a camera. I hope the pages that follow will help Americans overcome their preconceptions about the U.S. organ shortage and their misconceptions about what Iran has done to solve its kidney shortage. No debate over compensating kidney donors is complete without some insight into the stories of those who have bought and sold kidneys in the only country in the world where such transactions are legal. I have done my best to present an honest, unbiased account of the truth, unaffected by political or social agendas. If I have accomplished my goal, then this book should go a long way toward banishing the uninformed imaginings, both good and bad, over what caused the organ shortage in the United States and what solved it in Iran.

The Kidney Sellers

Introduction:
A Critical Need

Why did I feel compelled to take this trip to Iran? Because it was possible that tens of thousands if not hundreds of thousands of deaths among U.S. dialysis patients were preventable, but no one seemed to be looking for answers in the only country in the world where virtually everyone who needs a kidney transplant gets one.

From Innovation to Crisis

When we say "organ shortage," we must be clear that this is one of those problems we would have wished for half a century ago. We face an organ shortage because modern medicine makes it possible to transplant organs from one human body to another, meaning hundreds of thousands of people who a few years ago had no hope of survival now have a new lease on life. Until the 1950s, little could be done to save damaged organs. If diseases were caught early enough, potential deterioration could be slowed or curtailed by treating the underlying illness, but if a vital organ was damaged beyond repair, the patient would inevitably die—sooner rather than later. The one exception was kidneys. Because dialysis machines simulate, to some extent, the work of kidneys by filtering the blood, death could be forestalled for a few years, but not indefinitely.

Even now, the average lifespan on dialysis in the United States is only four years. Also, by most accounts, life on dialysis is not much of a life at all. The majority of dialysis patients leave their jobs within a few months of starting dialysis. Fewer than 10 percent of patients are still employed after six months on dialysis. They are too tired, too weak, too stiff, have too many medical appointments, and have to spend too much time watching their diets and getting dialyzed (usually three times a week, for three to four hours each session).*

---

* See www.ethical-solutions.org/projects/steve_lessin/ for a moving account of life (and death) on dialysis.

3

Attempts at transplantation are not new to medicine. Skin grafts, which are technically a form of transplant, probably took place as early as the second century B.C. Documentation of early efforts to transplant major organs also exist, but there are no reliable accounts of success until 1954, when Dr. Joseph Murray transplanted a kidney from a healthy living donor into his identical twin, who was suffering from renal failure.

Dr. Murray's experiment worked for two reasons: First, both donor and recipient could live with just one kidney. Most people are born with two kidneys that function in unison but can live normal, productive lives with just one. For example, my 25-year-old son Ian lost one of his kidneys to cancer when he was a baby. Ian now leads a normal life: No physical, dietary, or medical accommodations of any kind are necessary. Studies show that losing or donating a kidney later in life also does not have long-term detrimental effects. Most vital organs, like the heart or pancreas, can't be transplanted from living donors because the donors need them to survive. While part of a liver or a single lung can be transplanted from living donors, such operations are dangerous, and a donor's quality of life can be impaired—assuming the donor even survives the transplant. But live kidney donation involves a comparatively simple, low-risk operation.

Second, Dr. Murray's experiment succeeded because the transplant was from one identical twin into another: The recipient didn't reject the organ, meaning his immune system didn't attack and destroy the transplanted organ. Instead, the recipient's body accepted the transplanted kidney as if it were its own, allowing it to function normally. While Dr. Murray's operation was clearly an important medical breakthrough—it won him the Nobel Prize in Physiology/Medicine—it was limited in that it only worked for a very small portion of the population that needed transplants: namely, people who needed kidneys and had healthy identical twins.

Not until effective immunosuppressant drugs were developed in the late 1970s and early 1980s did the prospect of lifesaving transplants become a possibility for all patients who needed organs. Anti-rejection drugs not only meant surgeons could use kidneys from living donors who were not identical twins, but also opened the possibility of an endless supply of organs from the recently deceased. Because of this, transplant medicine in the United States and the world shifted its focus away from the use of living donors to researching more effective means of harvesting, preserving, and transplanting organs from cadavers.

As so often is the case, the optimism associated with a new discovery caused an overestimation of what realistically could be achieved. Great strides were made, and many lives were saved, but the transplant list grew exponentially. Practically everyone who potentially could be rescued by a transplant went on a waiting list to get one. It didn't take long for deceased organ donation to fall short of its exalted prospects, particularly when it came to kidneys. Soon demand outstripped supply, and the organ shortage was born.

The use of cadaver organs is still the only option when most major organs fail. But for kidneys, where living donation is a viable alternative, cadaver organs have proven to be second best. In the 1980s (when Congress started considering national regulation of organ procurement and transplantation) living kidney donation was common practice, but at that juncture in transplant history, people were hopeful that the growing supply of cadaver kidneys could eliminate the need to put living donors at risk, even if that risk was minimal.

The transplant community faced a harsh reality. Cadaver kidney transplantation was developing rapidly in the United States, yet in 1982 there were only 5,000 kidney transplants and cadaver organs had been harvested from a dismal 1 out of 10 potential deceased donors. By 1983, when Congress held its first hearings on how to solve the organ shortage, there were 70,000 Americans on dialysis and 10,000 or more actively waiting for a kidney.

It was in this climate that Dr. Barry Jacobs developed his business plan. He proposed that the government pay living kidney donors, many if not most of whom would come from developing countries. The government would have to spend relatively little to compensate such donors: For every $1,000 used to purchase a kidney, Dr. Jacobs calculated that $15,000 or more would be saved in dialysis costs.

His proposal sparked immediate outrage, and it was hard to see how it could not be viewed as inherently exploitive. The prospect that thousands of impoverished people would be shipped from developing nations to have their kidneys harvested by rich Americans read like the plot of an alarmist science fiction novel. And, indeed, if a system had been set up as Dr. Jacobs proposed, it would have presented serious ethical concerns.

In reaction to Dr. Jacobs' plan, witness after witness testified that there was no need to even consider organ sales, and some strongly urged Congress to ban any such enterprise on moral grounds. Dr. Paul Terasaki, president of the Transplantation Society, wrote on behalf of the three main American transplant societies that physicians "strongly condemn the recent scheme for commercial purchase of organs from living donors. *This completely morally and ethically irresponsible proposal is rejected as abhorrent* by all members of the Transplantation Societies" (emphasis added).

Witnesses argued that the kidney shortage could be solved without resorting to buying kidneys—the shortage could be solved with cadaver organs, supplemented by the occasional relative or good friend willing to do an altruistic living kidney donation. All that was needed was a national regulatory structure to make the existing fragmented deceased organ procurement systems more efficient.

Congress Demands, "Just Try Harder"

In response to the shock and horror of Dr. Jacobs' plan and the testimony that a deceased donor organ program would suffice, Congress passed the National Organ Transplant Act (NOTA) of 1984. The law prohibited paying for organs, imposing a potential fine of $50,000 and a maximum sentence of five years in prison. It also created the Organ Procurement and Transplantation Network (OPTN), which would provide the national coordination needed to increase the efficiency of the U.S. cadaver organ procurement system, and the Scientific Registry of Transplant Patients, which analyzes transplant data. In 1986, the United Network for Organ Sharing (UNOS), a non-profit organization, won the initial government contract to operate OPTN, and to this day UNOS is the only organization to manage OPTN.

At the time, what Congress did seemed reasonable, but over the following three decades, no matter how efficient the U.S. cadaver organ procurement system became, it could not satisfy the demand. Medical innovations keep people alive longer, and the ever-growing diabetes and hypertension epidemics continually increased the number of people who could benefit from a kidney transplant. Today the number of kidneys provided from cadavers could never be enough, even if every organ from every potential qualified donor could be harvested.

This is true because not every death results in useable organs. Organs can be diseased or injured, or the body can be dead too long before it reaches the hospital. Patients who die in the hospital after a car accident or similar trauma are the best potential organ donors because the appropriate medical equipment is at hand to switch gears from saving the patient to preserving organs for transplantation. Nevertheless, given what we know now, no matter how the process for retrieving organs from the dead improves, there will never be enough kidneys to meet the ever-growing demand.

Following the United States' lead, the World Health Organization (WHO) encouraged banning compensated organ donation, and most countries followed suit. But the rest of the world had just as much or more trouble than the United States in keeping up with the demand for organs, and before long, the out-of-control worldwide kidney shortage was accompanied by an equally out-of-control black market in kidney sales. So, ironically, policies that were intended to prevent exploitation of the poor have resulted in an ongoing tragedy of global dimensions.

Now, in ways Congress could not have imagined in 1983, the black market in kidneys exploits hundreds of thousands of people around the world. Those who illegally sell their kidneys suffer crude surgical techniques, infections, unsupervised recoveries, and the threat of criminal sanctions if they are caught—which is likely, if they seek follow-up care. All the while, they are also at the mercy of organ brokers who frequently don't pay what they've promised, if they pay at all. The United States is one of the greatest offenders, exploiting the poor and helpless in foreign black markets far more horrific than anything implied by Dr. Jacobs' proposed business plan. Now a thousand or more Americans purchase kidneys illegally every year (based on a 2012 estimate), and the worldwide market in human kidneys is somewhere between $600 million and $1.2 billion a year (based on a 2011 estimate).

What Next?

As the world's organ crisis grows, the United States is beginning to reconsider its strategy for solving the kidney shortage. The most common options involve tweaking the existing system of cadaver organ donation to make it more efficient. However, in light of the hard truth that cadaver organ procurement will never keep up with demand, the possibility of compensating living donors has recently reemerged as a possible solution. But can compensated organ donation work, or is such a system inherently exploitive? Is it possible to meet the pressing needs of recipients while at the same time protecting the health and well-being of those who might choose to donate? And what type of person might be willing to make such a difficult choice?

These questions cannot be addressed in a comprehensive way without looking closely at Iran, where a market in human kidneys has been legal for more than a quarter of a century, and where there has been no kidney shortage for over a decade. There is great resistance to looking at Iran because Iran and the United States have vast religious, cultural, and political differences. The fact that Iran is a closed society in constant confrontation with the West also makes information gathering extremely onerous.

It was because of these realities, however, that Iran's system of organ procurement followed a separate path. Shaken by a revolution and a war with Iraq that destroyed what little Western-style transplant infrastructure it had and crippled by sanctions and its own isolationist policies, Iran tried something different. Without the money, technology, or inclination to set up a Western-style system of cadaver organ procurement, Iran began condoning, regulating, and even encouraging compensated living kidney donation—that is, allowing the buying and selling of kidneys from living donors—as early as the mid-1980s.

Within 15 years, Iran had no kidney waiting list. And today, in most regions of the country, there is a waiting list for people wanting to sell their kidneys.

At this writing, over 400,000 Americans are on dialysis. Only a fourth of those are on the cadaver organ waiting list because the rest have given up or are too old or too sick to try. In 2012, fewer than 16,500 people received kidney transplants.

It is now clear that no matter how efficient the system becomes, cadaver organ procurement in the United States will never provide enough organs to solve the kidney shortage. Stem cell research and improvements in the artificial kidney, i.e. dialysis, are conceivable long-term solutions worth pursuing, but in the meantime, most Americans who could benefit from a kidney transplant don't get one. In the United States, an average of 20 to 25 people die every day waiting for a kidney. Of the more than 100,000 waiting, only 15 percent get transplants, and over 30 percent of those will lose that kidney within the first five years. Cadaver kidneys fail at such a high rate because patients have to wait too long—on average five years. Studies show the longer patients are on dialysis, the weaker they become, and the more likely their transplants will fail.

The heartbreaking cycle of desperation, disappointment, and death is played out daily among American renal disease patients. These are real people who far too often die hoping beyond hope, waiting for a kidney that with every passing day, even if it comes, is less likely to save them.

Americans Suffer

As a medical ethicist I have long known about the organ shortage and about the grim statistics of the waiting list. But knowing the facts is one thing; witnessing the human tragedy up close is another. When I first visited Steve Lessin—a friend of a friend, and a diabetic waiting for a kidney transplant—at his apartment in Arlington, Virginia, just outside of Washington, D.C., he was in good spirits. We sat and talked in his living room. We spoke about politics and philosophy, but also about dialysis and the kidney shortage.

"So why do you want a transplant?"

"I feel pretty damn awful, to be honest. I went from someone who worked full-time—you know, active runner, skier, etc., etc.—to somebody for whom just getting through the day has become a big deal … but I've done better than most people on dialysis."

And he had. For one, Steve was still working—only half-days (on the days when he could muster enough energy to leave the apartment)—but most dialysis patients don't have the energy to do even that.

"I love my job. I wish I could do more, but I've got only three, maybe four hours a day I can concentrate."

I got up to use the bathroom and accidentally opened the door to Steve's bedroom. In the middle of his unmade bed was a bloodstain close to three feet in diameter. The next door I tried was a room literally filled from floor to ceiling with dialysis and diabetic supplies. Finally, I found the bathroom, where four used dialysis bags lay draining urine-like waste into the tub, and the trashcan overflowed with used dialysis tubing. The smell of human waste permeated beyond the bathroom as if someone hadn't cleaned the toilet in months. The squalidness of Steve's everyday life was stunning. My stomach churned nervously. I paused to gain my composure, desperate not to show any reaction to what I had seen.

Steve called out, "Get me a soda, will you?" I took a three-step detour to the kitchen. Soda was easy to find: It was pretty much the only thing in his kitchen aside from a box of crackers.

"Steve, why don't you have any food?"

"Never have much. I'll go to the store later."

I looked at his cane dubiously. "How do you do it?"

"Just a bag or two at a time. One roll of toilet paper, one can of beer.... You get the picture."

I had to leave, so I started to get up and put on my coat.

"Hey, Sigrid," Steve said firmly. When I stopped and turned to him, he stood up with difficulty. He shook my hand, tubes dangling from his abdomen. "Dialysis may be better than the alternative, but it's not a solution."

"Can I come back and see you again? Is there anything I can bring you?"

"Yeah," he laughed, "a kidney!"

Steve was one of the first people to hear my stories from Iran. They made him smile, and they made him cry. Steve's situation, so commonplace among dialysis patients, moved me and motivated me to press on. Could I possibly find a way to help Steve? If I hadn't been on my way to Iran, I would have given him a kidney myself.

(1)

No Turning Back

Most of my friends and family tried to talk me out of going. My sister Ingrid cautioned, "Sisi, will you be able to keep that Smith-educated feminist streak of yours in check?" Jon, a friend who had just returned from Afghanistan, warned me that it would be dangerous, pleaded with me not to go, and even asked if my husband Bob wouldn't do something to stop me. I chuckled and told him, "Bob knows me better than that." But it would be a lie not to admit that I had serious misgivings. Although there was no precedent for any such action, there was a part of me that wanted Bob, Ingrid, Jon, and everyone who knew me to forcibly block my path, to keep me safe, protect me from my foolishness.

Iran Is the Enemy

It would be understandable if Bob did have concerns even though he supported my research. Iran and the United States have been at odds for as long as I can remember. Some of my earliest childhood memories are of my father fretting about instability in the Middle East and Iran's role in either maintaining or undermining peace. As a young adult, I remember watching along with millions of Americans as the turmoil brewing beneath the surface boiled over in Iran: Anti-West sentiments reached a fevered pitch and the Islamic Revolution of 1979 swept Ayatollah Khomeini into power.

We watched, horrified by the Khomeini government's complicity, as 52 Americans were taken hostage at gunpoint and held for 444 days. The Iranian student takeover of the American embassy allegedly even included Mahmoud Ahmadinejad, the president of Iran at the time of my trip. In 1980 the United States broke diplomatic relations with Iran and to this day has not officially reopened them. Instead, the U.S. government imposed economic sanctions on Iran, prohibiting nearly all investment and trade; consequently, for decades there have been very few if any reasons for Americans to go to Iran. So what was I *doing*?

I was sure that the only way to find definitive answers to the kidney-sales question was to go and see for myself, but was it too dangerous? Every year, for over 30 years, the U.S. State Department has issued travel warnings, recommending that Americans stay out of Iran. The list of dangers could inspire an action movie, including kidnappings, terrorist activities, public unrest (often directed toward Westerners), bombings, drug gangs, and government surveillance. Potential travelers are warned:

> Iranian authorities have prevented a number of U.S. citizen academics, scientists, journalists, and others who traveled to Iran for personal/cultural/business reasons from leaving the country and in some cases have detained, interrogated, and imprisoned them on unknown or various charges, including espionage and being a threat to the regime.

As if this wasn't sufficient to cause hesitation, the warnings go on to state that anyone who violates local Iranian laws, "even unknowingly," could be expelled, arrested, or imprisoned and that "public floggings" are common. At this point my qualms mushroomed into nightmares. One night I dreamt that I was tied to a wooden hitching post in a dust-smothered village square. A sea of dark-clad men and women jeered at me through cloth-bound faces as a huge man lashed me with a thorny whip, his robes billowing with each stroke. I struggled against my restraints, trying to escape, crying out in desperation, "What did I do? Let me go. I didn't do anything!" My tormenter bellowed to the crowd in Persian, "Down with America! All imperialist pigs must pay!" The crowd roared back, *"Allahu Akbar! Allahu Akbar!"* Then, jarred back to reality, a chill ran down my spine. In my waking hours the sound of the crack of that whip dissipated slowly as I became more engaged in the everyday preparations for my trip.

I must admit, the long history of U.S.-Iranian tension and the dour State Department warnings did give me pause—*Is going to Iran the only way to get the answers I seek?* Perhaps not, but I am not easily discouraged once my mind is made up. While I have never been entirely sure whether to consider this a strength or a weakness, I felt I had no choice in the matter. Someone had to do an honest, in-person assessment of Iran's organ procurement system, and if not I, then who? My plan was to educate myself about Iranian law and culture before I left, particularly rules regarding proper female attire and behavior. I needed to minimize the chance of drawing attention to myself or unintentionally breaking any laws.

As I tried to pull together a research team, I realized I wasn't the only one with misgivings about going to Iran. One person after another showed initial enthusiasm only to reconsider and pull out. I had envisaged a dynamic team heading east with me: a medical anthropologist familiar with Iran, a well-known documentary filmmaker, and an Iranian-American medical professor who specialized in treating kidney disease—a savvy crew of enterprising adventurers lighting out on a mission to discover the cure to the world's organ crisis. But by the time I left for Iran my team had dwindled to just two. I was initially excited that Diane Tober, a medical anthropologist whom I'd met through Professor Assefi's daughter Nassim, was interested in coming along. She studied family planning in Iran and was hoping to help me while she did research for her documentary film on famous Iranian women. Regrettably her visa application was denied.

I was also excited that I had managed to interest the distinguished filmmaker Rick Ray in my project. Among other things, he had made the bestselling *10 Questions for the Dalai Lama*. What a boon it would be to have him along! We had corresponded extensively and even met in person to work out the details of how to get him into Iran—we had decided that he would accompany me to the MESOT conference as my significant other. I had obtained a visa for him and was in the process of making flight arrangements when he called, just weeks before our scheduled departure. "I would have to miss a showing of *10 Questions* at National Geographic in New York that was arranged months ago ... and besides, my wife is worried it won't be safe." I was devastated. Who was going to film my interviews in Iran? How was the documentary I planned going to get made? Rick hurriedly helped me pick out camera equipment to purchase, and in addition to all the other things I had to do, I now had to find time to learn how to use the camera before I left for Iran.

In the end, my team consisted of only Dr. Bastani, an Iranian-American nephrologist and professor at the University of St. Louis Medical School, and me. Dr. Bastani already had an invitation to speak at MESOT, and he took a sabbatical to accompany me on my post-MESOT research trip. Yet, to my surprise, even Dr. Bastani had misgivings. He called a week before our scheduled departure with unsettling news. "Did you see the report about the Japanese tourist who was kidnapped for ransom just outside of Tehran? I would understand if you decided not to go." Dr. Bastani had also been warned by Iranian friends that he should be careful because he had been somewhat outspoken in the United States, at times lecturing on peace and the proper role of Islam in modern society. But despite all these reminders of why it might be dangerous to pursue my vision, I held firm in my conviction to go.

Safe Is a Relative Term

I planned and researched for eight months and developed a strategy for staying safe. Dr. Bastani was part of that strategy: He was a native Iranian, flu-
ent in Farsi, with many familial and professional connections in Iran. People
who had been to Iran recently told me it wasn't *that* dangerous—well, so long
as you laid low, didn't draw attention to yourself, and most definitely didn't
bring up sensitive political issues like women's rights, Middle East policy,
democracy, religious freedom, or any other human rights issue. I was getting
the picture: As long as I wasn't seen or heard, I *should* be OK, but how could
I conduct research in a state of invisibility? It seemed like I was supposed to
hold my breath for the duration of the trip. I was beginning to wonder if un-
folding events were aligning to tell me something—something glaringly obvious that I was prone to ignore: *Don't go, Sigrid! You might not return in one
piece, if at all.*

The prospect of being kidnapped worried me, but again I pushed my concerns aside with a plan. I would only take licensed, dispatched cabs if I had to
travel on my own, and people at both ends of the cab ride would be informed
of the cabbie's name, the cab's number, and my estimated time of arrival—no
hailing a cab off the street for me! But then again, what use was having the
cabbie's details if I was already secluded away in some hovel or dungeon? The
ability to trace the cabbie didn't necessarily mean that anyone would be able
to find me even if the cabbie cooperated. There were a lot of ifs in that line of
reasoning, but at least it was something.

My fears were slightly alleviated when I met with Dr. Ahad J. Ghods, a transplant nephrologist from Iran who was instrumental in developing the Iranian
organ procurement system. What a stroke of good fortune! After seven years
of trying to get a visa so he could speak at Yale Medical School, Dr. Ghods was
granted a visa in time for me to confer with him in person before my trip. He
was only allowed to stay in the country for four days and was not allowed to
leave the immediate vicinity of the university. Despite the briefness of his visit,
he generously spent a few of his precious hours in the United States speaking
with me. I drove up to New Haven to hear Dr. Ghods' presentation and met
with him afterwards to ask—as tactfully as I could—about whether it would
be safe for me to travel to Iran.

When Dr. Rastegar, the professor of medicine who organized the Yale event,
first introduced me, Dr. Ghods glanced to my right and left, looking for a
more suitable "Dr. Fry-Revere." I don't think he was expecting a woman. I extended my hand, and he shook it, somewhat overenthusiastically, as if an alien
limb was attached to him and he wanted to get rid of it. Then it was my turn

to be taken aback. We had barely sat down when he asked, "Have you ever lived abroad?" I couldn't help but feel insecure. *Is he trying to assess whether I'll be able to handle the culture shock? Maybe he wants to get a sense of whether I have enough perspective to objectively evaluate what I'll find.* I shifted in my seat, then leaned forward, determined to give a confident, self-assured response.

"I've lived mostly in the U.S., but I have traveled to 46 countries, including Eastern Europe and Turkey." He didn't seem impressed, so I added, "I've lived in Switzerland, Greece, and Argentina—for a year in Switzerland and Argentina, and for four months in Greece." At that, he seemed to relax just a touch.

"Was your father in the military?"

"No," I replied. "He was a political science professor."

No response. So I added, "My parents wanted to expose their children to other cultures, so they took us to as many places, as often as they could." When I was 8 years old, my father took an extended sabbatical, and we traveled around Europe living in one of the first motor homes: a Dodge truck chassis with a custom-built top, equipped with boat furnishings. "Moby Dick" was home for almost two years. We even lived in him after returning to the United States.

Dr. Ghods leaned back in his chair. "OK, what questions do you have?"

I felt extremely fortunate and thankful that Dr. Ghods was willing to take the time to help me make some critical decisions about my research trip. He told me Iran wasn't as dangerous as the American government made it out to be, probably no more dangerous than Argentina or any other more advanced developing country. I inquired about my list of potential research partners, which Iranian cities I should visit, safety tips. I was relieved to find out that Dr. Ghods knew Dr. Bastani and thought highly of him. I took his advice—all except the part about getting official permission to do my research and film my subjects. After careful consideration, I decided I didn't want to take the chance that permission would be denied, that my itinerary would need approval, that my interviewees would be vetted, or that I would end up with a government chaperone. It was better just to go on a lecture tour and do my research on the side.

As it turned out, the Iranian government refused to give me a visa to extend my trip more than a few days beyond the MESOT conference at which I was scheduled to speak, but Dr. Ghods and others suggested, "Go, make some Iranian contacts, and try again once you're already in Iran."

So that was the new plan: Go speak at the Iranian conference. Then, if I felt safe and could get my visa extended, I would change my flight and stay to do the lecture tour and, more importantly, my research. If not, then I would cut my trip short and return home.

Reality Check

Five days before leaving for Iran, Bob threw me a going-away party at our home in Northern Virginia. It was sweet of Bob to arrange the party although most of the time my mind was elsewhere, panicking in silence. With only a few days before my scheduled departure, my visa, which had been granted weeks before, still hadn't arrived. I needed to find a YouTube video on how to wear the Iranian head covering I'd bought. I needed to read more, a lot more, about Iranian culture. I took a sip of Chablis, swallowing consciously—it could be months before I held another glass of wine. Neither I, nor anyone around me, was blind to the fact that if I got my wish, I would leave all the people I loved for at least two months and would likely return a changed person.

Cathy, an intern at the Center for Ethical Solutions, pulled me back from my contemplative isolation. "Would it be safe for me to sell my kidney?"

The question caught me by surprise, particularly coming from Cathy, who was putting together a memo for me on organ procurement around the world that focused (at least in part) on the horrors of the worldwide black market in kidney sales. I must have knit my brow or otherwise looked confused.

She rephrased. "Is it medically safe to donate?"

"Oh, well, yes, it's safe." For over a decade, more than a third of kidney transplants in the U.S. have been from living donors rather than deceased donors. And studies from Scandinavia and elsewhere indicate that living kidney donors don't have an increased risk of kidney disease, or for that matter, any other form of illness.

I also told her how my son had lost a kidney to cancer when he was a baby and how, 24 years later, he has totally normal blood work—his remaining kidney has no trouble doing the work that would otherwise be done by two.

Cathy relaxed with relief, but the question as she first framed it nagged at me. "Didn't you say something about selling your kidney? What is that about?"

"Well," she hesitated, but went on to tell me that she was recently divorced, jobless, and had three children; that it was very difficult to make ends meet; and that she was at George Mason University finishing her masters in international policy, but as of yet, had no job prospects.

"So," I pressed, "what does that have to do with selling your kidney?"

That was when I first heard about Steve Lessin. Cathy met Steve through Match.com, but she sensed right away that something was wrong. He looked haggard, colorless—his online photo was only a few months old, yet he was a different man when she met him. They dated a while and both realized the relationship wasn't going to work, but Steve offered Cathy $90,000 if she were willing to give him one of her kidneys.

I shivered at the prospect that I almost let Cathy go without pursuing the question further. "No, Cathy, you can't donate your kidney for money. I thought you knew that it's against the law. You, Steve, and anyone else involved in the transaction could end up with a $50,000 fine and five years in prison."

"I know, I just thought maybe you knew a way around that."

"No," I said with enough emphasis that two nearby guests turned to see what we were talking about. I couldn't help myself—how could Cathy not know this?

I steered her over to what I hoped was a quieter corner. "It's even illegal to have the operation outside the country if the donor is compensated monetarily," I explained, not sufficiently convinced that I had gotten my point across. "Besides, even if you could hide the income, you wouldn't be able to hide the fact that you were missing a kidney. How would you explain that? Also, what would you do for insurance? Even if Steve or his insurance company were willing to cover all the transplant-related expenses, what happens if you have complications, or if something pops up years from now that arguably could be related to the operation? Or what if an insurance company denies you coverage because it claims you have a preexisting condition? A situation like that was just in the news."

I caught my breath. I worried I had overwhelmed Cathy. "Steve needs to find someone who will give him a kidney for free." Later, after Cathy introduced me to Steve, I considered donating a kidney to him myself, but I needed to wait until I was back from Iran.

I looked around. The number of people listening had doubled. I hoped I hadn't embarrassed Cathy. She avoided direct eye contact and added noncommittally that she had been pretty sure there was no way to make it work but thought it was worth asking, just in case. The last time she saw Steve, he had looked so ashen—"like he had one foot in the grave"—and this would have been a solution for both of them.

I felt for Cathy, and I felt for Steve. I knew exactly what Cathy was talking about: I hadn't been divorced, but I too had my own troubles with making ends meet, particularly when it came to paying for the expensive special ed program I wanted for one of my children. I also knew what she meant about Steve: I would see that skin tone myself when I met Steve, and I'd seen it two weeks earlier when I visited dialysis centers in Ann Arbor and Detroit to interview and film U.S. kidney disease patients for a possible documentary comparing the U.S. and Iranian kidney procurement systems. Once you've seen a few dialysis patients, you can recognize them easily. Anyone who has been on dialysis for more than a couple months has a grey, corpse-like tone to their skin. And there is almost always something in their demeanor that either defiantly cries, "I will live on!" or resignedly sighs, "I know I'm dying; leave me alone."

Most people don't know that dialysis, while lifesaving, is not a long-term solution. Dialysis filters out only about 10 percent of the toxins that a healthy kidney removes from blood, so people on dialysis continue to be poisoned by their bodies' own waste products. The decline, which may be a bit slower for some than for others, is nonetheless inevitable: Heart damage and other serious complications usually occur within just a few years. But the ashen skin tone is an early, telltale sign of the dire condition such patients face.

Most of the dialysis patients I visited in Michigan were affectedly upbeat. "God will provide." "I will get better." "I can be patient. I'll get a kidney from the waiting list eventually." In the four years since I did those interviews in Ann Arbor and Detroit, almost all of the people I interviewed have died, and none, as far as I can find out, have received a transplant.

Only one patient I interviewed in Ann Arbor seemed sincere. Lakesha had smooth, brown skin, a beauty mark beneath her lower lip, and unruly, coarse curls peeking out from under a purple mesh hair net. She was eager for someone to talk to during her tri-weekly, three-hour-long stint hooked to an unforgiving dialysis machine. At first, she was excited to talk about school and her boyfriend. But when I asked her about her hopes for the future, she pulled her blanket up over her face and hid from me as if she wanted to hide from the realities of her predicament. All the other patients I spoke to gave optimistic rationalizations about their chances of getting a kidney or talked about lasting for years longer—maybe even decades—on dialysis as they had once heard that someone somewhere had done. But Lakesha was obviously afraid and showed that she knew her chances of surviving more than a few years were slim. As I drove away from the dialysis center, Lakesha's final words reverberated in my ears: "The only thing worse than what I'm going through now, would be dying." Lakesha's honest wisdom made her more real and more alive to me than the other patients who, with their optimistic smiles and unwillingness to discuss the realities of what they were facing, seemed already half dead.

A Painful Truth

I got to know Steve Lessin better after I returned from Iran. He was not like the other dialysis patients I'd met. He was neither naively optimistic nor yielding to his fate. He moved slowly, but with purpose. He had worked hard all his life, and it had paid off—at least until now. Steve pursued every avenue he could to try to save his life.

"What is it like in Iran? Can I go there to get a kidney?"

I agonized uncomfortably for almost half a minute about what to say. Steve would see through me if I tried to sugarcoat the grim reality. I had to be honest. I sat down across from him in his little apartment, I on a chair and he on the sofa. I had to avoid the tubes stretching from his open-shirted belly to the next room, where his dialysis machine could be heard—*swish-tick, swish-click, swish-tick*—as if counting down the time Steve had left. I reluctantly explained that Iran does not allow foreigners (other than perhaps Iranian ex-pats) to purchase kidneys. Foreigners are welcome if they bring their own donors from their own country and are willing to pay for the surgery out of pocket, but they are not allowed to pay Iranians to be their donors. This restriction is strictly enforced, so much so that, in April of 2008, a transplant unit in Tehran suspected of allowing foreigners (Saudi nationals) to purchase kidneys from Iranians was shut down and all the physicians involved lost their surgical privileges.

"What about anywhere other than Iran?" Steve asked, knowing very well what my answer would be. He had done his research.

"Not a good idea—the black market is immoral, illegal, and risky."

In a rare moment of weakness, Steve started to rationalize a possible run at the black market. "Money isn't an issue. ... Maybe I could make sure the donor got his money; hand it to him personally or something."

I looked at him sympathetically. "And what about the other risks?"

Steve agreed he couldn't risk losing his job or being fined or jailed for violating the National Organ Transplant Act. He was also worried about how sure he could be that the donor would be healthy and wouldn't have hepatitis, malaria, or AIDS. And what about the medical facilities abroad and the chance of infection or other complications? "All legitimate concerns," I said. But even with all these potential dangers and complications, the drive to survive has motivated many a less cautious and far less scrupulous American to purchase a kidney on the black market.

Two days after the party, my visa arrived, and three days after that I was on a plane to Frankfurt, Germany, where I would meet Dr. Bastani for the first time. My apprehensions were dwarfed by excitement: I was finally on my way to Iran.

٢ (2)

Getting There

In the Frankfurt airport, a gentleman in the waiting area for the flight to Tehran set a compass on the floor. He carefully watched the needle spin and adjusted the compass a few times before stowing it in a velvet pouch in his backpack. He pulled a mat from his pack and placed it carefully between the rows of seats to face southeast toward Mecca. He set a small, flat, sand-colored stone in the niche and took off his shoes. Between announcements for boarding, while other passengers searched for tickets and gathered their belongings, he knelt, placed his forehead to the stone, and prayed.

As I waited in line, I silently joined him with a prayer of my own. *Please, God, let my going to a dangerous country where I don't speak the language with a man I have just met not be a mistake.* I wished I had arrived at the gate earlier. I would have had time to talk to Dr. Bastani, look him in the eye, and maybe pull out at the last minute if I really wanted to. But we barely had time for a quick handshake before boarding the plane, and we were seated aisles apart. I sank into my seat, wedged between two strangers, and quietly contemplated the books about Iran that I'd brought to read on the trip.

What the Tour Books Tell You

I knew Iran was an important Middle Eastern country, but not until I started preparing for this trip did I fully appreciate its significance. Iran lies smack in the middle of this vital region, with Iraq on its western border and Afghanistan to its east. Its other neighbors include Pakistan and Turkey, and nearby are Saudi Arabia, the United Arab Emirates, and the southwestern tip of Russia. Only second in size to Saudi Arabia, Iran is a full 636,372 square miles. While this is only about one-sixth the size of the United States, it is larger than Germany, France, Great Britain, Italy, and Austria combined. Iran's population is equally large when compared to its Middle Eastern neighbors, though not by Western standards: 77 million people live in Iran, compared with 314 million in the United States and 736 million in Europe. But there are only 30 million people in Saudi Arabia and about 35 million in Iraq. In the Middle East, only Egypt is larger than Iran with a population of 85 million.

Iran is resource rich, but its people are relatively poor. Iran has the second-largest oil and natural gas reserve in the world after Saudi Arabia, but its population is impoverished both by Western standards and by the standards of its oil-rich neighbors. The average individual income in Iran in 2009 was a little over $3,000 per year, compared with $20,000 in Saudi Arabia and $39,000 in the United States. All these statistics began to put into perspective what Dr. Ghods had told me about the Iranian kidney market. The going rate for a kidney in Iran is the equivalent of about $5,000 — more than most Iranians make in a year.*

While the geographic, demographic, and economic factors mentioned so far are important for understanding the context in which the Iranian organ market operates, religious and cultural factors also contribute to how Iranians see themselves in the world and are vital to understanding why Iran has developed such a unique organ procurement system. Iran is a Shi'ite Muslim island in a sea of Sunni Muslim states. Muslims are adherents of Islam, the religion founded firstly on the Qur'an, which is considered the verbatim word of God, and secondly on the teachings and normative example of the Prophet Mohammad. Up until the ousting of Saddam Hussein in Iraq in 2003, Iran was the only country where Shi'ite rulers governed a majority Shi'ite population. In every other Middle Eastern country, a Shi'ite minority — or even a majority such as in Iraq — was ruled by Sunni Muslims, the only exception being Syria where an Alawite (a branch of Shi'ism) minority rules over a Sunni majority. (Since my return from Iran, Syria has been engulfed in a brutal civil war, still raging at the time of this writing. Syria's Shi'ite rulers are barely holding on to power in smaller and smaller enclaves while fighters stream across the border from various Middle Eastern countries, including Iran.)

The Shi'ite/Sunni division goes back to the time of Mohammad's passing in 632 A.D. When Mohammad died, there was general agreement to continue

---

* Income figures fluctuate wildly in Iran because of inflation. Thus, coming up with accurate comparisons is difficult. Throughout this book I use the most reliable statistics I could find for the time period when I was in Iran. Please see the Notes section for Chapter Two for more on the difficulties of doing income, standard of living, and price comparisons.

the caliphate system of government he had established in Medina: a constitutional republic based on Sharia, or Islamic law. But those who later became known as the Shi'ites insisted that rulers put into power after the Prophet Mohammad's death be imams—that is, direct biological descendants of Mohammad who are "purified" and fully knowledgeable in religious law. The Sunnis didn't consider such qualifications necessary and instead chose their leaders from pre-Islamic Arab aristocracy without requiring a biological tie to Mohammad. According to Twelver Shi'ites, who comprise the majority of the Shi'ite population today, during the Twelfth Imam's Occultation (the time when he is absent or hidden from view), Shi'ites are supposed to follow the lead of their religious scholars in religious matters. This role was expanded to include political leadership by the late Ayatollah Khomeini, an expansion of power not considered legitimate by some Shi'ite religious leaders, especially those living in Iraq.

Since the 1979 revolution, Iranian law specifies that a supreme leader chosen from the class of scholars called "ayatollahs" should rule in the absence of the Twelfth Imam. Ayatollahs are highly trained in Islamic theology and jurisprudence (essentially mullahs with Ph.D.s). Iranian mullahs and ayatollahs who believe their lineage traces back to one of the twelve Shi'ite imams qualify to wear a black, rather than a white, turban and are often revered for their lineage in addition to their scholarly and religious achievements. The supreme leader of Iran, by law, must be an ayatollah, but not necessarily qualified to wear a black turban. The late Supreme Leader Ayatollah Khomeini wore a black turban, as does his successor the Ayatollah Khamenei.

Ethnicity is another important distinction for understanding how Iranians view their place in the world. Even among Muslims, many cultural and ethnic differences exist in the Middle East, but as far as Iran is concerned, the most important distinction is the Persian/Arab divide. Iran was the heart of the Persian Empire. Although modern Iranians have incorporated much of Islamic culture into their own, Iranians do not consider themselves Arabs—they are Persians.

Sunni vs. Shi'ite and the Persian/Arab Divide

As I sat wedged in the middle seat between two Iranian men on my flight to Tehran, it dawned on me how important the Sunni/Shi'ite and Persian/Arab differences are to understanding how Iran views its neighbors, and why Iran is so willing to develop its own policies in isolation from both Western and

Arab influences. Iran has strained relationships with the West, but its tensions with more immediate neighbors are just as significant.

Saudi Arabia and Afghanistan are predominantly Sunni, but Saudi Arabia is Arab, and Afghanistan is made up of Pashtun and Tajik tribes (among others) who speak languages derived from Persian. I imagine Iranians seeing Saudi Arabia as the big, arrogant, threatening stepfather, but Afghanistan more as an embarrassing half-sibling whom they alternate between wanting to protect and disown. Iran's keen interest in Iraq may have as much to do with the fact that Iraq's population is mostly Shi'ite as it does with the fact that the two countries share a border and were embroiled in the longest conventional war of the twentieth century. The Iraq-Iran War raged between 1980 and 1988, a war both preceded and followed by border disputes between the two countries.

Iran's sympathy toward and tendency to ally itself with Shi'ites could also explain why in Bahrain it supports the Shi'ite popular unrest directed at the country's Sunni caliph rulers, while in Syria it unwaveringly supports the Shi'ite rulers against that country's discontented Sunni majority.

Ancient Roots

It is impossible to understand the Iranian mindset without understanding that the Persian Empire was over 1,000 years old when the Arabs conquered it. While it never quite rose again to the hegemonic power it once was, Persia forced the Arabs out and ruled much of the Middle East for yet another thousand years before the more modern empires of Russia, Turkey, Mongolia, India, and Britain forced it into its current borders. In the twentieth century, Iran's rulers became all but puppets—first of Russia, then of Britain and the United States—until 1979, when Ayatollah Khomeini and his Islamic revolution put an end to both the last Persian Dynasty and to Western influence in Iran.

Iran was a powerful Persian empire for thousands of years, a leader in innovation and the establishment of cultural norms, with a proud population not afraid to think for itself. That culture has been constrained by the historical events described above, but isolation imposed from both within and without has also enabled Iran to develop an ideological independence that lead to a rejection of the rest of the world's universal ban on organ sales in favor of a totally different approach.

I stirred in my seat, accidentally nudging the elbow of one of my fellow travelers. He smiled at me, a little too broadly, when I apologized. "What are you reading?" Without looking up I said, "Just some history," and continued to read, trying to signal my disinterest in starting a conversation. Sitting there, pretending to read while he continued to stare at me, I realized that after a quarter of a century of isolation, I would be the first Westerner to take a close look at Iran's organ market. *What, I wondered, would I learn about solving the organ shortage?* Once I was sure my neighbor had given up on trying to engage me in conversation, I returned to my reading in earnest. I was beginning to understand that outside the confines of my research, I would have to mute my natural desire to engage in discussion and debate, lest I be enticed to give too much away and draw attention to myself.

I read that Persia did not become "Iran" through any conquest or revolution. Reza Shah Pahlavi, father of the last Persian Shah, Mohammad Reza Pahlavi, requested in 1935 that all foreign nations use the name "Iran" and "Iranian" instead of "Persia" and "Persian" in their official correspondence with his country. "Persia" and "Persian" are from the Greek, and he wanted to introduce instead "Iran" and "Iranian," the phonetic equivalent of what the Persians call themselves. The resulting linguistic disassociation of modern Iran from its ancient roots as the Persian Empire was inevitable, although probably unintentional. Some Iranians dislike this disconnect, particularly when their Islamic practices lead Westerners to assume they are Arabs. Those Iranians insist on calling themselves Persian and speakers of Modern Persian, instead of "Iranians" and speakers of "Farsi," but often they nonetheless end up having to explain that Persians are from Iran and that Modern Persian is just another way of saying Farsi.

As I looked at all the maps of different Persian dynasties, I couldn't help but be impressed: *Wow, these vast empires were ruled by the ancestors of modern-day Iranians.* And it hit home that the Persians must have had as much influence in the development of the greater Middle East as the Greeks and Romans did on the development of Europe. After all, at one point or another in Iran's history, the Persian Empire stretched from current-day Greece, Eastern Europe, and North Africa into what are now Russia, China, and India. The Empire even included the entire Arabian Peninsula's coastline. Persia was the largest empire the world has ever known!

Unfortunately, from my Western perspective, Iran's more recent history falls short of its glorious past. The history I am more familiar with is what I've witnessed on the news: Iranian students taking over the American Embassy, Iran's involvement in global terrorism through Hezbollah, its infamous Quds Force, and its grievous human rights violations, particularly its mistreatment of women. Most Americans nowadays are familiar with stories of the beating and arrest of women whose clothing allows more than their hands and face to show, Iran's discriminatory inheritance and divorce laws, and, among other inequities, the continued practice of stoning for adultery that is enforced and carried out against women far more than against men.

I dozed off for the last hour or so before we landed. Images of the past, present, and future Iran mingled with my dreams. I woke up to the sound of the landing gear engaging, a sense of falling, half dream-omen, half real. I braced myself for the adventure to come. I reminded myself: *I must hold to my resolve not to say anything about Iranian politics until I am safely back on U.S. soil.*

۳ (3)

Transplanting Organs and Ideas

Dr. Bastani and I were among the first to disembark at the Imam Khomeini International Airport in Tehran. Dr. Bastani was tall—my guess six feet, or even a little taller. He took his appearance seriously and was always dressed in a pressed shirt and neatly pleated pants. I never once saw him look disheveled. His slightly greying beard and hair were cropped short but left long enough to minimize the receding hairline and slight double chin that comes with age. He had a distinguished air, reinforced by the dark-rimmed spectacles he wore on a black cord around his neck. The cord created large distracting loops to the right and left of his face when he pulled his glasses down his nose to get a better look at me.

If I didn't know he was an American-Iranian medical professor, I would have guessed an Indian scientist working for NIH. He had that endearingly absent-minded, distant look of a researcher, but other features gave away his origins. He was formal almost to a fault and loved to quote poetry and tell tales from Persian mythology. And he wore a signet ring, a subtle but clear indication that he valued status and fine things: a common but not always immediately evident trait among Iranians. I also learned later that, despite the usual gravity with which he spoke, he possessed a keen sense for making people feel at ease. With his broad smile and humorous quips he could get almost anyone to take down their guard—even me.

Inside the airport, I was drawn to the families in the arrival area. The women and children bobbed up and down, straining to see past the men waiting in front

27

of them. The women wore dark tunics, slacks, and headscarves with an occasional colorful exception. The children looked like kids almost anywhere. Both girls and boys wore boldly colored coats and boots, but the girls also wore headscarves. Many of the women were carrying extravagant bouquets of flowers: Some blossoms were familiar, some unfamiliar, most tied with trailing ribbons. All were worthy of a wedding (or funeral), and the scent of freshly cut flowers permeated the airport. I was struck by kaleidoscopic energy—only a few sedate chador-wearing women were among them (*chador* in Farsi literally means "tent"). The crowd swayed with anticipation. I wanted to see how they greeted their relatives and friends, but I didn't want to lose Dr. Bastani, so I hurried after him as muffled squeals of glee burst out behind me.

Customs officials escorted us to a special room where 50 or so other conference attendees waited—MESOT organizers had paid a special fee for us to receive the white-glove treatment. Neatly dressed men in black jackets with silver buttons served us tea and apologized for the wait as we enjoyed an assortment of lemon- and pistachio-filled tarts. In total, tea was served four times between our arrival in Tehran and our arrival in Shiraz.

After my second glass of tea, as I began to wonder where the bathrooms were, a man in a blue uniform with official-looking insignia approached us and asked me—but not Dr. Bastani—to follow him. I glanced nervously at Dr. Bastani, but he motioned with his hand that I should go. *What now?* I thought. *Why me and no one else?* But as I was escorted out of the lounge, more uniform-clad Iranians, escorting two other conference attendees, joined us. I was relieved not to be the only one singled out and soon learned the others were also American—well, at least one of them was, because he kept nervously repeating under his breath in English, "I knew I shouldn't have come; I knew I shouldn't have come."

We walked down a small, dark corridor to a door with an official-looking Farsi sign that I couldn't read. I imagined it said something like "Do Not Enter—SAVAK," referring to the Iranian secret service under the Shah, or "Do Not Enter—SAVAMA," the "reformed" secret service started by the Grand Ayatollah Khomeini, which is rumored to be just as brutal, if not worse.

Both of my companions looked pale, especially the one still muttering under his breath. My heart pounded too, but unlike the others, I went through the door with my head held high, grinning at the guard on the other side of the threshold. I later learned to reconsider smiling at anyone in public, particularly men, because it is a cultural taboo in Iran for women to smile at men they don't know. Even making eye contact can be considered forward, but at the time it seemed like a good idea. The stone-faced official, who stood behind a high counter with glass panels, ignored me and requested our passports, taking those of the two men first. The official examined them one at a time, glancing up briefly to see if the faces matched those in the photos, and returned them. The uniformed men who had brought us there then motioned us to follow as they led us back to the lounge.

I was almost disappointed. *What, no fingerprinting, no questioning ... no getting hassled for being American?* In my heightened emotional state I was braced for a dramatic confrontation, but what I experienced was a kind of bureaucratic officiousness that could have happened anywhere in the world. I had encountered ruder treatment crossing the border into Canada—and would once again, when I tried to travel to Toronto shortly after returning from Iran. But my introduction to Iran was entirely routine. So my being pulled aside by uniformed men was not the stuff of high drama as I imagined it might be. At least on the way back I noticed where the bathrooms were.

A Quick Tour of Tehran

Mehrabad Airport in Tehran, which handles domestic flights, was all the way across town, and our flight to Shiraz departed from there. Once we stepped outside the Khomeini terminal, the city air hit me like a wall. I coughed, and my eyes, nose, and throat stung. I hadn't experienced such bad air quality since living in L.A. in the 70s. This would take some getting used to. It wasn't hot, maybe 60 degrees Fahrenheit, but unlike most of the car rides I would take in Tehran, this driver, in deference to his passengers, kept the windows up and the air conditioning running. *What would it be like in the summer when the temperatures in Tehran regularly reach into the upper 90s?*

Our driver, Hassan, was young, maybe in his late 20s or early 30s. He gave us a large smile and was quick to inform us that he had a master's degree in urban planning. "You will see," he said confidently, "Iran is different than you think."

In perfect English, Hassan shared that he'd been a tour guide for eight years and was proud to have a job. He pointed out city highlights as we made our way through the benzene-fume-choked streets. I looked out at the road signs and had a sinking realization that not only could I not read them, I couldn't distinguish numbers from letters. At least in a country like Greece, I could match up addresses with what I saw on a street or metro map. Here, nothing. All I saw were beautiful squiggles, undulating backwards—the enchanting hieroglyphics of a mysterious nation's psyche. I was simultaneously enthralled and guardedly aware of my vulnerability.

It took us nearly two hours of stop-and-go traffic to travel from one airport to the other. The whole way we negotiated speed bumps on every major thoroughfare—even highways, and I couldn't help but ask myself if our driver's urban planning degree might not be put to better use than giving quick tours of Tehran to foreigners.

"Over there," Hassan pointed, while we bounced our way over yet another speed bump, "is the Holy Shrine of the Grand Ayatollah Khomeini. And if you go that way, you see Rey City, where there is the Imamzadeh Shah-e Abdol-Azim, a shrine for a descendant of Imam Ali, and also a shrine for Hamzeh, the brother of Imam Reza, the eighth Shi'ite imam." He turned to look at me, clearly proud of his English vocabulary. "It is *magnificent!*" I began to wonder if all the attractions in Tehran were mausoleums. He continued to point right and left and left again. "If you go that way, you can see the University of Tehran, and that way, the grand bazaar to go shopping."

Then with a *ta-da*, Hassan energetically gestured toward the distant horizon where I could just make out the Azadi Tower—the iconic symbol of Tehran, much like the Eiffel Tower is for Paris. This was more than a job for Hassan; he clearly loved the city. He drove around Azadi Square twice to ensure I had enough time to admire its arches from all sides. "The Azadi was built as a monument to commemorate the 2,500th anniversary of the Persian Empire. It used to be called the Shah's Memorial Tower. It was renamed the Freedom Tower after the Islamic Revolution." There certainly was something impressive about the tower—classic yet futuristic—with four conjoined winged arches of white marble jutted into the sky as a reminder … of what? Our guide sat a little straighter in his seat as he explained the monument's history. I didn't dare put into words what I was thinking: *Do Iranians think the tower still represents freedom today?*

The tension Iranians feel between their Persian past and current-day culture dominated by Arab influences is omnipresent. I frequently experienced Iranians, despite the obvious contradiction, seeing themselves as keepers of the flame for the once and future Persian Empire. I thought to myself, *Sometimes memories of greatness are the most dangerous memories of all.*

The Final Leg to Shiraz

We were dropped off at Mehrabad Airport in front of a building labeled "CIP" (Commercially Important Persons) and treated to more fragrant tea. Trip-weary, I was glad to board the plane to Shiraz. As the flight attendants gave the safety briefing, which, like in the United States, everyone ignored, I looked around and noticed that the plane's signage was in two languages, Farsi and Russian. Dr. Bastani joked about how dilapidated the planes were. He pointed to a crack in the cabin paneling. "We could fall out of the sky at any moment." I visibly rolled my eyes. We laughed, and I realized Dr. Bastani and I were going to be friends.

Little did either of us know that within a few months of our return to the United States, two domestic Iranian flights did just that—fall out of the sky—killing everyone on board. I never heard the final official findings, but there was speculation in both instances that the planes were old and ill-maintained.

The Iran Air flight attendants, all female, wore navy blue uniforms adorned with beige-gold trim and a tiny Homa bird, a symbol of good fortune from Persian mythology. I noticed how young and attractive the women were and remembered my aunt telling me how after WWII, when commercial passenger flights first became commonplace, flight attendants were chosen for their looks and poise as much as for anything else. I know this is no longer true in the United States, but it seemed to still be the practice in Iran.

During our flight we were served naan (Persian flatbread), goat cheese, olives, dates and walnuts, and, of course, tea. As we chatted about the food, Dr. Bastani mentioned that his favorite meal was sheep's head soup. He looked visibly surprised when I told him, "I would love to try *kalepache*—I am curious to see how it compares to the calf's tongue and brains my mother used to make." Looking at me with disbelief, he remarked, "You really aren't like other Americans or, for that matter, much like other women, are you?" I chose to take this as a compliment.

Where Am I?

When I awoke the next morning, I was not sure where I was. The Homa Hotel looked pretty much like any other four-star conference center elsewhere in the world, but there were clues that I was somewhere different from any place I'd ever been. The light was different. The hue of most colors was richer and deeper than what I was used to, but when I looked at myself in the mirror I looked almost bleached. I was tempted to put on some makeup, but thought better of it—remembering that I was in an Islamic country where the authorities frowned on the use of cosmetics.

Outside my window, I saw more evidence that I was no longer in the United States, or any other Western country. There was construction everywhere—unfinished buildings, frozen in time, with girder beams and equipment rusting like giant metal dinosaurs after the ashes from an extinction-bearing meteorite had settled. I watched the men stroll, chatting and swinging their arms as they moseyed along. The women walked with purpose, eyes cast downward. Particularly if alone, the women proceeded with determination, as if their destinations reeled them in. Men in black suits with earpieces or walkie-talkies watched from the parking lot and stood at every street corner within several blocks of the hotel.

I enjoyed people-watching from my window and later through my camera lens. Iranian women wore mostly muted colors. The older women usually wore chadors, covered from head to toe in black robes with only their faces showing. Rarely did I see anyone wearing a *niqab*, the face covering or veil so common in Arab countries. The younger women wore dark slacks, long-sleeved tunics, and headscarves. Sometimes a woman dared to wear a touch of color—maybe a patterned headscarf, bold shoes, or an ornamental purse—but usually it was their makeup that showed signs of rebellion: bright nail polish, vibrant eye shadow, or deep red lipstick.

Desperate to fit in, or more to the point—not stand out—I decided to dress in the "uniform" as young Iranian women called it—black pants, brown and black tunic, and dark brown headscarf. Only later did I learn I should probably change into a plain black tunic because brown, or any color other than plain black, could be misunderstood as a sign of defiance, something like U.S. women in the 70s refusing to wear bras. I also realized the sandals I had brought would have to remain in my suitcase—women in Iran are allowed to show only their faces and hands, not their feet (it may not be illegal for a woman to show her feet, but it clearly was frowned upon. I never once saw a woman wearing sandals outside her own home). Once we returned to Tehran, I went tunic-shopping and bought myself the most ordinary-looking black manteau I could find. No matter what type of tunic I wore, however, my thick, waist-length braid refused to cooperate. It would not stay neatly coiled at the base of my neck, nor would it stay on my head without giving me a dreadful headache, and my scarf kept falling off. After several futile attempts, I decided to leave the braid hanging loose under my tunic, making me look like I had a deformed spine.

Curious Natives

Two of the tiniest old ladies I have ever seen were in the elevator when I got on to make my way to the conference. They must have been under five feet tall and were covered from head to toe in flowing black chadors. Their faces looked shrink-wrapped. They gave me the once-over in unison.

"Land?"

Are they asking what floor I want?

They tried again. "From?"

I see—"U-S."

Blank stares.

"U-S-A," I said with deliberate slowness.

Again, blank stares, but "United States of America" was greeted with an up-and-down nod.

"America!" One woman shot the other a look that clearly meant, "*I told you so.*"

The next day, I had another elevator encounter. A middle-aged Iranian woman stepped into the elevator. She was probably the wife of one of the physicians attending the conference (although she herself could have been a physician—Iran has a high percentage of female doctors). I greeted her with a "*Salaam,*" and she greeted me back with, "*Salaam alaikum.*" Then the doors opened again, and two more women joined us. They wore thick black under-robes, black chiffon over-robes, gold-trimmed headdresses, and bangles. The Iranian woman and I said, "*Salaam*" in unison, but the women didn't respond. Instead, they silently turned their backs to us and faced the elevator doors. *Wow*, I thought, *that was impolite—acting as if we didn't exist.* The Iranian woman looked at me, raised an eyebrow, and smiled. I realized these must be Arab women, and I had just experienced a touch of the animosity commonly felt between Arabs and Persians. By the time I left Iran, I had seen many a colorful headscarf, even some clearly imported from France as evidenced by their fleur-de-lis or Parisian monument motifs, but never another gold-trimmed hijab.

The MESOT Conference

The conference was well organized; I was told there were a thousand attendees, including a surgeon from Turkey who flew his team in by private jet. There were dozens of presentations to choose from, most of them medical, but I attended the few that dealt with transplant ethics. One such presentation was by Dr. Francis Delmonico, who lectured on the Istanbul Declaration, the World Health Assembly's 2004 resolution prohibiting the sale of organs, and the evils of compensating donors. He encouraged Iranians to reform their system to phase out kidney sales altogether.

Our MESOT hosts did not skimp on the entertainment. The final dinner featured traditional Persian food and music. In mid-November I was sitting at a cane table in a huge white tent under a warm, starlit sky. I had a buffet of new tastes to sample: saffron rice with *zereshk* (barberries); lamb, chicken, and beef kabobs; a variety of sumptuous meat-, vegetable-, or fruit-based curries; salads; herbs; and of course, an assortment of desserts, many featuring pistachios. The stage near my table continuously vibrated with singers and dancers who were mesmerizing, albeit at times a bit somber.

It was hard to take my eyes off the lovingly crafted traditional Persian instruments, many making vaguely familiar but haunting sounds. One man played the *santur*, a wooden instrument like a hammered dulcimer; several of the musicians had guitar-like instruments—a *kamancheh* (bowed lute) and an *ud* (fretless lute) but also a sitar (which is originally from Iran, though usually associated with India by Americans) and possibly a *tanbur* (another long-necked fretted instrument). There were at least a dozen drums, some of the *daf* (framed) type and others of the *tombak* (chalice-shaped) type. The music was vibrant and often tribal in its rhythms. I couldn't help but think that a few female singers and dancers might lighten the mood a bit, but of course, women are not allowed to perform in public in Iran.

Getting to Know You

Dr. Bastani and I didn't spend as much time together at MESOT as I would have liked. I was still a little concerned about setting off to do research with someone I barely knew. We both had to prepare for our presentations and had different talks and meetings to attend, but we did manage to find the time to have a few moments to cement our plans for how to proceed after the conference.

Dr. Bastani soon learned that I was a neophyte when it came to Persian culture. He was a natural teacher, and I was a willing student. He took me around to the shops in the Homa Hotel lobby and showed me how to recognize a high quality carpet—silk over wool, and the more knots per square centimeter, the finer the carpet. He also showed me beautiful marquetry made with inlaid woods of various kinds, bone, shell, bronze, silver, and gold that are arranged in intricate geometric patterns on boxes or picture frames. The best marquetry uses no paint at all: The colors are achieved by the variety of materials alone.

He offered to purchase a box with marquetry sides and painted peonies on the cover. I declined. Later he offered to purchase for me a small bowl inlaid with night-blue lapis lazuli. I declined again.

"Sigrid, you know it is customary in Iran to give people gifts as a way of sharing our culture."

"I'd rather not accept gifts from you."

"Why not?"

I hesitated, thinking I would say something akin to, "Just because." But then I realized I was planning to travel with this man for the next seven weeks; I had better be upfront with him. "Well, in my culture, accepting gifts from a man can give the wrong impression. Men tend to expect something in return."

He chuckled dismissively. "Let me buy you this one little box. You say you like horses; it has horses on it."

"OK." I nodded and gingerly took the delicately inlaid box from his hands. "But nothing else; I don't have room in my suitcase."

Persepolis: I'm the Target?

One of the outings arranged by conference planners was a visit to Persepolis, the great capital of the first Persian Empire. I was so taken by the magnificence of these ancient ruins that I went twice. Darius the Great began construction of the capitol palace complex in 518 B.C. Ill-fatedly, the Greeks destroyed it in 330 B.C. when Alexander the Great, after giving homage to Cyrus the Great, set fire to the city. By some accounts the nearly all-consuming conflagration was unintentional, but the damage was nonetheless unforgivable. The city's structures were mostly made of stone, but the roofs were of wood, and when they burned, the intense heat melted the iron and lead clamps that held together the roofs and adjacent structures.

The city was never rebuilt, but still standing today are hundreds of foundations, columns, doorways, staircases, and incredibly well-preserved stone reliefs. Also remarkably well preserved are cuneiform inscriptions in several ancient languages, including Ancient Persian, Neo-Babylonian, and Elamite, an ancient language unrelated to any of the Semitic, Sumerian, or Persian languages.

At the entrance gate to Persepolis, an inscription in the name of King Xerxes reads, "By the favor of Ahura Mazda I built this Gate of All Nations." And a gate to all nations it was. Persepolis included housing for ambassadors, dining halls, and bas-reliefs that depict the arrival of delegations—men wearing clothing and armor from various regions, bearing gifts (or paying taxes) to the Persian "king of kings." Archeologists have identified these people as including Ethiopians, Arabs, Thracians (ancient Greeks), Indians, Parthians (rulers of northeastern Iran), Cappadocians (from current day Turkey), Elamites (from just east of Mesopotamia), and Medes (from what is now central Iran).

Zoroastrian symbols of winged lions with human heads, bulls with bearded human faces, griffins, eagles, lotus flowers, and winged circles of light (or the sun) ornament the ruins, as do frequent references to the god Ahura Mazda. "Ahura" means light and "Mazda" means wisdom. The god Ahura Mazda is first among gods, the "uncreated" god of Zoroastrianism. I can't help but wonder if Ahura Mazda inspired Alexander the Great's teacher Aristotle when he famously described god as the "unmoved mover." An inscription on the palace of a hundred columns implores Ahura Mazda to protect the city from "famine, lies, and earthquakes." If only King Xerxes had known to also ask for protection from fire.

I walked around Persepolis with my mouth agape. I spent a brief but formative part of my life in Greece, and I have always been a great admirer of ancient history. Here I stood before the greatest monument in the world to the Persian counterpart to the Hellenic powers. Unlike the glories of Greece and Rome, however, these ancient architectural, cultural, and linguistic treasures are rarely seen by anyone other than Iranian schoolchildren and a few privileged foreigners. I was excited beyond belief to be there, but I felt sad for all those other lovers of archeology who would never be given the opportunity to see what remains of the greatness that was ancient Persia.

The sophistication of this ancient world mesmerized me, but the modern one kept intruding. I paused to take a photo, concentrating on capturing the velvet sunset smoothing the fissures in the griffin-crested columns, when an unwelcome hand found its way under my tunic. I spun, nearly hitting the grinning museum guard in the face with my camera. After a startled frozen instant and an angry locking of the eyes, I regained my composure, straightened my tunic with obvious intention, and resentfully headed for the refuge of our humming Mercedes Benz tour bus. Sitting high above the Persepolis parking lot, I looked down at the middle-aged conference-goers, carrying their cameras and sun hats, rocking the bus gently as they climbed onboard.

Again I was reminded of the realities of modern Iran, when on our way back from Persepolis, we had a three-car police escort leading and following our bus. As dusk fell in an inky cloak, their silent flashing lights held my attention, blurring my vision to the passing landscape. *We aren't dignitaries*, I thought, *but I guess we are potential targets. All of us?* There were two or three Americans on the bus, but the rest were Middle Easterners, mostly from Arab countries. *Yes, I suppose all of us.*

As far as I know, neither Dr. Delmonico nor any of the other Americans attending the conference other than Dr. Bastani and I ventured into Shiraz or the surrounding areas beyond the impressive MESOT-organized outings. After the conference, Dr. Bastani and I moved out of the Homa Hotel and into hospital housing, kindly arranged for us by Dr. Tabei, the head of the Department of Pathology and Medical Ethics at Shiraz University Medical School. At once, I realized the *real* visit to Iran was about to begin.

۴ (4)

Law, Hypocrisy, and the Black Market

Shiraz is known as the city of poets, wine, and flowers. Wine hasn't been legal in Shiraz since the Muslims conquered Persia in the seventh century A.D., but one can easily see why the city and its environs inspire poets. It was 70 degrees Fahrenheit in November. The sun shone brightly, but quite unlike the unforgiving desert sun I'd expected; the light glistened like diamond facets—both ephemeral and timeless, both soothing and exacting. There was a faint scent of citrus in the air. Palms, canna lilies, magnolias, and orange trees hung with fruit lined the streets; magpies were as common as sparrows. Shiraz served as the capital for several Muslim dynasties, and Cyrus the Great built his famous Persepolis in a neighboring valley. Even Genghis Khan spared Shiraz because of its allure. It was hard to concentrate on my research with so much beauty and history to explore.

"Toto, I've a feeling we're not in Kansas anymore"

The two-story apartment building where the university was kind enough to let us stay was located toward the back of the hospital complex with the other support facilities. We were given the phone number of a driver to call anytime, whether to tour the city or to take us to our speaking engagements and research interviews. Hospital housing in Shiraz was nothing like the four-star MESOT accommodations. There were no men in black suits with walkie-talkies roaming the grounds, no romantic gardens, no shops where silk carpets were sold for thousands of dollars, and no chicly robed Arab women gliding through marble lobbies. But the crows in spats and tuxes didn't discriminate: They were just as prevalent in the orange trees and palms surrounding this building as they had been at the Homa Hotel.

A demure, middle-aged woman, in full chador but no veil, greeted us at the entrance. She spoke briefly to Dr. Bastani, then, satisfied, retrieved two keys from a wooden cubby on the wall. She pointed down a brightly lit hall to the left as she handed Dr. Bastani his key, holding it out by the wooden room plaque so he could take the key without touching her. Then she motioned for me to follow her down the hall to the right. Dr. Bastani called over his shoulder, "Meet you in the lobby at 8 A.M. sharp!" The matron ushered me into my room, leaving my key on the table. She started to say something but stopped, probably realizing that asking me in Farsi if I needed anything was futile, so she exited, gently closing the door behind her.

The room reminded me of a college dorm before anyone had moved in, down to the musty smell of disinfectant. The room was furnished with a bed, a table, and a chair, but the walls were bare. Unlike a dorm, though, a white china bud vase with blue plastic-petaled daisies brightened the room. And although I didn't realize this until later, my room had the exceptional luxury of a Western-style toilet—a *clean* Western-style toilet, something I learned to appreciate during my stay in Iran. Iranian toilets are generally tiled holes in the floor with footrests and a hose for flushing—no commode, no seat, no cover, and no pressurized flush, not even a wall tank with a pull chain.

After leaving the Homa Hotel, I could no longer have my clothes laundered. Instead, I washed them with hand soap in the sink and hung them over the towel rack. I was amazed: Everywhere except for Tabriz, the climate was arid enough to dry my clothes in a few hours. I was glad I had brought olive butter for my skin.

I went to bed thinking Iran wouldn't be too different from what I had experienced while living in Argentina or Greece, but that night I awoke, disoriented and frightened, to the deafening sound of helicopters. There were at least three of them flying just above the housing complex. Wild thoughts raced through my mind. *Should I hide under the bed? Should I open my door and see if anyone else is panicking? Do I need to put on my hijab?* But before the last aircraft passed, I sank back into bed with the realization that the choppers sounded different than what I was used to: They weren't American-made. *I'm safe. It's not a U.S. or Israeli attack. At least not this night.* Nonetheless, throughout my stay in Iran I felt a sense of hyperalertness—a need to be an ever-vigilant observer in case my ignorance of the country and its people stumbled me into danger.

Lovers or Research

The next morning I got up, eager to begin my research. After a hospital-sponsored breakfast of naan, a boiled egg, a slab of creamy feta cheese, and walnuts, Dr. Bastani and I stepped outside to meet our driver. Adel was a jovial middle-aged man who was constantly asking Dr. Bastani questions about everything under the sun — our research, America, the upcoming Iranian presidential election, and even his personal aches and pains.

Adel took us to Namazi Hospital where Dr. Bastani and I gave our presentations. I can't follow a lecture in Farsi, so while Dr. Bastani spoke, I asked to check my email. A female doctor of about 30 accompanied me to a bank of computers and helped me access the Internet, but instead of leaving, she sat down beside me. I wondered if she was there to prevent me from accessing "forbidden" websites.

"I'm just checking my email."

She nodded. "Why are you here?"

"In Iran?"

"Yes. Iran is not an easy place for women."

It was evident she wanted to talk; my email could wait. "What do you mean?" I asked, thinking she might delve into a litany of women's rights issues from dress codes to inheritance rights, but she didn't. Instead, she wanted to know if I had children. "Yes, four," I said as I took a photo of my family out of my briefcase.

She pointed to Bob in the photo. "And you have a husband?"

"Yes, he—"

She cut me off. "But you are here with Dr. Bastani. It is hard for a lady-doctor to find a man in Iran."

I chuckled, seeing where the conversation was going. "No, Dr. Bastani and I are just research partners."

She furrowed her brow. "But he's so handsome!"

"Yes, but I'm married, and to me, my husband is more handsome."

She looked confused. "And he let you go to Iran with another man?"

Wow, I thought, *how can I explain in so little time?* I leaned over and placed my hand on hers, smiling. "I come from America. I discussed my project with my husband, but whether or not I go to Iran is not for him to decide."

I paused and watched her. I knew what was going through her mind, but how could I explain? *Only a person devoid of emotion doesn't on occasion feel temptation. The question is, what does she do when it happens? It helps to remember that a lack of foresight is at the root of most immorality.*

At that moment, a young man called from the doorway. "Dr. Bastani is waiting for you." As I got up to leave, my unmarried companion was so steeped in thought she forgot her manners and remained seated. When I said goodbye, she looked up at me and said in a quavering but forceful—almost scolding—voice, "If I had a husband and children like yours, I would stop being a doctor. I would never leave them."

Hospitality, Iranian Style

Later, Dr. Maryam Moeini and Dr. Mohammad Mehdi Sagheb treated us to lunch and showed us around Shiraz. Dr. Moeini reminded me of Forouzan, the first Iranian I remember meeting. Forouzan was a petite, feisty 19-year-old with large brown eyes, long lashes, and slightly unruly black curls. We were both in Geneva, Switzerland, for our college junior year abroad, and she had missed the first month because her visa was initially denied. At the time, the Iranian Revolution was young, and I asked her how she felt about the Ayatollah Khomeini. Her features hardened.

"You would never understand."

The assumption bothered me, given I had just met her, and although I did try to ask her again, she never said more than, "It's complicated." Since then, I frequently read about Iran, but when I finally got there, I never dared to ask anyone other than Dr. Bastani about the Revolution. I feared my inquiries might draw unwanted attention or raise suspicions about my motives for being there.

Dr. Moeini, like several women throughout my trip, pulled me aside and asked if I needed anything: shampoo, deodorant, feminine products?

"Yes, I need chocolate," I joked with a wink.

She gave me a knowing smile.

"No, no," I protested. "I don't need anything. I'm kidding." But the next morning, I found a shopping bag outside my door. I hesitated. *Sigrid, proceed with caution—there could be something dangerous inside. Poison gas? A bomb?* Then I glimpsed a dark brown and silver wrapper that gave Dr. Moeini away: a Hershey bar. The bag contained a dozen assorted candy bars, most with packaging immediately recognizable as Mars, Twix, and Hershey's. Dr. Moeini had left a note in Farsi, probably "It was nice meeting you. *Bon appétit!*" I smiled from ear to ear and bit into a Snickers before retreating to my room to take inventory.

I did enjoy the sweets, but I wondered if Dr. Moeini had intentionally brought me "American" chocolate—was there such a thing as Iranian chocolate? I saw some European-looking truffles in a pastry shop in Tehran, but none of the cookies, pastries, or desserts served at meetings, restaurants, or private homes contained chocolate. I later read a news report about a man who was sentenced to have his hand chopped off for stealing chocolate. A blogger commenting on the report pointed out that under Sharia law, the ordered amputation was non-negotiable because it was based on an explicit statement in the Qur'an: "As for the thief, both male and female, cut off their hands. It is the reward of their own deeds, an exemplary punishment from Allah." I couldn't help shuddering at the thought, but I reminded myself that such barbarism didn't diminish Dr. Moeini's sincere show of hospitality.

The whole time I was in Iran, people went out of their way to show me around and make sure my every need was met. I didn't know these people, yet they treated me as if I were an old friend. The only other place I ever felt this welcome was Greece. One of my favorite memories comes from a trip to the island of Mykonos. The day before Easter, my family took our motor home "Moby Dick" by ship to the island and parked on the beach. Easter morning we awoke to find a basket by the door filled with breads with whole eggs baked into the top of each loaf.

That same day, we were invited to dinner. We climbed a ladder up to the second story of a white plaster home to be greeted by the smiles of a middle-aged couple. I closed my eyes and breathed in deeply the aroma of roasted lamb. The woman of the house noticed, tapped my mother on the shoulder, pointed at me, and mimicked my obviously appreciative reaction. They both laughed. I was amazed by how the adults managed to communicate without a shared language: they gestured, pulled out wallet photos, and even drew on paper. Once I had eaten my fill of lamb and rice wrapped in grape leaves, I rested my head on my mother's lap and concentrated on a hand-woven, meander-patterned rug that hung over the doorless entryway. The rug moved ever so slightly in the breeze, allowing me to glimpse the measured advance of a single cloud floating across an azure sky.

In Iran, I also spent much of my time watching rather than listening. I rarely understood the details of conversations, but I did understand that Iranians were reaching out to a stranger, eager to bridge the gap of otherness in a way I had never experienced in Argentina, Germany, Switzerland, or France and rarely experience in the United States. Dr. Moeini's sweet gift was one such example; many more were to come.

I Stand Corrected

One of the sites Dr. Sagheb showed us was Hafez's tomb. The gardens around the mausoleum were fragrant and well tended. The weather was so lovely I could hardly believe it was November. People were silent, treading softly around

Hafez's sarcophagus, ebbing and flowing in and out of the sanctuary as they showed their respect, leaving roses as if he were a saint. I was prone to worship Hafez myself: My favorite poet, Goethe, called Hafez the greatest poet the world has ever known.

I was fascinated by a Sufi wise man offering advice in a corner of the museum shop. Dr. Bastani helped me ask if I could take his picture. The old man examined me stone-faced for 30 seconds or longer before agreeing. I knelt on one knee and aimed my camera while Dr. Bastani pulled out some money to pay the sage for his time.

When I got up and turned around, Dr. Sagheb was only a foot away. We both stepped back, but he stretched out a hand heavy with a volume of Hafez poems.

"For me?"

"I couldn't let you leave here without."

I fingered through the gilded pages of Arabic script and side-by-side English translations. I avoided making eye contact with Dr. Bastani as I accepted, thanking Dr. Sagheb profusely.

When Dr. Sagheb went to get the car, Dr. Bastani whispered with an impish note of triumph: "Room in your suitcase?"

"For Hafez?" I grinned up at him. "You bet!"

Drs. Moeini and Sagheb told us not to miss the Vakil Bazaar, so it was the first place we explored after they left. Reminiscent of something from *The Arabian Nights*, the Vakil is a maze of cavernous tunnels lined with shops under arched porticoes. Vendors sell everything from spices, jewelry, and rugs to housewares and ladies' undergarments. The colors, smells, and sounds drew us in.

Like most traditional Iranian bazaars, Vakil is divided into districts — it made me think of European guilds from the Middle Ages. Each type of merchant had his own section of the bazaar: sometimes a row in the main tunnels, sometimes an adjacent courtyard with homes above the shops. One section sold cooking pots, pans, and utensils, all aluminum and most big enough to feed a village. Another section sold jewelry, lacy pieces of gold and silver with semi-precious stones. A third sold inlaid boxes and picture frames made with the Khatam-kari style of marquetry: The workmanship I saw at the Vakil was as good or better than anything I saw in the shops at the Homa Hotel.

Wafting fragrances gave away the spice district long before we got there. Open burlap sacks were piled to overflowing with mounds of green and black cardamom, reddish-brown cinnamon, yellow and red saffron, and a seemingly never-ending variety of herbs I didn't recognize. The dazzling, rich hues brought bold flavors to mind. At home, spices are sold in tiny containers usually no bigger than a pill jar—I'd never seen so much cinnamon, let alone saffron, in one place. A football field's worth of the saffron crocus flower is needed to produce one pound of saffron. At home the spice can cost anywhere from $500 to $5,000 per pound, and I was looking at small mountains of it sitting out in the marketplace.

Other regions of the bazaar proudly displayed nuts and dried and candied fruit nearly overflowing their baskets, boxes, and glass jars. Still others had hookahs and tobacco, Persian paintings, and elephants, camels, and horses sculpted out of brass and tin. Some had printed textiles and madras bedspreads, placemats, and napkins hanging from the ceiling, and yet other regions revealed intricately woven Persian, Kurdish, and Ghashghaee carpets. I took pictures while the shopkeepers looked on, amused but possibly a little annoyed because I wasn't buying anything.

Next I stopped at an arch filled with garments that could have come straight from the Frederick's of Hollywood catalog. Mannequins lined the storefront, some wearing prom dresses with silk bows, while others sported lacy black and red bras, teddies, stockings, and garter belts. I pointed, curious. "So, Bahar, is this what Iranian women wear under their chadors?" My mind raced with questions I didn't dare ask out loud. *Why hasn't the government shut the store down for selling wares that lead to "unacceptable Western debauchery"? Where does the shop get its inventory? And when and where do Iranian women wear such things?* Dr. Bastani pretended not to hear my question, and I let it pass.

While Dr. Bastani shopped to replace a signet ring he'd lost, I started filming the echoing catacombs of people chatting and haggling. Some shoppers walked purposefully through the windowless tunnels with a particular find in mind, but others walked leisurely, relaxed, taking in the view as I did. *Why are things so different here than out on the main street? Are there morality police I haven't seen? If yes, why wouldn't they also come into the bazaar?* I wanted to capture the scene: the paintings of the Grand Ayatollahs Khomeini and Khamenei above the arches, the caged canaries hanging askew from hooks on the wall, the 8- or 9-year-old girl in an orange dress and purple headscarf dragging a white pillowcase filled with who knows what. Then with no warning, I felt a sharp slap on my arm. I steadied my camera with both hands and turned to see a young man's face, contorted in rage, much too close to mine. I could feel his breath. He was saying something loudly while gesturing toward the area where a woman sat on the floor with two children.

He demanded in broken English, "You film her?"

I quickly explained, "No, no—only the bazaar." I made a wide sweep with my arm and with shaking hands showed him the last screen shot in my camera's viewfinder.

A few people stopped to watch; others hurried by. But when Dr. Bastani strode over, the young man turned with a huff and disappeared into the churning masses. He wore no uniform; he carried no gun. He was just an average-looking young man in brown slacks and a mustard-colored anorak. I was stunned, frozen among the nebulous hustle and bustle, struggling to understand what had happened. *How can I protect myself from people like him?*

I realized then that playing tourist might jeopardize my research: I needed to be careful not to put my camera at risk. After Shiraz, I was more attentive to how my actions might be perceived, rarely filming anything other than our interviews.

Strangled by My Hijab

The next day we attended the dedication ceremony for Iran's first doctorate program in medical ethics. The elevator was out-of-order, so we had to trudge up four flights of stairs. It was not the last malfunctioning elevator I would encounter in Iran, but it was the first, and I had pridefully overestimated my fitness. Dr. Bastani carried most of my camera equipment for me, but by the time I reached the third flight of stairs, I desperately wanted to shed my tunic and hijab. Most of the time I wore a *maghnae* instead of a headscarf because my hair was all but impossible to keep under control and hidden with just a scarf. My *maghnae*, made of a stretchy, elastic material, fit tightly around my face and covered my neck under my tunic, allowing me to feel secure about not violating any laws by accidentally showing too much hair. But now, climbing in a hot, stuffy stairwell, sweat pooling at my temples, I wished I could tear off the itchy synthetic cowl.

By the time we reached the fifth floor, my distress was evident: Most people were drinking tea, but a kind nurse fetched me a glass of tepid water. *How do Iranian women survive in the summer?* My guess is that most don't wear a *maghnae*, but they still have to wear long sleeves and long pants or long robes and head coverings in temperatures that can exceed 100 degrees Fahrenheit. *How on earth do they manage? Do they even go out during the day? They probably know better than to climb four flights of stairs in the heat with no air conditioning!* Dr. Bastani later confirmed that Iranian women do tend to avoid the sun, so much so that many suffer from vitamin D deficiency with its consequent bone loss and muscle pain.

I relaxed into my seat in the small conference room filled with faculty, some in suits and ties and others in white lab coats. Also present were several members of the press with cameras and notepads poised. And then there was the gentleman at the front of the room, looking stern and being shown great deference.

The West Treats People Like Animals

I could not understand Dr. Ali Akbar Velayati as he gave his impassioned speech in Farsi. Dr. Velayati, professor of pediatrics at Tehran Medical School, foreign minister immediately after the Iranian Revolution, and currently an advisor on international affairs to Supreme Leader Ayatollah Khamenei, was there as spokesperson for the Iranian Ministry of Health and Medical Education (Ministry of Health). He personally didn't look all that unusual in his white button down shirt and grey jacket, but he was accompanied by a dark-robed mullah in a black turban and full beard—an ayatollah probably present to ensure this ceremony to inaugurate an ethics program didn't stray from Islamic principles, or perhaps to give it religious credibility.

All the other men present wore a closely cropped beard and mustache like Dr. Bastani's, or the Shi'ite five-o'clock shadow, and no one other than the ayatollah wore a robe or turban. The "need a shave" look is normal in Iran. It is the minimum length required to show adherence to Muslim rules for wearing a beard. The Prophet Mohammad said that men should grow beards, so mullahs grow long beards and the pious Sunni will wear a beard of at least two inches, but for the Shi'ites, any beard at all will do. So most of the men in the room that day, like most Iranian men in general, wore a beard that looked more like stubble.

Dr. Velayati raised his arm and gesticulated with his index finger, shaking it up and down or circling it in the air. Suddenly, he looked directly at me as he spoke. I had no idea what he was saying, but Dr. Bastani discreetly jotted something down on a notepad and slid it sideways to me after Dr. Velayati moved on to another topic. Like many doctors, Dr. Bastani's handwriting was difficult to decipher, but I got the gist of the message: "He says the West treats humans like animals, BUT in Iran, we will teach our doctors to follow the dictates of the Qur'an and treat patients with the respect they deserve."

At a round table discussion after the ceremony, I was peppered with questions about medical ethics in the United States. I did my best to answer but also managed to squeeze in a question or two of my own. "How does following the Qur'an mean people are treated with more respect than in the West?" It was explained that in the West we usually think of humans as evolved animals, while Muslims place human beings in a different category from animals, emphasizing that people deserve a special degree of respect because they are God's representatives on Earth. It was also tactfully pointed out to me that in Iran, patients and medical staff share the same cultural and religious perspective—so unlike in the United States, the chances of violating someone's religious beliefs is slight.

This latter point ran counter to what I understood about Iran. I was under the impression that Iran was quite diverse with significant ethnic, cultural, linguistic, and even religious minorities. There are Kurds, Azeris, Turkmen, Lors, Baluchis, Nomads, and Arabs as well as considerable numbers of Christians, Jews, Sunnis, Zoroastrians, and Baha'is, all of whom (except the Baha'is) are officially tolerated. I realized that it would be unwise to bring up that Iran is like the United States in any way, but there were similarities. After all, both have to deal with a variety of different religions and cultures living side-by-side. Instead I timidly pressed the issue of informed consent: "Isn't informing patients important regardless of potential religious or cultural differences?" But it seemed even that was a mistake.

One of the physicians reacted viscerally, responding in an unusually emphatic tone for an Iranian professional. To the agreement of some and the embarrassment of others, he launched into a tirade about how the West has no comprehension of what it means to practice medicine in Iran. As I listened, I realized he didn't have a philosophical objection to informed consent; he had a practical one. "I already work every hour available in the day. How can I be expected to spend time explaining procedures and answering questions?"

I was acutely aware that there was an arc of stillness forming around us — people had stopped drinking their tea or taking notes and were listening intently. "Informed consent in principle is good," he scoffed, "but it is enough that patients consent to my treating them and using my best judgment." He grew more impassioned as he gained momentum, encouraged by other physicians nodding their support. If he took the time to answer patients' questions, or "Allah forbid, the questions of family members," the process of providing treatment would get bogged down — enough so that he and his colleagues could not see as many patients as they currently did. Some people would not be seen in time, and others might not be seen at all. "People would die!" *Perhaps*, I wondered in silent frustration, *but why can't an oil-rich country like Iran train more doctors and maybe some nurse practitioners?* But I'd caused enough turmoil for one afternoon — probably more than I should have. Stoking their suspicions about Western ethical imperialism wouldn't help me get access to their patients.

Dr. Bastani later explained that immediately after the Revolution there was an acute physician shortage and many hospitals are still short of staff. Of his medical school class, fewer than a third remained in Iran, and for those who remained, life was hard. Among the challenges they faced were poor facilities and a lack of supplies. He even told me that one of his classmates was stoned to death for having sexual relations with a patient.

It started to dawn on me that many of the freedoms and rights we take for granted in the West are luxuries in Iran. Doctors shouldn't have to choose between providing treatment and taking the time to let patients ask questions. Yet, in developing countries like Iran, physicians make appallingly difficult resource-allocation decisions every day that Americans rarely have to face. Can we honestly blame them if they decide treatment comes first and that they don't have time for detailed explanations, let alone the formalities of informed consent?

That night we ate dinner at the home of Dr. Mahvash Alizadeh, a female physician who teaches patient-care ethics at the University of Shiraz. I asked what she thought of the informed consent debate we had witnessed earlier that day. She acknowledged the problem and told me, quite ironically given what Dr. Velayati had said at the dedication ceremony, that she spent much of her time trying to teach medical students to treat their patients like people, not like widgets in an assembly line. "It only takes a second or two," Dr. Alizadeh tells her students, "to say 'hello' and give someone a smile before diving into the chore at hand."

She pointed out that Iranian culture would need to change before a Western-style informed consent could be implemented. I was reminded of what it was like in Argentina where I often watched my grandfather with his patients. He told me, "Rightly or wrongly, patients and their families don't ask many questions: The ethos is one of trust. To tell them they should be asking more questions would make them suspicious." The same was true in Iran. Dr. Alizadeh went on to say something that comes to mind every time I struggle to maintain perspective: "Sometimes your Western sophistication gets in the way of real-life solutions." *Is Dr. Alizadeh right?* I wondered. *Could this insight apply to how the West views the Iranian solution to the organ shortage? In the West, people die waiting for kidneys, and anyone who tries to encourage donation by offering more than a "thank you" risks jail time and a hefty fine—where's the ethics in that?*

After such a profound discussion about the allocation of medical resources and patients' rights, I felt guilty for having to bring up a mundane problem, but I needed help figuring out how to store my video. The incident at the Vakil Bazaar brought some urgency to the situation: If I didn't take steps to preserve my work, all could be lost. At home I would have consulted one of my teenagers, so I asked Dr. Alizadeh if any of her children could help, and, not unexpectedly, one of her sons was impressively tech-savvy. Mosab was fascinated by my Sony Blu-ray HD camera and laptop (the exportation of Blu-ray capable devices to Iran is banned under the Western technology embargo), and he eagerly explored how to help me preserve my video in the highest resolution possible. He spent over an hour teaching me how to download and code film data, and he even went out and purchased several small external drives so that I could easily store and hide my raw video footage.

A Government-Regulated Kidney Market Is Born

There was so much I needed to learn to understand the cultural and historic context for how Iran became the only country in the world to legalize kidney sales. As the Iranian system evolved, it ended up taking several approaches to solving the organ shortage. Among more recent developments is the Western-like approach taken by Shiraz where kidney sales are de facto illegal.

In most countries, compensating donors for anything beyond expenses directly related to the donation is illegal. In those countries where the practice of selling kidneys is not explicitly outlawed, it is nonetheless frowned upon. In all countries except Iran, kidney donors can only be paid on the black market, leaving both donors and recipients vulnerable to scam artists and neither with legal recourse if cheated.

In the 1960s and through most of the 1970s before the Islamic Revolution, Iran was part of the Eurotransplant Network. Iranian patients often went abroad for transplant operations at government expense. As program relationships developed, cadaver kidneys were sometimes sent from Europe to Iran for transplantation. But after the Revolution, Iran's relationship with the Eurotransplant Network collapsed. Due to sanctions and financial constraints, Iran had to develop an independent solution to its kidney shortage. Iran didn't have the infrastructure or resources to develop a cadaver organ program, so a system based solely on living donation evolved. Recipients began to pay non-related living donors. Because the medical community didn't want to see patients die, doctors and other medical professionals initially looked the other way when it came to donor remuneration, but with time they hesitantly condoned compensation.

By the mid-1980s, Iranians began talking about regulating the practice of compensated kidney donation. The medical community discussed possible guidelines, while the families of kidney disease patients pressed for government regulation. The Red Crescent (the Iranian equivalent of the Red Cross) was matching donors and recipients, but kidney disease patients felt the process needed streamlining. First and foremost, they wanted a stronger intermediary to vet donors and help ensure honest dealing and compliance with contractual obligations. Some recipients had trouble with donors taking deposits and then reneging on their promises to donate; others paid for donor testing only to learn that donors didn't qualify to donate because they had lied about their health status. And many recipients felt strongly that donors needed more compensation than recipients could offer—among other things, recipients wanted donors to receive non-monetary compensation in the form of health insurance.

As so often happens, it took a shocking incident to motivate government to act. Not long after Dr. Jacobs' misguided proposal to start a living kidney donor import business and the U.S. Congress' subsequent decision to ban organ sales, a grim story hit the Tehran newsstands: A transplant recipient's family was brutally attacked by a donor for no apparent reason, and two of the recipient's children were stabbed to death. The transplant community was galvanized into action, and for political reasons the national government had no choice but to act. The *Majilis*, the Iranian parliament, granted approval for the formation of non-governmental organizations (NGOs) to work with kidney disease patients as intermediaries to help depersonalize the process, standardize procedures, and generally see after the interests of kidney disease patients.

These non-profit NGOs were staffed by Iranian volunteers who themselves were mostly kidney transplant recipients, though some were kidney donors. They focused on helping kidney disease patients find donors and medical and social assistance but also quickly realized the value of trying to keep donors happy. Satisfied donors were more likely to share their good experiences with others, who in turn might be less hesitant to donate themselves. These organizations have official names like "The Iranian National Kidney Foundation," "The Association for the Protection of Kidney Patients," and "The Charity for Special Diseases." Iranians generally referred to them simply as the *Anjomans*, literally, "the associations" or "the institutions."

For over 20 years, the *Anjomans* have worked closely with the medical community to improve the lives of kidney disease patients. They've institutionalized practices that facilitate the donor/recipient matching process. They've achieved benefits for kidney disease patients and their families, ranging from subsidized donor payments to dental benefits. For donors, so far they've successfully lobbied for the national government to provide an *issar*—a gift of one million tomans (approximately $1,000 at the time I was in Iran, but with the purchasing power equivalent of $3,000 to $4,000* if used to cover everyday living expenses). Additional government benefits for donors include one year health insurance and an exemption from Iran's mandatory two-year military service for men.

One watershed development happened in 1992 when the Ministry of Health decided to prohibit the sale of kidneys to foreigners. At first Iran had no restrictions

---

* Please see Notes section for Chapter Two for a discussion of how difficult it is to estimate purchasing power.

on who could receive or donate a kidney other than the obviously necessary medical constraints. With time, however, it became evident that Iranians were being exploited as a kidney resource for the rest of the world. Worse still, high-income foreign transplant recipients were pricing Iran's own kidney disease patients out of the market, so the Iranian government took steps to restrict its kidney market to its own citizens. The Ministry of Health implemented rules that limited kidney sales transactions to people of the same nationality. Foreigners, including refugees, could bring a donor of their own nationality (paid or unpaid) to have a transplant operation in Iran, but they couldn't purchase a kidney from, or sell a kidney to, an Iranian. A corollary guideline allowed refugees to continue receiving the same free dialysis services provided to Iranian citizens, but unlike Iranian nationals, they could not have transplant operations at government expense.

Beyond these overarching national regulations and guidelines, each individual province, hospital system, medical team, and *Anjoman* maintained considerable latitude in how to implement the national requirements. As a result significant variations have developed. One recent development is a concerted effort to increase the supply of cadaver organs.

As I was about to learn, the province of Shiraz deviated furthest from what is commonly called "the Iranian model." Of all the provinces I visited, Shiraz's system is closest to how organ procurement is practiced in the West. The Shiraz transplant community prohibits recipients from paying kidney donors. Instead, the *Anjoman* promises donors only the one million tomans provided by the national government and refers to that payment as a gift intended to help defer donation related expenses, not a payment for the sale of a kidney.

Getting to the Point of My Trip

After several days of sightseeing, dinners, lunches, innumerable teas where we were served cucumbers, oranges, and pastries, and many interviews with doctors, transplant coordinators, dialysis patients, and a few transplant recipients, I plucked up the nerve to ask, "When do we get to interview kidney sellers?" Dr. Bastani gave me an indulgent smile and counseled patience. I was feeling time-conscious and slightly agitated, worried that the days were ticking by without my achieving my objective.

I've always been an "up and at 'em" kind of person, and while I was enjoying learning about Iranian culture, I was beginning to wonder if I would ever get the chance to interview kidney sellers directly. I knew Dr. Bastani meant well; after all, this was his culture, not mine. But all these formalities were costing me precious time. Yet, there was nothing I could take into my own hands to move things forward. I had to restrain my impulses, sit back, and rely on Dr. Bastani. Without him, there would be no interviews at all.

I gradually learned the routine: We gave the lectures we promised, enjoyed our hosts' hospitality, and then, once we had met all our obligations and they had the chance to evaluate our motives, we could ask for access to the transplant wards and to be introduced to *Anjoman* administrators. Then at the *Anjoman*, the process would repeat (albeit in abbreviated fashion) before we could interview kidney sellers in various stages of the process: inquiring about compensated donation, checking the status of their applications after deciding to donate, undergoing medical and psychological evaluations, processing payment, and receiving services after the donation.

My good fortune in having Dr. Bastani's assistance did not escape me. He arranged and handled all the meetings with acumen. His orderly and methodical manner demanded respect and reflected his stature and reputation as a professor of medicine. He was uncannily successful at timing his requests so that hardly any were denied. I was impatient but forever grateful.

The Shiraz *Anjoman*

For five days we did interviews at hospitals and dialysis centers with mostly transplant administrators and support staff. Finally on November 26, we had our first interviews at an *Anjoman*. We had trouble finding the place because the building had no sign. We walked around, trying to get our bearings. This part of Shiraz was not one to inspire poets. It was balmy, as elsewhere in Shiraz, but there were no palm trees to provide shade and no picturesque lawns with magpies or even crows. Sunglasses were a must, not only against the bright light as elsewhere in Iran, but also against the dust.

Dust rarely intruded in affluent areas of Shiraz where vegetation was well watered and lush, but in this less well-kept area of the city, it was everywhere: on the cars, windows, rooftops, even on a solitary stray cat pressed against a wall, which wore its dust-crusted coat with indignation. I'd never seen anything like this townscape, swathed in beige and a disconcertingly alien silence.

I fumbled under my tunic for the lip balm in my pant pocket as Dr. Bastani studied a scrap of paper with the *Anjoman*'s address. We were relieved when the stillness was broken by a woman rounding the corner. She almost didn't stop, but when Dr. Bastani explained that we were lost, she softened and guided us to the *Anjoman*.

It was hard for me to believe that this was an official workplace of any kind, let alone the Fars Province headquarters of the Iranian National Kidney Foundation. The office was in the upper level of a townhouse in a bad part of town—well, at least not a good part of town. It was a neighborhood overlooked, ignored, forgotten, and surrounded by narrow streets and graffiti-covered walls, the occasional shuttered gate, and a few listless saplings someone had over-optimistically planted along the street.

Once inside, we climbed a steep, narrow staircase. I gripped the wrought-iron rail for support and felt the uneven texture of paint over patches of rust. I briefly feared the door at the top of the stair would be locked, but it opened easily onto a tiny lobby that looked more like a large landing. Nurse Ehyako-nande was up from her desk and greeting us before we even had a chance to make inquiries. A round, ruddy-faced woman, she approached with the stiffness characteristic of a dialysis patient.

The office was clean but dingy, filled with a hodgepodge of desks and furniture that must have been donated from a variety of sources. None of the office doors matched: One was blue with a milky windowpane and the other solid brown. I couldn't place the malodor—maybe cat, but I didn't notice any food or litter box. Nurse Ehyakonande smiled as she ushered us into a conference room, but she seemed nervous, even anxious. I hoped we weren't the cause of her distress.

I sank into the worn-out sofa cushions with the uncomfortable feeling that getting up might require more coordination than I could gracefully muster. Weary but excited to finally begin, I maneuvered myself to the edge of the sofa and was pleased to discover how well the hot tea moistened my dry lips. Several members of the *Anjoman* staff perched on dining room chairs around a low coffee table, looking as awkward as I felt as we sipped tea from mismatched glasses. A black, potbellied gas heater stood in the corner, and there, leaning against the wall by the stove, was the missing sign. Arabic script encircled a stylized twelve-petaled lotus flower like eddies of water—the sign read "The Fars Kidney Foundation."

By contrast, the National Kidney Foundation office in Ann Arbor, Michigan, which I had visited only a month earlier, was a free-standing brick building with a two-story solid glass front, a turnabout with flower beds full of mums, ornamental grasses, bushes, and a flag pole. Red maples and yellow sugar-gum trees were carefully choreographed on hills of lawn that surrounded the building. I remember pausing for a moment to take a deep breath of crisp fall air and letting the soft sunshine stroke my face before entering. The Michigan NKF headquarters had all the modern conveniences of a twenty-first century office building: recessed lighting, computers, Xerox machines, a high-tech video conference room, and furniture specifically designed for office use. Nothing mismatched, teacups or otherwise, and although I have no idea how old the building was, a certain newness still lingered. But the contrast wasn't all negative. The Shiraz *Anjoman*, however dilapidated, had its own charm, a homiiness that no modern office building could ever achieve.

After introductions and several glasses of tea, it was time to start filming. Nurse Ehyakonande initially refused to be interviewed, but after other staff members kept asking her questions, we impressed upon everyone that she should be included. Camera-shy, she carefully positioned her chair several feet to the side and slightly behind the men, not realizing that if I wanted to I could easily focus my lens on her alone. I heard voices out in the lobby and wondered if we were missing a valuable opportunity. The voices came and went, but when our interview was done and the door was left open, I saw someone else come into the *Anjoman*.

My First Kidney Seller

Ismail entered the lobby tentatively as if unsure he had found the correct place. Nurse Ehyakonande spoke to him briefly and then ushered him into the conference room.

Dr. Bastani welcomed Ismail with a reassuring smile.

"This will only take a few minutes. Ismail, right?"

Ismail nodded but stood ill at ease in the middle of the room. A hunched elderly man I hadn't seen before appeared with an offer of fresh tea and oranges. Dr. Bastani offered Ismail a seat. We accepted tea, but Ismail did not; he darted glances in my direction, not quite sure what to make of me. I looked down, grateful to have a tea glass to examine. His gaze shifted from me to the doorway, as if to ensure an avenue of retreat should he need one.

That his name is an Arab variant of the Hebrew Ishmael didn't escape me. The Ishmael of my favorite American novel *Moby-Dick* introduced me to the world of whaling; perhaps this Ismail would introduce me to the world of kidney selling.

My video camera was a necessary evil. This research was my idea, and because I didn't speak Farsi, I needed to record as much as possible for future translation. But my being a woman helped: clad in "uniform" (the standard hijab, long-sleeved dark tunic, and long black pants worn by most young professionals at work) I blended in quite well. And because it wasn't culturally acceptable for anyone, particularly not men, to do more than acknowledge my presence, my camera and I were generally ignored and quickly melted into the background.

Dr. Bastani began with his usual opening: "Hello, my name is Dr. Bastani. We've come from the United States to conduct interviews regarding the process of kidney transplants in Iran."

Ismail shrugged, and Dr. Bastani gave me the go-ahead. As I set up the camera, Ismail watched me with a mixture of uneasiness and curiosity, but Dr. Bastani skillfully redirected him. "Don't worry about the camera; just talk to me."

Now, behind the lens, I could take a good look at Ismail without violating any social norms. He was young, maybe 25, with wavy black hair, intense eyes, a faint smile, and a silver wedding band on his left hand. His khaki-colored pants were frayed at the cuffs, but his sweater—an open crew neck striped in light blue, navy, and white—looked new. The sweater seemed out of place given how warm it was, but his black open-toed sandals did not. His hair was neatly cut, slightly dulled from working in the sun. He had a mustache of respectable thickness, but his beard was only stubble—the Muslim five-o'clock shadow so common in Iran.

Dr. Bastani considered becoming a surgeon, but instead specialized in nephrology so he could have more interaction with patients. That Dr. Bastani is a people person showed in how quickly he put Ismail at ease. As they spoke, Dr. Bastani began to translate for me, but I told him there was no need to interrupt the flow of conversation. I had everything on tape, and he could tell me the highlights after the interview.

Dr. Bastani was totally focused on the task at hand, barely glancing at his notes before leaning into the discussion. Their melodic banter reminded me of French or Italian. I let the sound of their voices wash over me as I took mental notes of their tone and manner of speech, Ismail's demeanor, the way the room smelled, and any other goings-on around us the camera might miss. This was why I had come to Iran!

"They told us that you want to donate your kidney. Would you introduce yourself and talk to us?"

"In the name of God, my name is Ismail. I want to donate my kidney because I have troubles in life and financial problems."

I couldn't help but wonder, when Dr. Bastani later told me what Ismail had said, if his honesty would cost him the opportunity to donate—Shiraz forbids non-altruistic kidney donation, and Ismail had admitted he needed money.

Ismail's Mistake

The University of Shiraz's transplant team, which performs all transplants in the region, requires that potential kidney recipients try to find an altruistic donor or wait for a cadaver kidney for at least six months after beginning dialysis before pursuing a non-related, paid, living kidney donation. In Shiraz, like in the West, we often heard that getting paid for a kidney is unethical and that it is best to use cadaver organs to avoid exploitation, but I think the motivation in Shiraz is quite different than in the West.

Although preemptive transplants from living kidney donors have been shown to produce the best outcomes for recipients, other types of transplants are usually done with cadaver organs. Heart and pancreas transplants are totally dependent on a supply of cadaver organs, while others, such as liver transplants are usually performed with cadaver organs because live donation can be dangerous for the donor.

For historic, economic, and religious reasons, cadaver organ donation has been sorely neglected in Iran. Because over 90 percent of all transplant patients need kidneys, Iran had focused on kidneys to the detriment of other types of transplants until Dr. Malekhosseini became head of surgery at Shiraz University Medical School in 1989. Dr. Malekhosseini wanted to encourage cadaver donations to create a source of organs for liver, heart, and pancreas transplants. His solution was to require that kidney transplants be done with cadaver organs. That way, potential kidney recipients and their families would encourage the cadaver organ donations needed to benefit both themselves and patients needing other organs. Dr. Malekhosseini's program performs almost all the liver and pancreas transplants in Iran, with an emphasis on liver transplants. Dr. Malekhosseini estimated that in 2008 his team did 180 to 200 liver transplants and only 140 to 160 kidney transplants.

Ismail, unlike almost all of the other potential donors we spoke to in Shiraz, didn't know he was supposed to lie about his motivations. Unfortunately, one of the *Anjoman* administrators was present when Ismail shared his financial woes:

> I'm just a laborer; I do whatever job I can find—with my problems in life, I have to. It's almost winter, and I can't save enough money; life is so difficult. I can't ask somebody every day to let me borrow money. That is why I have to give up part of my body. It is for my wife and child.

Ismail was in debt to family and friends, and his parents and in-laws were also barely scraping by. He was hoping for five or six million tomans,* enough to purchase a used car to start a taxi business like his father's. Incongruously, the *Anjoman* told us the going rate in Shiraz for a kidney is four million tomans, three million from the recipient in addition to the one million provided by the national government—information they willingly shared with donors and recipients though they also informed them that they are not allowed to admit to any money changing hands.

"What is your hope for the future?" Dr. Bastani asked Ismail.

"My hope is that I am able to earn a decent living for my family, so I don't need to ask anybody for help. I need to earn bread for my wife and child so I am not ashamed of myself in front of people."

"Do you think donating your kidney for money is a good way, or would it be better if, as in other countries, it were illegal to donate for financial incentives?"

Ismail blanched. But as the color incrementally returned to his face, he shifted forward in his chair and continued in a steely tone, "What should a poor laborer do? When our society is not helping its young people, you have to sell your organs. Other countries probably help their people somehow." His voice wavered then regained its resolve. "Otherwise when I am hungry and have no money, I am going to become a thief. … I can't predict what will happen when someone runs out of money. What's left? They go stealing or killing for money."

Dr. Bastani asked what Ismail's parents and in-laws thought about his donating a kidney. Ismail replied that it was none of their business, but also that it would be hard to keep them from finding out.

Dr. Bastani probed further, "Why don't you want them to know?"

"Helping a sick person get well is surely a deed praised by Allah," Ismail said, "But they will know I'm a failure for having to resort to selling part of my body. It means I'm not a good provider, not a good man."

---

   * See notes to Chapter Two at the end of the book for a discussion of how much this is in U.S. dollars and how to determine the purchasing power of 5 million tomans.

When I saw how upset Ismail was getting, I asked Dr. Bastani what was going on, and he translated for me. With Dr. Bastani's help, I wanted to know why Ismail's wife didn't donate instead. Ismail responded that she had the baby to take care of and, as the man, it was his responsibility to bring in money, not hers. "Besides, people will think badly of her too—like, what will she sell next?"

There was a knock on the door, and Nurse Ehyakonande told Ismail that his wife was there. A young woman in a saffron-colored headscarf opened the door a crack, and I saw a baby girl, maybe 9 or 10 months old, dressed in a pink jumper, chewing on her own fist. The baby gurgled. The woman scolded Ismail, while instinctually bouncing the baby on her hip. He literally leapt out of his seat, rushed past us, and left the *Anjoman*, wife and child in tow.

I must have looked puzzled because Dr. Bastani quickly filled me in. "Something about, 'Why was he taking so long?' and that the baby needs milk."

The Charade

Several nurses we interviewed later at Namazi Hospital told us that money almost always exchanged hands. Other medical professionals and *Anjoman* administrators told us if people were paying for kidneys, they didn't know about it and didn't want to know. Because both donors and recipients had to sign statements on their applications to participate in the matching program that said there would be no payment, most of the donors we spoke to lied or said all they wanted was the one million tomans they were getting from the national government. Something my father used to say came to mind: "Bad laws can make liars out of even the best of men."

I couldn't help but wonder whether this system was any better than a black market. But then I realized donors are guaranteed one million tomans and one year of health care from the government, and while this is little compared to the benefits donors receive in other parts of Iran, it at least provides donors a modicum of protection—something that doesn't exist when donors sell their kidneys on the black market as they do in other countries. But in Shiraz, like on the black market, if recipients refuse to pay the agreed amount, donors have no legal recourse to help them collect.

We have no way of knowing how often recipients renege on their promises to donors; all we know is that recipients are not legally obligated to keep their promises—in fact, as far as the law is concerned, they're obligated not to. Mr. Badei, the head of the Shiraz *Anjoman*, said he was familiar with a case where a donor was arrested for harassment when he claimed his recipient hadn't paid as promised.

Dr. Bastani asked Mr. Badei not to exclude Ismail simply because he was honest, but we never found out if Ismail donated his kidney, whether he was able to purchase a car to become a taxicab driver, or whether he found a job. Two-and-a-half years later, we tried calling him, but the cell phone number he had given us was no longer valid. Ismail may have come back to the *Anjoman* and, being the wiser for having had the interview with us, said nothing about his financial situation. And maybe the *Anjoman* staff, as was evidently their practice, would let him sign the sworn statement that he was motivated by altruism alone without probing any further.

We asked Mr. Badei if Ismail could go to another region in Iran to sell his kidney, but he informed us that forum shopping is against Ministry of Health regulations and impractical. If Ismail had relatives in another province, it would be possible to establish a temporary residence for the sake of arranging a kidney donation, but that would mean more time away from work (or from looking for work) and time away from his family. In addition, he would have to absorb all the costs of traveling to the region not just for testing, transplant surgery, and post-operative care but also for benefits provided by the contracting *Anjoman* such as healthcare services, job counseling, and household goods. The potential difficulty of taking advantage of such benefits at a distance rarely makes it worth the effort of registering to donate in another district.

What about Money for Cadaver Organs?

Maryam, a petite, soft-spoken young woman who worked on PR for the Shiraz *Anjoman*, enthusiastically told us all about the Shiraz deceased donor program. She shared how kidney recipients from Shiraz had won in Iran's version of the Special Olympics and how she personally had persuaded hundreds of people to sign up to be cadaver organ donors. During our interview, I noticed some of the telltale signs of a transplant recipient: Maryam had peach fuzz on her cheeks and slightly pock-marked skin, all potential side effects of anti-rejection medication. But she also had large ebony eyes with long, pronounced lashes—a feature that she accentuated with dark eyeliner and plenty of blue eye shadow. Dr. Bastani teased her about her eyes and how beautiful they would look on film. She flushed apricot and suppressed a girlish giggle.

Maryam explained that it would not be possible in Iran to give money to the families of deceased donors, but valuable non-monetary gifts are quite common. A headstone, resolved medical bills, free transportation of the deceased's body to the burial site, and a medical staff representative speaking at the funeral are all things regularly provided in Shiraz. Maryam explained that it would be unthinkable to give money directly to the family of a deceased donor—unconscionable to set up a system that allowed family members to benefit financially from the death of a loved one. To do so, Maryam stressed, would destroy cadaver organ donation in Iran: "It would become a dishonorable enterprise if families were given cash, even if such cash were supposedly to cover donation-related expenses."

"This is not true for living donation, because living donors decide for themselves to give of their bodies to save another," Maryam explained. On the black market, where desperate Americans sometimes purchase kidneys, the potential for someone being hoodwinked into donating by a third party (or even drugged or forced to donate unwillingly) is all too real. But in Iran, where donors are protected by law, it isn't a third party who decides to take a donor's kidney for the third-party's benefit—it is donors who decide for themselves.*

Bad News for Nurse Ehyakonande and Maryam's Dilemma

That day, before we left the *Anjoman*, the ruddy-faced Nurse Ehyakonande pulled Dr. Bastani aside and showed him some lab results. Bad news: The kidney her older sister had given her 20 years ago was failing. This explained both the stiffness I mistook for her being on dialysis and her anxious and distracted manner. Nurse Ehyakonande had more important things on her mind than

---

* The basic principle that individuals should be able to consent to give *of themselves* for money, but that others should not have the right to do so, is as true in the United States as it is in Iran. After all, we pay many kinds of self-sacrificing heroes: military personnel, emergency medical teams, firefighters, and other rescue workers, who risk life and limb for the sake of others. In the United States, like in Iran, it is acceptable to help oneself (e.g., get paid) for helping others even at great sacrifice to oneself. However, compensating the relatives of potential cadaver organ donors, while perhaps not dishonorable like in Iran, would nonetheless result in potentially problematic conflicts of interest in the United States. It could create perverse incentives for family members to make treatment or non-treatment decisions in order to hasten death and/or improve the chances of preserving organs to ensure payment. And, even if paying relatives did not actually create such perverse incentives, it could nonetheless create an impression of impropriety.

visitors from America. Her doctor said she needed a new kidney, but she hoped the "big" doctor from America would see things differently. Regrettably, Dr. Bastani could not change the facts. The labs were clear: She would need a new kidney soon.

Patients, staff, and doctors would frequently ask Dr. Bastani for his opinion on everything from a patient's diagnosis and treatment to reviewing academic papers or whether Dr. Bastani could help someone get a visa to come to the United States. Later that day, Dr. Bastani was even asked to act as marriage counselor.

Maryam, the PR coordinator who had graciously answered our questions about cadaver organ donation, asked Dr. Bastani if he could tell whether her kidney, which she had received from a deceased donor a decade earlier, would fail like Nurse Ehyakonande's. Dr. Bastani borrowed a stethoscope from Nurse Ehyakonande and gave a fully-hijabed Maryam a once-over, taking her pulse and listening to her heart through her clothing. He then reassured her that, as far as he could tell, she was fine. Then she piqued our curiosity by asking if she could come speak to Dr. Bastani that evening at the hospital housing where we were staying—what she had to say, she shyly whispered, could not be discussed at her place of work.

When Maryam arrived at our housing complex, Dr. Bastani called me from my room. Proper etiquette prohibited Dr. Bastani from speaking to Maryam alone, so I came and sat with them, the door to the hallway open. I couldn't understand what they were discussing, so I reminisced about tales of yore from my alma mater, Smith College, where supposedly a hundred years ago students were not allowed to have male guests in their rooms unless they had a chaperone or left the door open and kept both feet on the floor at all times. But this wasn't a hundred years ago, and Dr. Bastani and Maryam weren't college students: This was a physician, speaking to a patient.

I could tell by the cadence of her voice that Maryam was alternating between apologizing and thanking Dr. Bastani profusely for giving her an audience. At times she spoke hesitantly, her words tinged with concern; at other times she cooed in soft, dulcet tones. Later, I learned from Dr. Bastani that Maryam was in love and wanted to get married, but her parents worried that her kidney would fail under the stress of having children. Dr. Bastani told Maryam that there are always risks associated with pregnancy and childbirth, but that her priority should be to see after her own happiness. That explained why, when they were done, Maryam all but skipped out of the room, grinning infectiously at both of us.

Sheep's Head Soup

Dr. Bastani had promised me we would go out for *kalepache*, a traditional soup made of ... yes, sheep's heads. And coincidentally, the day we went was Thanksgiving. I hadn't realized going out for sheep's head soup would mean getting up at 6:00 A.M., but *kalepache* is a working man's breakfast that in many restaurants is served only in the early morning. Dr. Bastani told stories of enjoying a meal of sheep's head soup before heading off to a long day of medical school classes. On this Thursday morning, it would be our start to a long day of interviews.

Adel was waiting and ready to take us to his favorite place for *kalepache*. We drove up to a small storefront where we saw people lined up out the door and down the street. Many of them were carrying pots—I assume for taking the *kalepache* home rather than eating it at the restaurant. Once we were inside, Dr. Bastani led me to a small table in the corner. It was a wooden table that seated four, covered with a clear plastic sheet; in the center was a pitcher of water, a lemon-juice dispenser, and a red plastic basket filled with freshly baked naan. Everyone in the room turned to look at me—I was told later it was not so much because I was a foreigner but because most Iranian women wouldn't be caught dead eating *kalepache*.

I sat down, ignoring the stares, and directed my attention to the mustached man in a white button down shirt ladling broth over the sheep's heads that peered at me over the rim of an immense pot—a slightly unnerving way to start the day and certainly different from the typical muffins and coffee we have for Thanksgiving breakfast at home.

The soup was not quite ready, so the patrons waited patiently in line, as did Dr. Bastani. The sheep's heads looked as one might expect: white skulls with sinewy pink and beige flesh hanging from the bones. The mustached cook gave a nod to a fully chadored, apron-wearing woman behind the counter who was probably his mother—she looked too old to be his wife. He started to transfer the greyed heads, meat falling off the bone, from the bottom of his pot to hers, taking the time to scoop loose morsels from one pot to the other. The previously visible heads sank below the surface to simmer. She took her pot over to where customers were waiting and started filling orders, scooping meat and broth into the pots of the patrons to take home. She then produced smaller tureens from under the counter for those like Dr. Bastani who were eating in.

There were bones in our pot, but thank goodness, not a whole head. Dr. Bastani had ordered the choice morsels of cheek, eyes, tongues, and brains. He showed me how adding lemon juice made it possible to use a spoon to scoop out and discard some of the excess fat. We then added naan to our bowls to sop up the broth and ate the naan and meat together. Dr. Bastani cautioned me to watch out for little bones and ocular lenses. I was particularly fond of the tongue and eyes, less so of the cheek meat and brains. Later, while in Tabriz, we went out for *kalepache* again, but at a more upscale establishment where the brains, tongues, and eyes were neatly arranged in a star pattern on a plate with herbs, and the brains were tinted yellow with saffron. While very good, I must say I preferred the less sanitized experience, where I was allowed to hunt for my favorite morsels in a mélange of meat, naan, and broth.

It being Thanksgiving Day back home, I grew wistful, thinking of the Rockwellesque meal my husband's family would be enjoying in southern Illinois: turkey, homemade mashed potatoes, green bean casserole, pecan pie, and of course, the perennial debate over whether Cool Whip is as good or better than real whipped cream. I could see in my mind's eye my family talking and laughing, all stuffed with food to the point of discomfort. I missed them terribly.

My melancholy was eased by an invitation to dinner at the home of Dr. Sharifkazemi and his wife Roya. There were several types of curried dishes (the curries I experienced in Iran were spicy, but not as hot as Indian ones), rice with barberries, and pistachio pudding. The only thing I could have done without was the *doogh*, a salty yogurt drink. I'm sure if I were dying of thirst in the desert it would be quite refreshing, but no matter how many times Dr. Bastani had me try different varieties, I couldn't get used to the taste or consistency. Plain yogurt is fine — Iranians eat it with all sorts of meat and rice dishes, and it is a delicious complement to spicy or dry foods, but I just could not get used to drinking watery, salty yogurt.

Dr. Sharifkazemi had two sons. The younger son, Mahdi, who was 10, rattled away at me in English. His fluency amazed me, and before I knew it, he was asking me to come see his video collection. I went to be polite and also to give the adults a chance to converse in Farsi — they had been struggling to speak in English for my sake. Some of the games Mahdi had were ones I knew from my sons' shelves at home: *Age of Empires* and *World of Warcraft*. I recognized the boxes and realized I could read the titles — they were in English. Others were in kanji or some other Asian script I didn't recognize.

"Are you learning English in school, Mahdi?"

"No, just from playing videogames. None of the good games are in Farsi," he lamented. "Just English or Japanese."

"You also speak Japanese?" I sputtered.

He wrinkled his nose. "Well, not all that well. My Japanese is only as good as my English." He expressed disappointment at not being able to master his videogames to the proficiency he would like, but his language skills were exceptional. Suddenly I saw videogames in a new light. I wouldn't object at all to my children playing videogames if, like Mahdi, they learned foreign languages in the process.

My own foreign language skills, some German and French, served me well in Iran. Almost all the physicians I met were trained in Europe or the States at some point in their careers and could speak at least a modicum of German, French, or English. They seemed to be particularly impressed with the Germans, and Dr. Bastani would play into that admiration, telling those who wondered about my name that I was German. This made me a little uneasy: I am of German heritage on my mother's side, but I was named "Sigrid" after my Norwegian grandmother, and I was born in the United States.

Dr. Farshid Saghila and his wife Dorna were also at Dr. Sharifkazemi's dinner party. Their 3-year-old daughter Mina chased Mahdi around the room. I think Mahdi latched on to me in part to escape Mina, but I did manage to find time to speak to both of Mina's parents once she fell asleep on the couch.

Mrs. Saghila, a doctor like her husband, shared a complaint common among professional women all over the world. She worked full-time as a physician but also had to find a way to care for Mina and the household—responsibilities that culturally fell to her even though she admitted her husband helped more than most. Her husband asked me in detail what I hoped to achieve with my research. He was worried I might find things that would embarrass his profession, but he added thoughtfully, "When you finish, please share with us what you find so we can learn and improve."

In our seven days in Shiraz after the MESOT conference, we visited Namazi Hospital, Saadi Hospital, Abu Ali Hospital (in nearby Sadra City), and the Shiraz *Anjoman*. We conducted 21 interviews, but of all the people we spoke to, my thoughts kept drifting back to Ismail. Once I'd returned to the States, I witnessed the tragedy of several friends dying, waiting for kidneys that never came, and I was ashamed that America was contributing to the exploitation of impoverished foreign donors through the black market. But here in Iran I was feeling sympathy for a young man at the other end of the shortage: a man who might not be allowed to help his family by selling his kidney. Had Ismail's fated interaction with us "saved" him from himself? I am sure some, like Dr. Delmonico,* would think so, but I was conflicted. My firsthand encounters with people like Ismail were beginning to answer questions, unraveling uncertainties and preconceptions—and my journey of discovery had only just begun.

---

* Dr. Frank Delmonico is an outspoken critic of compensated kidney donation. He spoke both at the event I organized for Cato and at the MESOT conference I attended in Shiraz.

۵ (5)

Bargaining for Body Parts

I left Shiraz with a heavy heart. It was provincial but beautiful, full of history and warm people. Shiraz was nothing like what I had feared Iran would be like — what if Tehran were? But I knew I needed to go. One-fifth of Iran's population lives in the capital's metropolitan area, so naturally Tehran is where the majority of Iranian kidney transplants take place. Also, my visa was almost up, and I needed to get permission to stay in the country. I couldn't bear the prospect of being sent home with only a fragment of my research done.

Basic Needs

Back at Tehran's Mehrabad Airport, our first order of business was to get some Iranian rials. Without rials we would be unable to pay for transportation or food. Our research would be limited to where Dr. Bastani's closest friends and relatives lived. But currency exchange proved harder than expected. We had tried the airport money-exchange booth at Khomeini International when we first arrived, but they limited our exchange to $100. We had tried at our hotel and two banks in Shiraz; now we were trying the airport again, but no luck. We then tried several banks in Tehran, always with the same result. Not until Dr. Bastani's father found a friend of a friend, who was a "businessman," were we finally able to exchange our dollars. What exactly it meant to be a "businessman" in Tehran wasn't altogether clear, particularly when it came to those willing to deal in dollars, but I didn't ask. We needed Iranian currency, and there seemed to be no official avenues of exchange willing to take our money.

After barely an hour in Tehran, my eyes began to water and my throat started to spasm. Industry on the outskirts of the city and a vast fleet of aging cars spewed emissions into the air. A wind off the Caspian Sea could help, but on this day, the Alborz mountains blocked any relief, trapping a blanket of smog that weighed heavy on the lungs.

I wouldn't end up in the hospital with an asthma attack—but it was hard to stay inconspicuous while incessantly sniffling and coughing. According to Dr. Bastani, the air in Tehran was never good, but it seemed to be particularly bad at the moment. As a child I was accustomed to breathing toxic fumes: It was just part of life with a chain-smoking mother. But since I left home, my lungs had grown accustomed to healthier fare. Thank goodness Dr. Bastani brought Allegra—it allowed me to film without adding my own cough track.

We drove through the hazy streets of Tehran with the heat of day closing in on us. The windows were open, but nothing you might call a breeze passed through the vehicle. The car crawled along from speed bump to speed bump as pedestrians swarmed around us at every slow-down, whether we stopped or not and whether there was a cross-walk or not. People on small motorcycles and mopeds wove in and out of traffic. One man had a carpet strapped crosswise to the back of his moped. The carpet all but swung through my open window and almost decapitated a pedestrian crossing in front of our car. There were shouts and the waving of fists, but the moped driver just continued on, ignoring the agitated pedestrians and annoyed drivers left in his wake.

We arrived for our meetings at the medical school a bit shaken, but Dr. Reza Malekzadeh, head of medical research at the university, immediately put us at ease. He gave off an aura of gravitas reinforced by his nearly white beard, but his eyes shone through his spectacles, cordial and humanizing. I could tell that he knew more of the world than most. He shook my hand and smiled, a Western greeting that made me feel at home. Later, he wrote a letter recommending that my visa be extended.

Research Associate, Really?

Dr. Bastani assumed I would stay at his parents' apartment, but once he called home, his mother showed some hesitation, and I had to sleep, at least initially, in a hotel downtown. I was put up at the Alborz Hotel on Vesal Shirazi Street, not too far from the University of Tehran's main campus. Dr. Bastani delivered me to the hotel to make sure the staff understood my situation—that I was a guest of the university and that I couldn't speak Farsi.

At first glance the hotel seemed innocuous, no different from similarly priced hotels in Europe. My impression soon changed, however, putting the Alborz more on a par with the lodgings I'd experienced when I lived in Argentina. A piece of plywood that connected the street and the entryway bowed with every step; beneath it, the sidewalk was crumbling and overrun with the weeds of its undoing. A green indoor-outdoor carpet like a Putt-Putt green that had seen better days lined the steps. Once inside I saw to my left a small paneled reception counter with a Formica top, followed by a café of four small square tables. Across from the entrance was a heavy wooden bench under a mural of a peacock and to its right, a small caged elevator, barely big enough for two, let alone luggage.

I braced myself for a bumpy ride. The porter strategically placed my suitcase between us and clanged shut the exterior accordion door. He slid the elevator door shut with a rubber-suctioned thud. He pressed the brass button for the third floor, and we lurched upward to the *cling, clang* of chains and pulleys. The elevator stopped, and the porter drew open the door and sighed. The doorway was almost completely between floors, a kind of no man's land. Above the divide, I got my first glimpse of the floor where I would be staying: more Putt-Putt green carpet and a heavy, once-white door with numerals I couldn't read. (The Hindi numerals used mostly in the Middle East are not like the Arabic numerals we use.) The elevator door reverberated as the porter shut it with measured exertion.

We travelled down to the second floor and up again, but no luck: Three feet still separated us from the actual floor. The porter hesitated. *He can't possibly expect me to climb through the opening, can he? I'm adventuresome, but really ... is he going to push me from behind if I don't have the strength to pull myself up?* I gave him a look that said, "Don't even think about it." Resignedly we headed back down. On the way, he tried the second floor, but no luck there either. The floor beneath our feet hit the lobby level with a resounding bang, and I was relieved the hotel didn't have a basement. I got out and gladly followed the porter as he begrudgingly plodded up the stairs.

My room was so tiny that I could barely bend over to pick up a dropped shoe without backing into the bed or a wall. The desk had no chair and bravely bore the weight of a small TV, but its legs were precariously crooked. I was afraid if I bumped the desk, the TV would come crashing down. Light shone through the closed top edge of the tinted window. The yellowed paint curled freely from the wall where persistent exposure to the elements had lowered its resistance. I wondered if water came in when it rained.

Then there was the bathroom, no different from the Iranian-style bathrooms I'd used at hospitals and restaurants. But until we had pulled up to the hotel, I'd held out hope for a Western-style commode. I reminded myself that Western conveniences were irrelevant in the greater scheme of things. A hole flanked by white ceramic foot supports was better than a bare hole in the ground, and a hose to flush with was better than nothing at all. But while I was thankful to have running water, drinking it and taking showers were out of the question. The faucet spewed liquid the color and consistency of creek water after a rain, and it smelled vaguely of something dead. It eventually cleared, but I decided to brush my teeth with bottled water. While my room was a hotel room in name only, I was a willing inmate. This was a research trip, and the quality of the accommodations didn't matter as long as I had a reasonably safe place to stay.

Not Afghanistan

I turned on the TV and watched the news. I couldn't understand the words, but I could gather the general gist from cutaways. One of the top stories was that Taliban militants in Afghanistan had doused schoolgirls with acid. Images of the schoolyard and the girls at the hospital, burned on their arms, shoulders, and faces, flashed by. I'm still haunted by what they must have gone through—the terror they must have felt trying to free themselves of their acid-soaked hijabs.

The next day when I mentioned the report to Dr. Bastani, I heard something often repeated: "That is Afghanistan, not Iran." He explained, "In Iran, girls get educated—as a matter of fact, right now, there are more women in college than men." Iranians emphasized this point with me many times even though I never once made the comparison. But I know Americans frequently do. Even my worldly friend, Jon, made the mistake of assuming the conditions in Iran were similar to what he had experienced in Afghanistan.

Of all my friends, Jon was the most ardently against my going to Iran. Jon once told me that while he was in Afghanistan, he saw a woman dressed in a burqa (fully covered from head to toe including a veil) beaten mercilessly by paramilitary thugs simply because she was out without an escort—or maybe because they knew they could get away with it. Not only did passersby ignore what was going on, but Jon had no idea whom to call for help—the police in Afghanistan do all they can to avoid confrontations with Taliban types. Maybe Iranians rightly feel thankful their country isn't like Afghanistan, but hardly a day went by where I didn't feel equally fortunate that the United States isn't like Iran.

I didn't see any militia walking down the streets in Shiraz. Yes, there was security at the MESOT conference, but that was different—discreet business suits but no blatant shows of force, no AK-47s being waved around. In Tehran, almost every day there was at least one instance where Dr. Bastani would change direction to avoid passing armed men in fatigues. Dr. Bastani didn't say much about the politics of the Iranian Revolution, but he did say, "It's a bad idea to set teenage boys with guns loose on a population."

Later, in Isfahan, Dr. Bastani warned me to expect a heated political debate at his cousin Mansoor's house. The evening started pleasantly enough, with amicable greetings and hospitable smiles and refreshments. We sat around in a cool, brightly lit room with ten of Dr. Bastani's relatives. Several of his nieces wore short Western-looking skirts and snug-fitting tops. His great-aunt, who must have been close to ninety, wore attire that was undoubtedly equally daring for her generation. She was cloaked in a long-sleeved, full-length dress and headscarf, but they were navy blue with large white polka dots.

At dinner, as Dr. Bastani had predicted, the tension began to mount. Most of the conversation, particularly once agitation set in, was in Farsi, but I did catch snippets. My hosts probably wouldn't understand it in these terms, but I recognized their conversation as the Iranian version of the perennial post 9/11 discussion on individual freedom versus security. Most of Dr. Bastani's family felt the government was too repressive, but some disagreed.

Other than Dr. Bastani and his artist nephew, Hamid, none of Dr. Bastani's family had had run-ins with the government. Hamid told of how, when an exhibit of his sculptures underwent a routine preview by censors from the Ministry of Culture, he was told a ceramic pair of cowboy boots could not be included. Hamid explained that they were just a sculpture of his girlfriend's boots, but the censors' decision was final. Hamid chuckled with disbelief. "Maybe they thought the boots were a statement of support for American imperialism. Who knows?"

He talked about the randomness of censorship: It didn't matter what the artist's intentions were; what mattered was whatever the censors imagined. "Artists in Iran know to avoid subjects associated with the West unless they want their work banned, or worse, to be thrown in jail. But the bigger problem is that innovation itself is controversial—and what artist doesn't want to create something new and unique? Unfortunately, anything outside the ordinary or the traditional risks drawing too much attention and a censor's ire."

Mansoor, the head of the Isfahan branch of Dr. Bastani's family, repeated emphatically that a sometimes-repressive regime is the price Iranians pay for peace on the streets. Speaking in English for my benefit, he exclaimed, "Iran is not Afghanistan, and we have the strong hand of the government to thank for it." I nodded but thought to myself, *It's not that simple. Might Mansoor think differently if those "peace-keepers" decided he posed a threat? What if a meddlesome neighbor or envious colleague lodged a groundless complaint against him? Without due process as we know it in the West, Mansoor could find himself paying hefty fines, under house arrest, in jail—or even worse, facing unethical interrogation techniques used to try to get information he didn't have or a confession about something he didn't do.* Without the checks and balances that control power in the West, one man's peace-keepers are another man's oppressors.

Stick the Rich Foreigner

Back at the Alborz Hotel in Tehran, I came downstairs to a lobby filled with commotion. A young man, tall and lanky with smooth alabaster skin—clean-shaven save for an attempt at a mustache—stood in the middle of the lobby in a gold-trimmed purple bathrobe. He was speaking loudly, gesticulating wildly, and seemingly threatening the manager. I approached the teenage girl behind the desk (who was pretending to ignore the situation) and handed her the address Dr. Bastani had written out for me so she could help me call a cab.

When she saw me looking curiously at the young man, she volunteered, "He's Saudi. He says he left many thousand rials in a suitcase under the bed and that the money is gone. He says he is going to call his father." I saw the manager shrug, obviously saying he knew nothing about the theft. The girl continued to whisper, doing her best to suppress a smile, "Reza told him he can have his father send him more money." I smiled at her but felt a pang of sympathy. His misfortune was all too familiar, and my own experience told me that no matter how much he struggled, he would not find his way out of this net.

I had been caught similarly once. On a fragrant spring morning, my friend Vickie and I loaded our motorbikes onto a train to France from Switzerland, where we were students at the University of Geneva. We got off at Toulon and started up the Mediterranean coastline of the Gulf of Lion. Drunk with excitement for the adventures to come, we stopped in Marseille and got a room at a bed and breakfast. It started raining, so we decided to go out to a movie. We weren't totally naïve, both having lived in Paris, so we decided not to take all our money in case we got mugged. We hid most of it in metal film canisters behind the heating element in our room and headed out. But we were about to learn a lesson that had nothing to do with the streets of Marseille.

We returned to our room at about 11:00 P.M., exhausted but relieved the rain had stopped. We were enthusiastically discussing what we would do the next morning when I noticed the suitcases we had left on the bed were askew. I opened mine to find things out of place—a shirt was ill folded, my cosmetics bag was in a different corner of the suitcase. Both our cameras were gone. I darted to the money behind the radiator. Thank goodness it was untouched. We bemoaned the loss of our cameras and decided to confront the lady of the house.

"Excuse me, has anyone been in our room?"

"No."

"Our cameras are missing."

Expletives in French were followed by, "How dare you accuse us of theft. You horrible Americans!" If a rolling pin had been handy, I'm sure she would have shaken it at us. "You always think you can push people around."

Ignoring her guilt-ridden defensiveness and hoping to offer her a way out, I calmly implored, "Please just help us find our cameras." I hesitated, pressured by her unresponsive gaze. I added, "Or we'll have to go to the police."

She all but pushed us out the door. "Go, go to the police!"

It took us a while to locate the police station and to convince a policeman to come back to the bed and breakfast with us. In retrospect, I think he was bemused by the whole situation. Maybe this wasn't his first trip like this. He tipped his hat to the lady of the house, "*Bonjour!* Sorry to disturb you." She saw us and started once again shouting profanities while the policeman stood outside the door with us. He suggested we find another place to stay.

"But our things!"

The lady of the house invited the policeman in politely. He stood by the door, holding his hat in both hands, rocking back and forth, heel to toe. She watched us with dagger eyes as we hurried to our room to collect our things, including the money behind the radiator.

Returning, we told the policeman, "We would like our money back—what we paid for the room."

"You dirty, self-important Americans—get out of my house!"

As we hurried out, the policeman turned on one heel and tipped his hat. "*Bonsoir*, Madame."

She smiled, "*Good evening*, officer."

Outside on the street, we asked the policeman, "What now? Do we file a report?"

He patted me on the shoulder condescendingly. "Instead, why don't you have Daddy send you money for a new camera?"

By this time it was two in the morning. Exhausted, defeated, and coming to the shocking realization that the police would do nothing, we pressed the policeman about where we should stay the night. The officer just pointed toward *Rue de la Republique.* "Try down there," he said and nonchalantly strolled off in another direction, leaving two 19-year-old women to fend for themselves in the middle of the night.

I felt for the Saudi "prince," but I was glad that the few thousand dollars I had with me were carefully hidden away: some in a money belt, some in a pouch around my neck, and even some in my bra and in one of my shoes, but none in my room at the hotel. If someone mugged me, the plan was to hand over the pouch around my neck and not admit to having money elsewhere. I hadn't taken such precautions in Shiraz, but it was becoming ever more evident that although Tehran was not Afghanistan, it also wasn't Shiraz.

Not Shiraz

Many things were different in Tehran. Most people were not as willing as Dr. Malekzadeh to break protocol to make me feel welcome—generally the people I met in Tehran didn't offer to shake hands. After all, you never know who might be watching. At one point I inadvertently extended my hand to a physician. He recoiled, putting his hands in his lab coat pockets and grimacing as if he were afraid of catching some disease. I withdrew my hand promptly, bowed ever so slightly, and muttered an apology. The corners of his mouth contorted with disgust; he turned away from me and gave Dr. Bastani a curt "*Salaam.*" Dr. Bastani threw me a glance that told me not to worry.

Dr. Bastani's knowing demeanor often reassured me. He did so, not necessarily with words, but with slight, almost imperceptible gestures that would go unnoticed by others: a confident nod, the trace of a smile, a glance in my direction. I had the sense that these gestures, while invaluably calming to me, were made with a repressed sense of fun—having me along somehow tickled Dr. Bastani. Yet, I'm sure he knew how indispensable he was to my research.

Thanks to Dr. Bastani I recovered quickly, and minutes later when we were introduced to a representative from the Ministry of Health's Transplant Coordination office, I repressed the reflex to extend my hand. The official reacted to our inquiries in a way I was beginning to expect in Tehran. He was quite willing to share information but requested that I not film him or use his name—lest someone misunderstand his interaction with us as "cooperating with the enemy."

In Shiraz, men and women tended to sit in groups in different parts of the room, but the segregation wasn't strictly enforced. In Tehran there was an invisible and inviolable line down the middle of classrooms and lecture halls. No matter how many people there were of one gender or the other, no one dared to cross the line. Before one of Dr. Bastani's lectures, a man politely asked me to move over two seats to the women's side of the room.

Even meals were handled differently: In Shiraz, physicians had invited us out to lunch. In Tehran we usually ate lunch in a secluded conference room or in a physician's office away from peering eyes. On one occasion, Dr. Bastani was taken to lunch while I was left behind to eat in the segregated hospital cafeteria, where I knew no one and no one was instructed to help me. I'm not sure whether the lack of deference was due to my country of origin or the fact I was a woman, but even after I stood for a long minute turning in circles trying to decide where to start, no one came to my assistance.

I realized a disregard for strangers might be xenophobia or a big city indifference I'd also encountered elsewhere. But there was something more going on. This was a major metropolis in a developing country, where the contrast between rich and poor was far starker than what I'd experienced elsewhere, except perhaps parts of South America. There the wealthy live behind high walls and drive down beautiful shop-lined avenues in their expensive cars, seemingly oblivious to the squalor only a couple of blocks away. Tehran's backstreets were far too sedate to qualify as squalid, but there was a telling tenor to how people interacted—an emotional distance different from what I was used to at home.

As I got up to carry my tray away, a woman approached, pointed to the rice on my plate, then pointed to herself. I nodded yes and watched her scoop the rice onto her plate while we stood in the middle of the cafeteria. She returned to her table where she transferred her newly-acquired prize to a Tupperwaretype container that she pulled from her bag. *Curious, I thought, that she should have a container handy. Does she make a habit of asking people for their leftovers?* I stood watching her much longer than was polite, but the second she noticed, I quickly turned, hurried over to set my tray on the dirty dishes conveyor belt, and left.

Here I had been feeling sorry for myself because I had to eat alone, and then it struck me in a way it hadn't in a long time: I was the lucky one.

When I lived in Bariloche, Argentina, as a child, I remember a boy about 6 or 7 years old who was furtively following us at the market. I stumbled over the uneven cobblestones, trying to keep up with my mother. I took in as much as I could, looking up from my feet whenever possible. The building in front of us looked like an airplane hanger, rusty and dented, its industrial-size doors wide open. The cars parked haphazardly in the square seemed smaller than those back in the United States. The air had a chill coming in off the lifeless glacial lake, Nahuel Huapi. An assorted bouquet of raw beef mixed with baked goods and over-ripe fruit wafted from the building. My ears were filled with the sound of buzzing flies and my shoes clacking on the cobblestones. I remember the strangeness of no birds calling, not even seagulls.

I never heard him; I only saw him. If I had been close enough, I probably could have smelled him. A flash of grey-blue shirt, a glimpse of torn slacks smudged with dirt, and a matted pitch-colored head that peeked out from behind a car. He had no coat—shoes, but no socks. I was as curious about him as he was about me.

When I pointed him out to my mother, she took a quick look, then stopped and knelt to meet my eyes. "Accident of birth, my dear." She smiled. "You are warmly dressed, holding your mother's hand, shopping at the market. And," she glanced over at the boy again as he peeped out from behind a different car, "you have glasses."

Why is she talking about glasses? I looked at the boy again, following my mother's gaze. One eyeball was surrounded by skin stretched thin, yet wrinkled like a baby's head crowning at birth. He had been given an adult-sized glass eye—probably because his family could not afford to have one made that would fit a child.

"Accident of birth." She squeezed my hand. "You were born in Washington, D.C.—not here, and not in a poor town in Mississippi. You are one of the lucky ones. You had an eye operation and now wear glasses. God only knows where his mother is."

She paused, "You know, sweetheart, he might even be one of the lucky ones—at least he has a glass eye. It's big, but he'll grow into it."

I pulled myself closer to her. I never saw that particular boy again, but in the year I lived in Argentina, I saw considerable misfortune of a kind not prevalent in the United States. I can't claim familiarity with the more severe poverty of places like sub-Saharan Africa, but I saw enough to understand how little can make someone privileged.

There was much about Iran that reminded me of Argentina, and the woman in the hospital cafeteria who wanted my leftover rice was one of them.

Many of the people we spoke to in Tehran seemed nervous, their comportment belying their words—I sensed they were uncertain whether they wanted to be seen with us, or at least with me. For the first time in Iran, some doctors, nurses, and administrators refused to be interviewed or, if they let us interview them, refused to be photographed. Others showed concern that we might get ourselves in trouble with the government, the morality police, or even come to harm at the hands of unscrupulous members of the general public.

When we left Dr. Haghighi's office, he was shocked to learn we planned to take a taxi. Shooting a glance over at me, he whispered to Dr. Bastani, "It is not safe," and ordered his personal driver to escort us to our next appointment. This was more like the Iran I'd been warned about—I needed to be careful and certainly not do any more exploring on my own as I had done near my hotel that morning.

The dangers were real—maybe no worse than in any other similar developing country, as Dr. Ghods had said—but real nonetheless. Several people joked about the dangers of capricious governance: "Sure, we are free; we can do anything we want. We just don't know what might land us in jail." And when responding to questions about my husband's profession—he's a free-speech attorney—I would get, "Oh my, that must be dangerous." No indeed, this was not the West, but it wasn't Shiraz either.

Precautions and Hospital Security

Obstacles aside, Dr. Bastani continued to work his magic opening doors and getting us worthwhile interviews. The routine of teas, meetings, lectures, and round-table discussions continued, but now I was more patient. I knew to sit back and appreciate learning about the people we met even if they weren't necessarily the kidney sellers I had come to interview. I understood that with time, we would get the interviews I needed.

I started downloading my video to an external drive and erasing my camera's internal memory every chance I got, sometimes more than once a day. This proved a wise strategy and served me well the one time we ran into security problems in Tehran. At Shariati hospital, when we were about to wrap up for the day, a security guard approached and requested that we accompany him. Dr. Bastani followed, and I followed Dr. Bastani. We walked down several flights to the security office near the hospital's main entrance. Dr. Bastani gave the security chief the names and phone numbers of our contacts at Tehran University Medical School. Calls were made, but the chief still insisted on reviewing the footage on my camera. I started playing back what I'd taped on my viewfinder. But he shook his head and sent a junior officer out of the room. The officer returned almost immediately with another officer, whom the chief directed to take my camera. Anxious, I held on.

Dr. Bastani asked, "Can Dr. Fry-Revere come along to show how the camera works?" After a brief exchange of words, the young officer sat down beside me instead of taking my camera to another room. I gingerly opened my viewfinder, turned the camera on, and handed it to him.

I tried hard to act normal but was worried that even if the footage didn't bother them, my possessiveness might make them suspicious. Wild thoughts raced through my head. *Will they take my camera? They don't have Blu-ray in Iran, do they? What if they check with the Ministry of Culture to see if I have permission to film? Thank goodness this footage doesn't include anyone criticizing the government. But I do have some interviews with kidney sellers that might look bad to outsiders. ...*

The director of security and Dr. Bastani spoke while the young officer zipped through my footage—he knew exactly how to fast forward and open files from the index. Later Dr. Bastani shared with me what the chief of security had told him: A few months ago, a journalist from the Netherlands had filmed a woman going into labor in a crowded hallway outside the hospital's maternity ward, which made the hospital look bad. The Ministry of Health sent out a directive to all Iranian hospitals not to allow foreigners to do any filming. Dr. Bastani explained that our situation was different: We weren't journalists; we were doing research, and Dr. Bastani is Iranian. We were only filming to keep accurate records of our interviews for data-collection purposes.

Getting a sense of what Dr. Bastani was saying before I actually knew the details, I maneuvered my MESOT-logoed canvas briefcase onto the table so the officers could see it, hoping it might provide visual confirmation. I offered that I had no intention of embarrassing anyone and that if they saw anything objectionable in the footage I had taken, I would erase it.

The young officer closed my camera and returned it to me without ceremony, and I could see the chief telling Dr. Bastani, with a nod to me, "Oh, no, that is fine. Sorry for the inconvenience." The only other time we were ever questioned by security was once in Tabriz, when a hospital guard thought the tripod I was carrying might be stolen hospital equipment.

Once again it was clear that Dr. Bastani's contribution to my research was indispensable. It was he who gave my project legitimacy inside Iran, and it was his contacts at the various universities and hospitals that made both the interviews and the filming possible.

A Trip to the Police Station

The next day, it was Dr. Bastani's turn to sweat. My visa was about to expire, so it was imperative that we go to Tehran's main police depot to get it renewed, a task Dr. Bastani clearly did not relish. It seemed a bit odd that visa renewals required a trip to the police department, but that was how it was done in Iran. Armed with a letter from Dr. Malekzadeh stating that my lecture tour was a legitimate reasons to allow me to stay in the country, we headed across town to the main police station.

Getting around Tehran was almost always an ordeal. Traffic was clogged at all times, except maybe between 2:00 and 5:00 A.M. Even when the traffic had a chance to move, things were slowed down by the ever-present speed bumps. I never once saw anyone use a turn signal, and I nearly had a heart attack the first time a taxi driver, having missed his exit, put the car in reverse and zigzagged backwards against oncoming traffic. Twice cabdrivers pulled over, took a rock from the side of the road, and struck something under the hood. I still have no idea what might be wrong with an engine that hitting it with a rock would remedy.

Being a pedestrian was just as dangerous. Crossing the street was like playing a game of chicken. People on foot advanced in tiny increments negotiating cars that jolted forward or stopped, depending on whether the traffic in front of them was moving. Drivers often gestured or screamed at the people on the street to get out of their way—well, at least they yelled at me. The last time I had such pedestrian troubles was in Paris when I crossed four lanes of traffic on the Champs-Elysees to reach the Arc de Triomphe, not realizing there was an underground passageway I was supposed to take. I saw a few overpasses for pedestrians in Tehran, but most people seemed not to use them or the crosswalks where they existed.

This particular drive to the police station seemed longer and more tortuous than other trips we'd taken. I was feeling queasy, perhaps as much from thinking about what might happen at our destination as from the driving, but Dr. Bastani was also quieter than usual. He was somewhat of a hero in the medical community during the Revolution, and I think the encounters he had with the authorities back then had soured him on the notion of visiting the police station.

Dr. Bastani could write a book of his own on what happened to him during the early years of the Iranian Revolution. In the beginning he was one of the pro-Revolution intellectual elite. In 1980, one year into the Revolution, he completed his residency training and became the director of the health department for the city of Jahrom, 125 miles south of Shiraz. During the three years that followed, Dr. Bastani had multiple run-ins with extreme conservatives in the health department, the revolutionary guard, and phalangists—culminating in a midnight attempt on his life. The final straw came when in early 1984, a few months into his faculty position at Tehran University at Imam Khomeini Hospital, he was informed that he was no longer eligible for hire at any government-run agency or medical school. Dr. Bastani attributes being blacklisted to his having protected some of his employees and political dissidents from conservative elements and angry mobs who wanted to harm them. He fled Iran with his young family and didn't return even for a visit until more than 15 years later. I'm sure there must have been times when he was haunted by those experiences, and taking me to the police station was an unwelcome reminder.

Huge billboards lined the highway, many bearing the face of Ayatollah Khamenei, the current Supreme Leader of Iran, not to be confused with the Grand Ayatollah Khomeini, leader of the Iranian Revolution and the first Supreme Leader of Iran. The Supreme Leader of Iran has full authority over all three branches of the Iranian government (the judiciary, the parliament, and the president), and even the armed forces, the Revolutionary Guard, and the *Basij* militia—a hard line, heavily-armed volunteer morality police that operates independently of the official police and is accountable only to the Supreme Leader.

"What does that sign say?"

Dr. Bastani glanced out the window and then, without looking at me, replied, "Together we can win against the superpowers."

Great, I thought. *How reassuring, given our destination.* We continued in silence. At times, I thought I could hear Dr. Bastani's breath but found it was my own, trapped and muffled in my ears. Dr. Bastani looked so calm. *Is his heart racing like mine?*

To say the least, it was disconcerting to pass through several sets of gates and to check in with guards toting AK-47s just to get to an administrator who could review my request for a visa extension. It felt like we were entering a maximum-security prison. I was grateful that Dr. Bastani was with me to do all the talking, but I knew this couldn't be easy for him. His acclaim among fellow doctors must have given him some solace from the memories of what had happened so many years ago, but asking Dr. Bastani to go into a compound filled with armed police officials was asking a lot. He could have arranged to have someone else go with me, but he didn't. I mused that the same courage that served him well during the Revolution must be serving him well now. I was afraid but impressed, and I felt my fate couldn't be in better hands.

The police captain was a big man—as tall as Dr. Bastani but younger and more muscular. His uniform was well pressed, and his curt, authoritative manner made it clear he took his office seriously. He guided us into a tiny room with bare walls. Dr. Bastani and I sat down on a well-worn sofa that reeked of cigarette smoke. I could see dust motes dancing in a stream of light from the window behind the desk. With no tea offered, I wasn't sure what to do with my hands. I put them on my knee and looked down, at first turning my wedding band idly, but then, thinking better of it, I uncrossed my legs, put my hands in my lap, and sat completely motionless. Dr. Bastani presented the captain my passport and the letter from Dr. Malekzadeh. The officer remained standing. He inspected my passport, inspected me, and then leaned over his desk and scribbled something across my visa. He handed it to Dr. Bastani and just like that, I had permission to stay in the country until the end of the year. *That's it?* I don't think he even took the time to read Dr. Malekzadeh's letter. *No questions? Thank you, Dr. Malekzadeh. Thank you, Dr. Bastani.*

On our way out, our pace picked up. Dr. Bastani and I walked faster than we probably should have, taking short measured breaths as if we had gotten away with something. Dr. Bastani looked relieved once we rounded the corner outside the police station. The tension lifted, he handed me my passport with a humorous flourish, "Madam, your visa."

"Thank you," I said with as much meaning as I could muster. Then I returned my passport to its safety pouch under my tunic and looked up at Dr. Bastani, beaming with gratitude. "Now for some groundbreaking research."

He smiled back in his usual understated manner. "Glad to help."

Is It Time to Flee?

After that first night in Shiraz, I never heard another helicopter overhead, but more than once an Iranian pulled me aside and wanted to know, "Are the Americans coming?" or "Should I move my family out of Tehran?" I was taken aback. The first time, I simply said I wasn't in a position to know. But the next time, I tried to reassure. "Would I be here if I thought there was going to be an invasion?"

Despite my best efforts, my response rang hollow; after all, only a week earlier I had awakened in a cold sweat at the sound of helicopters overhead, wondering if they were American or maybe Israeli. The United States had attacked Iraq with less provocation than Iran's not-so-secret support of Hezbollah and Hamas and its pursuit of nuclear power in violation of repeated United Nations Security Council admonitions. In retrospect it is ironic that in Iraq we found no government support of Al-Qaeda, no weapons of mass destruction, and no enriched uranium, but in September 2011, Iran defiantly put its first nuclear power plant online. The tensions that people felt when I was in Iran at the end of 2008 must be ten times worse now.

Not an NGO

We visited five different hospitals (Hasheminejad, Shariati, Sina, Labafinejad, and Imam Khomeini), the Hasheminejad Dialysis Center, the Tehran *Anjoman*, the Labafinejad Clinic, and the Ministry of Health's Center for Special Diseases. In Tehran we interviewed ten healthcare professionals, four *Anjoman* administrators, six dialysis patients, 34 transplant recipients, and 15 kidney sellers. We heard stories of donors who were satisfied with their decisions, even many years later, but also stories of donors who felt cheated and mistreated.

The Center for Special Diseases is a government-funded institute started by Fatemeh Hashemi Rafsanjani, the daughter of the fourth president of Iran Akbar Hashemi Bahramani Rafsanjani. It is through this center that the government-sponsored *issar* of one million tomans is distributed to donors.

One reason the government started paying donors one million tomans in 1995*—perhaps the paramount reason—was that the medical community was hoping to take haggling out of the donor/recipient equation. But their success at achieving a more congenial system of kidney selling was short lived. Within only a few years, Iran's high inflation rate depreciated the one million *issar* to the point where renewed bargaining for kidneys became inevitable. Not infrequently someone suggests a hike in the *issar*, but to date, the government contribution has not increased.

The existence of both an *Anjoman* that is a non-profit NGO charity and a government-sponsored Center for Special Diseases causes some confusion particularly because the priorities of the two organizations are different. The traditional NGO *Anjoman* in Tehran, which calls itself the "Iranian National Kidney Foundation," is the flagship organization for more than 100 *Anjomans* around the country, all of which have at least a tangential relationship with the Tehran *Anjoman*. The government-sponsored "Center for Special Diseases" has only the one office in Tehran and is not a charity organization: It relies on government funding to sponsor research on genetic and rare diseases (including kidney disease), to administer various social service programs (such as the national benefits available to kidney donors), and to distribute health insurance benefits, but it does not match kidney donors and recipients.

In addition to being the government office where donors collect their *issar*, the Center for Special Diseases is also where donors can pick up a certificate exempting them from military service, or visit the center's post-operative clinic. While we were there the center also had a data-collection study underway that paid donors to come to the clinic for basic follow-up tests.

We were told that most tradtional *Anjomans* don't collect long-term data on donors. Even efforts to follow-up by phone are generally unsuccessful because as many as 80 percent of donors change their contact information within a year after donating without leaving forwarding information. Our own experience with doing follow-up interviews confirmed this.

The success in collecting post-operative donor data experienced by the Center for Special Diseases is owed to its methodology. The center provides a small, but not insignificant, payment to donors who are willing to return for post-operative check-ups. Donors who submit to the requested physical and an-

* The Iranian Ministry of Health budgeted funds and started paying some donors as early as 1987–88, but payment wasn't officially sanctioned by the Iranian parliament until 1995.

swer researchers' questions receive 10,000 tomans, enough to feed a frugal person for a few days. It is important to note that this creates a selection bias in the data collected—such a small payment tends to attract donors who continue to be desperate for money after selling their kidney; the process also self-selects donors who live in or near Tehran because others wouldn't want to make the trip for so little money.

Disgruntled Donors

We spoke to seven donors at the Center for Special Diseases; six of them were unhappy. One of the major sources of dissatisfaction became evident as we sat in the waiting room listening to donors compare notes about how much they had earned for their kidneys.

One happy donor, Mohsen, had given his kidney to a friend of his father and received seven million tomans from the recipient in addition to the one million *issar* from the government. He didn't need the money the Center for Special Diseases offered for follow-up interviews, but he suffered some anxiety after the donation and was there to check his blood pressure. He summed up what he felt about those he heard complaining:

> Before the donation the psychologist would ask us, "Why are you doing this? Will you regret this decision?" to see if we have properly thought this out and if our mind was set. Everybody has his own reasons. Someone can be in very difficult financial times and, with the money he receives, can solve some problems. Afterwards, he may encounter other problems and say, "Oh why did I sell my kidney?" So I would say to that person, "If you're going to regret it later, don't donate." This is why the psychologist asks—to prevent people from doing something they will regret later.

Many donors, however, weren't unhappy about their decision to donate per se but resentful that they weren't paid more. Some donors received as little as three million tomans (including the one million *issar* from the national government) even though that amount was nowhere near enough to solve their financial problems.

Our selection of interviewees was not pre-arranged by anyone. I made a conscious decision not to seek permission from the Iranian Ministry of Health or the

Iranian Ministry of Culture to do my research. I didn't want the government interfering with how Dr. Bastani and I interacted with our subjects. This meant we had to be careful who we asked for assistance in arranging interviews. It also led to a situation at the Tehran *Anjoman* where, after a few visits, the staff thought better of giving us unfettered access and demanded we bring a letter from the Ministry of Health to confirm our project's legitimacy. We never followed up with the Ministry of Health, but I did promise and follow through with sending the Tehran *Anjoman* a copy of all the footage I took at its office. (I sent a copy of the footage once my research material and I were safely back in the United States.)

Because we were doing our research under the radar, we planned things so that the hospital wards, clinics, and *Anjomans* rarely had more than a few hours' notice that we were coming. We simply interviewed the donors and recipients who were there or who walked in the door while we were there. Occasionally people did not want to be interviewed or did not want to be filmed, but over 95 percent of the people we approached, recipients and donors alike, agreed to an interview.

Rajab, a 28-year-old Iraqi living in Tehran, told us he had no medical complaints but that he should not have agreed to donate for less than it would take to solve his financial problems. He sat down for his interview eager to share his story. He was dressed as if he had come from a construction site, but he said he hadn't worked in months. Rajab complained that he was eight million tomans in debt at the time of the donation and thought, when he first made inquires, that he could get 10 or even 20 million tomans for his kidney. In the end, all he received was 3.5 million: 2.5 million from the recipient and one million from the government.

"If I had known it would be this amount, … I would not have come at all, but once I started the process, I had to continue."

"Why didn't you back out?"

"The guy, the recipient, was a good man, and I couldn't pull out for his sake." Rajab went on to tell us that he and the recipient had become friends. The recipient would help him if he could, but he had financial problems of his own.

Rajab continued to tell us with a heavy heart that people discriminated against him when they found out he had sold a kidney. "The nurses and doctors saw me and said, 'Oh, he sold his kidney; he's not a good person.'" He went on to complain that potential employers shied away from hiring him. He speculated that maybe employers thought he was a bad person, that he was unhealthy, or that he couldn't work as hard as others because he had only one kidney.

Muhammad-Reza had a similar story. His bronzed round face and thick black eyebrows posed a stark contrast with his starched white button down shirt. His dress signaled self-assurance, but his demeanor said otherwise. He slouched and frowned. His wife, who had accompanied him to the center, sat erect next to him in a brown and tan floral-patterned headscarf and black coat. She spoke little, even when directly spoken to, but Muhammad-Reza had no problem sharing his woes. Shortly after we started our conversation, he sank into a litany of self-pity.

Muhammad-Reza donated a kidney two years earlier, when he was 24. "They put a big hat over my head!" he exclaimed—the Persian version of *They pulled the wool over my eyes.* "I didn't know I could negotiate. The *Anjoman* told me I would get three million tomans, and I accepted that." Muhammad-Reza moaned that he had fallen on hard times. He had lost his job, gone into debt to friends and lenders, and wanted to get married. "I stayed in bed for a month and gave away part of my body for a pittance—three million tomans, just two from the recipient and one from the government. Then later I learned people were selling their kidneys for 12, 10, 8 million."

He went on to express feelings of discrimination. "The *Anjoman* treated me as if I had sold a shirt, and that's it—I'm gone. Now I have kidney stones, but no one is taking care of me." He frowned, and his wife took his arm and patted it in anticipation of what she knew was to come: "They need to inform people. They need to make people stronger in their hearts. They should say, 'Come and save a person's life, and we will take care of you.' But they don't do that. I gave my kidney and did all that stuff and paid 750,000 tomans for insurance, and they said, 'Good riddance.'"

I felt for Muhammad-Reza, and I was disappointed that the *Anjoman* social worker didn't do a better job of helping both Rajab and Muhammad-Reza solve their problems. Also Muhammad-Reza's point that there should be more of a social sense of responsibility to take care of donors was well taken, but I couldn't help but feel Muhammad-Reza needed to move on—to get over what had happened to him and build a life with his new wife. He was at risk of defining himself in terms of his misfortune. He showed bad judgment, selling a kidney to pay for a wedding and getting married when he was unemployed. I also couldn't understand why, with an excess of potential donors to choose from, the *Anjoman* had accepted him. I hoped that someone at the center would provide him with the guidance he needed although I was told that was not part of their job description. He would have to go to a regular charity *Anjoman* for that.

Another donor, Morad, had a different type of story to tell. He stood politely in the doorway until Dr. Bastani asked him to come in and sit down. He spoke softly, staring past me into the distance. Even before he started to tell his story, I wondered if he was depressed. At 21 Morad had donated a kidney to his adoptive father, who died on the operating table. Money had been an issue for Morad at the time of his donation, but it wasn't at the root of his dissatisfaction.

Morad's adoptive parents had found two potential paid donors through the *Anjoman*, but each was excluded during the final round of testing, so Morad insisted on donating despite his adoptive parents' misgivings. He had lost his birth parents when he was only seven and had no relatives who claimed him. Morad felt he owed his adoptive parents a great deal. The least he could do was give his father a kidney, but he also felt guilty that his father, who was not doing well on dialysis, died during the operation. Morad was conflicted: "Could my father have stayed alive on dialysis? Maybe he didn't actually need the operation."

Morad was also disillusioned about how people reacted to his having donated a kidney: When he returned to the university, fellow students wondered if he had sold his kidney to support a drug habit, and he lost one of his best friends because of the stigma associated with kidney selling. "Outside when people find out that you have donated, they start looking at you in a different way. They start keeping their distance from you."

Like Rajab and Muhammad-Reza, Morad was having trouble finding work. He started training at several jobs, but supervisors changed their minds about finalizing their offers once they saw his medical record. At the time of our interview, Morad was working part-time at a bank because someone at the center gave him a letter making it clear that discriminating against donors was illegal and that there was no reason, health-wise or otherwise, not to hire Morad.

I wanted to suggest to Rajab and Muhammad-Reza that they ask for a similar letter, but they had already left.

Kidney Prices, Privacy, and Personal Worth

The bargaining that goes on for kidneys in Iran clearly sets the stage for both donors and recipients to feel cheated. There is no doubt that Rajab and Muhammad-Reza both felt exploited, as did three others of the seven donors we interviewed at the Center for Special Diseases. But it is also worth noting that they said much of their displeasure was linked to the amount of compensation they received and that they might have felt differently if they had been paid more.

On the other hand, recipients also sometimes felt exploited. Most recipients we interviewed spoke of gladly paying whatever they could to get a kidney, but a few spoke of being blackmailed or swindled. At the Labafinejad Clinic, Mustafa told us he negotiated a two-million toman fee with his donor and put that amount into escrow at the *Anjoman*—a common practice to ensure donors will receive the promised payments. But the night before surgery, the donor came to his house and demanded an additional 1.5 million. The *Anjoman* later told us that such behavior is strictly prohibited. If they hear that a donor has asked the recipient for more than the negotiated price, that donor will be blacklisted and prohibited from donating. One member of the Tehran *Anjoman* board of directors even remembered an incident where a donor was arrested and jailed for extortion.

Mustafa confided in us that he knew the donor was doing something wrong, but his family didn't want any more delays, so they paid. Nonetheless the donor's actions sullied the whole process for Mustafa, and he never wanted to see him again. Khadijeh, a different recipient we interviewed at Labafinejad Clinic, told us the first donor chosen for her kept calling and asking for more money, so her family told the *Anjoman,* and a different donor was arranged.

It was hard to tell what would constitute a fair exchange given the broad differences in donors' needs and recipients' ability to pay. When the average going price for a kidney is between four and five million tomans (on top of the one million given by the government) and there are donors who receive anywhere from 0–10 million from their recipients, I couldn't help but wonder: *Who is exploiting whom? And how does one determine a fair price when someone's life or financial well-being is at stake?*

In addition to the dissatisfaction among donors over how much they were paid, another trend was emerging that repeated itself in every city: Most donors didn't want people to know they had donated. Despite their awareness that they had done an honorable deed, they saw having sold a kidney as proof that they had fallen on hard times. Understandably, most people, whether kidney sellers or not, aren't in a rush to share their misfortunes with neighbors, friends, or even sometimes their families. Sadly, people like Morad, who didn't donate out of financial desperation, were caught up in the stigma that all kidney donors are kidney sellers, and that only drug addicts or people who are otherwise failures in life sell their kidneys.

In the United States, the Washington Regional Transplant Community (WRTC), for which I serve as the ethicist on their Organ and Tissue Advisory Committee, holds regular "Donate Life" events in celebration of cadaver organ donors and their families. These events are attended by members of the medical community, organ recipients, and the families whose loved ones' organs helped save lives. The recipients and medical community are there to say thank you. The donor families are there to honor their deceased loved ones and to be reminded that at least something good has come of their loss.

But living kidney donors in Iran face a different social dynamic than the families of deceased organ donors in the United States. Dr. Malakoutian told us the medical community and *Anjomans* in Tehran tried to arrange donor-appreciation events, even advertising them on television, but those efforts were a total bust. Mrs. Mirzayee, one of the social workers at the Tehran *Anjoman*, confirmed this. Both said donors are not interested in plaques, letters of recognition, or any other form of acknowledgment of their good deed. Most donors have made up their mind about what they want even before they come to the *Anjoman* and hardly listen to options. After their kidneys are removed, they usually just want to get their money and go.

At first this surprised me, but after some thought, it made sense. Donors in Iran uniformly told us that saving another's life by donating a kidney is a praiseworthy thing to do, but they were also keenly aware of the stigma associated with selling a kidney. Most of our interviewees, in fact, did fit the stereotype: They were in the throes of some form of financial crisis that they would prefer to keep secret. And while a few donors who were not in economic straits didn't care what people thought, others were bothered by the possibility that someone might assume they were donating because they had mismanaged their finances. The stigma of monetary ruin, desperation, and social failure (including drug use) all combined to explain why some donors, particularly in Tehran, requested that we use their data for research purposes only, not use their names, or obscure their faces if used in the documentary film I was planning.

I left the Center for Special Diseases dejected. Haggling over kidney prices clearly had detrimental consequences. Donors felt deceived and forced to choose between standing their ground to get enough money to solve their own problems and saving someone's life. Repeatedly in Tehran, and later elsewhere, we heard, "I needed more, but the recipient was too poor to give more," or "I felt too sorry for the recipient to ask for more."

It is tempting to assume there is a direct correlation between compensated kidney donation and dissatisfied donors, but in fact, the negative correlation is not with selling itself, but with the negative social consequences that are associated with the assumptions people make about donors. The negative stigma exists not because of the exchange of money per se, but because so many donors have acted out of financial desperation and an inability to meet social expectations in a conventional manner.

The social onus associated with being a kidney donor in Iran is not unlike that of being poor anywhere in the world. Ismail, whom we interviewed in Shiraz, put it succinctly: "My hope for the future is that I am able to earn a decent living for my family so I don't need to ask anybody for help. In this society, I must earn bread for my wife and child so I am not ashamed of myself in front of people." Arman, a donor we interviewed at Hasheminejad hospital, made a similar point when he stressed that donating a kidney is better than getting a handout or going on government assistance, and maybe even better than borrowing money from family and friends. But he also said he felt wanting to help another person should be just as important, if not more so, than being paid: "If I had understood that I could save someone's life by selling my kidney, I would have donated sooner."

But the stigma associated with being in need didn't answer all the concerns I was hearing. People seemed to harbor the idea that even donors without an obvious financial need had something else going on that they weren't being forthright about. (I'll adress the misconception that donors are all drug users in Chapter 8.) Perhaps there was a karmic debt they were trying to pay off or a sacrifice they had to make because of some gross misdeed they weren't divulging. There were hints of this type of condemnation in several of the interviews we did in Iran, but the clearest expression of how donors sometimes faced this type of misconception came in an interview I did in the United States.

Shortly after my return home, I interviewed Larry, a lawyer with a wife and three children who had donated a kidney to his best friend, Steve Lessin. (Steve was the dialysis patient I visited in Arlington, Virginia, who had tried to buy a kidney from Cathy, one of the interns at my center.) Larry had donated a kidney to Steve ten years earlier without hesitation. It was Larry's kidney that had recently failed and landed Steve back on dialysis. Larry felt distress, a vague sense that he had somehow let his friend down, but he didn't feel that way in the beginning. With time though, like Morad and others who had donated to friends and family in Iran, Larry developed mixed feelings about the donation—not because the transplant ultimately failed but because of the way people treated him when they learned of his donation.

People didn't see Larry's sacrifice as he thought they would. At first he enthusiastically mentioned that he had donated a kidney, thinking people might find it interesting or praiseworthy, but he soon stopped. "Everybody's just at a loss for words. They don't know [what to think]. They question whether Steve and I were having a homosexual relationship or whether I was nutty or did I owe him a load of money or something like that. They don't have anything to grab onto. They just couldn't comprehend it."

Larry told me a family member had asked him what he had done that was so wrong that he had to donate a kidney to make up for it, and others he told about the donation also made similar inquires, asking if Larry owed some kind of karmic debt. He was totally flabbergasted and taken aback that his motives could be so misunderstood. When I wondered out loud if anyone ever acknowledged that Larry had done an honorable deed or that Steve was fortunate to have such a good friend, Larry's eyes were at the brink of welling up with tears. "Never," he said softly, shaking his head almost imperceptibly. "Never."

Good Deeds That Pay Off

The majority of kidney sellers we came across in Tehran (and in Iran in general) were donating because of some kind of financial predicament, but most did not regret their decision.

On November 29 we interviewed Farid, who had just been admitted to Hasheminejad Hospital and was being prepped to donate his kidney the following day. Farid's situation was superficially the same as Muhammad-Reza's, but ultimately distinct because of his attitude. Both young men sold a kidney because they needed money to pay for their wedding (or to pay the traditional "bride price" which is a little like the Western notion of a dowry). Both were in debt and both had loving fiancées. But Farid and Muhammad-Reza approached their difficulties in totally different ways.

Farid was confident, self-assured, and forward thinking. Unlike Muhammad-Reza, Farid wasn't going to marry until he knew he could be a good provider. Another difference between the two men was that Farid was—well—stunning! Not that Muhammad-Reza was ugly, but Farid was extremely handsome. Dr. Bastani joked that he looked like the Iranian actor Fardin. He didn't have any particularly unique features—dark curly hair, faint sideburns, a wisp of a mustache, a square-cut beard, and olive skin—but none of these identify what made him attractive. I think it was his eyes. They were exceptionally large and expressive. His voice was soft but strong, and his whole face was animated when he spoke. Or perhaps it was his smile. He had that inscrutable Mona Lisa smile that makes a person want to learn more about someone. Whatever the root of his attractiveness, he exuded optimism.

Farid was about to be married when his successful electronics store was raided and his inventory and savings confiscated because he had some CDs by Haide and Mahasti—famous Iranian female vocalists. It was just another reminder that I was not in Kansas anymore; it's illegal in Iran to sell CDs by female singers. Farid was working on rebuilding his business, but his in-laws-to-be were getting impatient. Farid still owed the government 3.5 million tomans in fines, needed to find a way to finance his wedding, and wouldn't marry until he had purchased at least some inventory to reboot his business. So he and his fiancée agreed that he should sell a kidney.

While the misfortune that led Farid to donate was clearly tragic and unjust from a Western perspective, there was no reason to believe that the five million tomans he had negotiated for his kidney wouldn't supply the capital he needed to get married and restart his business. My only concern was that he would need to take special care to stay clear of the Iranian morality police, which may be easier said than done if one wants to be successful in the CD-selling business.

When Dr. Bastani mentioned how other young men we'd interviewed had felt ashamed about donating, Farid responded, "In the Qur'an, it says there is nothing wrong with helping yourself by helping others." His face broadened in a smile as he looked at both of us. "I feel good about what I'm about to do, and as long as my fiancée doesn't think less of me, which she assures me she won't, that is all that matters." Farid's story lifted my spirits, and I felt his fiancée was assuredly one lucky lady.

Another story that touched me was shared by Minoo, a kidney recipient at Labafinejad Clinic. Minoo was a sympathetic-looking 56-year-old woman in a midnight blue manteau. Her grey and baby-blue paisley scarf sat more than three inches off her hairline. Like many middle-aged women in Tehran, Minoo proudly displayed what she could of her dyed black hair in defiance of both age and the morality police. She wore sets of silver bracelets on both wrists that clinked when she moved. Minoo told us that four years ago she received a transplant from a boy of 19. She smiled when she said his name and shared that she had saved him from debtors' prison. "He is like a son to me."

It was not uncommon for recipients, like donors, to talk about how they saved their transplant partner. Minoo's donor owed a tort judgment (a *diye* in Farsi, which literally translates as "blood money") for having injured someone in a brawl. She gladly paid for all transplant-related expenses and gave him the five million tomans he needed on top of the one million he got from the government "so that he could pay off his debt to society." Minoo told us that since her transplant, she had seen her donor regularly and given him material support in the form of food, clothing, and household goods whenever she could.

Minoo's story was not atypical; many recipients we interviewed felt an affinity for their donors. It is interesting to note that out of the 23 recipients we interviewed who had received kidneys from non-related paid donors at least six

months prior to being interviewed, almost half said they had ongoing relationships with their donors. Three of these recipient/donor pairs were young
men close to the same age, but most were older recipients who had a good relationship with much younger donors. These older recipients kept referring
to their donors as sons and daughters.

A few of these pairs involved an older female recipient like Minoo, but most
involved older male recipients. In each case, recipients eagerly took on the role
of benefactor for their young donors. Sohrab, a 51-year-old teacher we met at
Sina Hospital, was a good example of this type of relationship. Sohrab felt a
strong attachment to his donor. "I have two sons, and it is as if he is my third.
I have promised God that as long as his kidney is working in my body, I will
be his servant. I would do anything for him." Later in the interview he told us,
"Just tonight my wife called and said that we are going over to his house for dinner." I was struck by the fact that the recipient was going over to the donor's
house for dinner, not the other way around—the friendship was obviously
mutual.

If the donor and recipient were closer in age, and particularly if they were
of the opposite sex, there was little likelihood of a lasting relationship between
them. I did hear of two instances where recipients married their donors, but
I am sure these were an anomaly. In none of the cases Dr. Bastani and I came
across where recipient and donor were of the opposite sex and close in age was
there—or did they think there would be—a lasting relationship. My guess is
that this has to do with the general social taboo against fraternizing with individuals of the opposite sex, the one sanctioned exception in the kidney donation context being a simulated parent-child relationship.

It is important to point out that I found fewer donors and recipients who were
satisfied with their donation in Tehran than elsewhere in Iran. It was only in
retrospect, after having traveled to Isfahan, Mashhad, Tabriz, and Kermanshah, that I started to piece together some of the factors that helped guarantee long-term satisfaction on both sides of the transplant equation.

Half of the donors and recipients we interviewed in Iran believed it was better if their relationship was just an economic one with no long-term ties. Donors
clearly wanted to put their current crisis behind them, and for some, that
meant not maintaining a relationship that would be a reminder of their fail-
ings. For recipients, it could be that some were influenced by the horrible incident in 1987 where a donor came to the recipient's house and attacked his family,

stabbing several of the recipient's children to death. But most recipients had a more mundane reason for not wanting a long-term relationship with their donor: They saw a mutually agreed-upon financial transaction as having a finality that would prevent the interminable feeling of indebtedness they feared would result if the donor became a friend. This latter concept of endless indebtedness came up several times in our interviews with recipients and was explained in depth by the Ayatollah Mohaghegh Damad in my discussion with him toward the end of our stay in Tehran.

Kidney Sales to Foreigners

Another issue that I was curious about was foreign participation in the Iranian kidney market. Organ purchases by foreigners, a practice initially allowed in Iran, was banned in 1992. The president of the Iranian Society of Nephrology, Dr. Behrooz Broumand, a dapper gentleman in his 60s, who wears a fresh orchid in his lapel and smiles invitingly when he speaks, told us that, in the beginning of the program, sales to foreigners weren't uncommon, but now they are rare. There are occasional cases where surgeons or the *Anjoman* make private deals to help foreigners (usually Arabs) get a paid Iranian donor, but they do so at great risk.

Dr. Broumand personally was tangentially involved in one such scandal: The Saudi ambassador's wife was his patient, and the ambassador offered him $30,000 to help find her an Iranian donor. Dr. Broumand refused, but the ambassador found someone else who was willing to help before Dr. Broumand or the authorities could stop him. He told us this incident happened shortly after the ban was initiated and that now the medical community is better at policing itself. Dr. Ghods told us of just such an incident. Earlier in the year I was there, it was discovered that surgeons at one Tehran hospital were arranging illegal transplants for foreigners. The physicians involved lost their surgical privileges, and the whole transplant unit was shut down.

A Tehran *Anjoman* social worker told us that in the current political climate it would be institutional suicide to get involved in arranging kidney sales to foreigners. If such activity came to light, the government would revoke the organization's NGO status. One *Anjoman* intake clerk told us that it would be difficult, albeit not impossible, to forge an Iranian ID card and come up with fake letters of reference and a fake proof of residency. Other *Anjoman* staff and medical professionals we consulted emphasized that everyone involved in processing a donor's application and pre-op testing would have to actively look the other way not to recognize a foreigner even if he or she spoke excellent

Farsi or claimed to come from a region in Iran where a different language, for example Kurdish or a Turkic dialect, is spoken.

Given these discussions I was surprised to hear one *Anjoman* board member volunteer some potentially incriminating information. I never directly asked the *Anjoman* board of directors about kidney sales to foreigners, but I did ask if the Tehran *Anjoman* had any contact with the U.S. National Kidney Foundation. They said they had interacted with the NKF at conferences, and then one board member mentioned totally out of the blue that they had even helped an official from the NKF get a kidney in Iran. I contained my surprise and let the conversation proceed without interruption, planning to ask Dr. Bastani when the opportunity arose if I had heard correctly.

Had it happened before or after Iran outlawed selling kidneys to foreigners? Actually, why had it happened at all, given that the NKF has openly condemned compensated kidney donation? Clearly, fear of death is a strong motivator—apparently, stronger than convictions about policy. Many a good American has unwittingly contributed to the horrors of the black market kidney trade; at least this NKF official didn't do that. I wondered, but had no way of knowing, if he (or she) was one of the few NKF employees I'd met who, at least behind closed doors and off the record, were willing to say the United States should consider compensated donation.

I gathered up my courage and came back to the question after we had all but finished our discussion, but the board members sensed I was fishing, and my bringing it up was a conversation stopper. Our interview was over, and returning to the issue may have been one of the reasons why the *Anjoman* later had second thoughts about letting us do a third day of interviews.

An obvious loophole in the law against foreigners shopping for kidneys in Iran involves Iranian expats. Technically, the compensated kidney program is available only to resident citizens. One *Anjoman* staff member told us that if an expat claimed to be living with a relative in Iran and had an Iranian ID card, it would be all but impossible to keep that person from entering the system.

But no one seemed to think expats availing themselves of the *Anjoman's* services was much of an issue—they seemed to consider it a minor infraction not worth the effort it would take to stop. Dr. Bastani knows three American Iranians who bought kidneys through *Anjomans* in Iran. He said they came to him for post-transplant follow-up treatment because their American pre-transplant nephrologists refused to keep them on as patients. The U.S. doctors these

American-Iranians were seeing before their transplants were concerned that treating patients who obtained kidneys in Iran might be understood as a violation of the National Organ Transplant Act, which prohibits taking part in any transplant where the donor received any form of "valuable consideration," namely any compensation in the form of money, goods, or services that is more than a token gift.

The one sanctioned exception to the Iranian prohibition on sales to foreigners is that several of the *Anjomans* we visited willingly helped Afghan refugees. It is legal for foreigners to bring donors from their own countries to have their transplants done in Iran, but it is technically illegal for them to avail themselves of *Anjoman* services to help them find a donor. Refugees, like foreigners, are supposed to find their own donors, but most *Anjoman* include resident refugees in their databases and are willing to match them with each other. The government will not help pay for the transplant or the donor's fee for refugees, but several *Anjomans* we visited would help Afghan refugee recipients find charity funds to pay their Afghan refugee donors and to pay for the transplant and related medications.

We came across four Afghan refugees in Tehran who under Iranian law could receive free dialysis treatment, but who as non-citizens weren't eligible for a government-funded transplant. Hanieh at the Hashiminejad Dialysis Center hoped that someday she could afford a transplant, but in the meantime she was deeply grateful to the Iranian government for providing her with dialysis.

She said that in Afghanistan there were only two dialysis machines for every 50 patients. The machines were in such high demand that she had to make an appointment a month in advance and pay the equivalent of 80,000 tomans every time she was dialyzed. Hanieh's condition deteriorated to such an extent that her family carried her, comatose, across the border to an Iranian hospital. It took four months of regular dialysis before she could walk again. For the past year and a half, she and her husband have lived in Iran while their three children remain in Afghanistan. When Dr. Bastani inquired about her plans, she said, "I don't know. … Right now, we are here." She seemed relieved just to be alive.

Hoda, a 28-year-old Afghan woman living in Kashan, Iran, told us a different type of refugee story. We met Hoda at Shariati Hospital where she described the hardships her family suffered coming to Iran, but those hardships were not related to her kidney disease. She didn't get sick until many years later. She had a transplant two months before our interview and was back in the hospital because of complications. Her donor was an Afghan refugee who had registered with the *Anjoman*, but they had never met because he was an illegal immigrant and shy of all but the most necessary meetings. To pay for the operation, her family sold the land they owned in Afghanistan and their house in the Iranian village where she had lived for more than nine years. The rest of the funds she needed were raised by her Iranian neighbors. In total, including testing and her donor's payment, she had spent 25 million tomans.

Hoda was wearing a surgical mask to prevent infection, and her black bangs peeked out from under a faded blue headscarf. She looked older than her biological 28 years, tired and weary. Her skin, abnormally translucent, looked prone to tear, like tissue paper. I feared I might see her eyes through her eyelids when she blinked. Her fingernails were chalky white. She spoke so softly I could barely hear her. Hoda was beside herself with grief because so many people had been generous, and her family had sacrificed so much. And now it looked like her transplant was failing. She seemed to be fading before my eyes, and I was overtaken by a profound sadness. *Would Hoda get another chance?* In the United States, so many people don't even get a first chance.

Beyond issues of who qualifies to receive a transplant, there are numerous regulations and guidelines promulgated by the Iranian Transplant Society and the Iranian Ministry of Health that cover almost every aspect of the donor-recipient matching process. Included are things such as the preferred age ranges for donors (20 to 40), instructions on how to carry out urine and blood tests to ensure addicts are excluded and that samples are not misrepresented, a prohibition against forum-shopping, and principles mandating informed consent. (In spite of these guidelines, most donors said they weren't informed about the possible risks of donation until well after they had already committed to donate, usually when they met their surgeon.) While everyone was bound by national laws, regulations, and standards, we were soon to learn that many details, particularly the range of potential benefits available to donors and recipients, were determined at the regional or even the *Anjoman* level of administration.

Before we moved on to other cities, however, there were still important questions about the Iranian system that could best be answered in Tehran. Next on our list were Ayatollah Mohaghegh Damad and Dr. Mohammad Reza Khatami. We would look to the Ayatollah for guidance on the philosophical and theological underpinnings of kidney procurement in Iran; and we would turn to Dr. Khatami, a nephrologist like Dr. Bastani, who happened also to be a former member of the *Majilis* and brother of the fifth president of Iran (Seyyed Mohammad Khatami), to give us a sense of the political future of the Iranian organ procurement system.

Selling a Kidney Is Like Selling a Qur'an

Ayatollah Mohaghegh Damad holds a law degree and a doctorate in Islamic philosophy and has achieved the highest degree in divine law available from the Islamic Seminary in Qom. He is the ethicist for the Iranian Academy of Medical Sciences, head of Islamic studies at the Iranian Academy of Sciences, and a member of the Iranian Ministry of Health Ethics Committee. He graciously invited us to interview him at his home in Tehran.

My excitement about the interview got the better of me, and I arrived half an hour early. I didn't want to impose, so I decided to explore. I walked along Ayatollah Mohaghegh Damad's street, which, like most residential streets in Iran, was flanked by two sets of high walls with doors opening into individual courtyards. Occasionally, at the end of one wall, there would be a few feet of narrow alleyway before the next wall. Through one gap I could glimpse Tehran in the valley below, shrouded in a mist of its own making.

I was enjoying the view when a buzzing caught my attention, then a rank odor. Across the alley, two sheep's heads lay next to an overflowing dumpster. Swarming insects conjured up images from *Lord of the Flies*. The stench drove me on, but I couldn't escape the feeling that someone was watching me. I scanned in all four directions, thinking I might have missed someone standing in a doorway. Then I looked up. There they were, two German shepherds walking along the top of a 20-foot wall—no fence, no owner at the other end of a leash, just the height of the wall between me and the dogs. I stood transfixed, looking from one dog to the other, trying to assess whether they saw me as a threat. I felt an odd desire to converse with them in Farsi, fearing my American tones might incite an attack. When they resumed pacing the wall, I quickly crossed the street and started back toward the ayatollah's house. I felt their eyes on me the whole way. I stayed steadfastly fixed on my course, moving deliberately and steadily so as not to provoke them.

Once inside the ayatollah's house, I felt right at home. The stoic style of his furnishings appealed to my Scandinavian sensibilities. The walls were decorated with artwork by his daughter and some of his friends, much like my farm-house walls in Virginia. The ayatollah wore a black turban, several layers of black and blue robes, and an impressive light-blue-gemmed ring on his left hand. I thought of the signet ring Dr. Bastani had lost and how Iranians, even the intentionally demure clergy, saw fit to adorn themselves with traditionally aristocratic symbols. His beard was grey and peppered black. Ever-patient with my questions, he readily shared important cultural and historic insights into why Iranians accept compensated living kidney donation as ethical.

Ayatollah Mohaghegh Damad explained that Sharia law—Islamic law—evolves, just like any other system of jurisprudence. Sharia is based on precepts set forth in the Qur'an, examples set by the Prophet Mohammad, and their interpretation and application in Islamic jurisprudence. Under Sharia law, he explained, it is unacceptable to gain from something that has no value: Essentially, it is immoral to cheat people by trading or selling something by implying it has value when it does not. His voice had a soft harmony, a cadence not typical in English, like a distant Gregorian chant. "Sometimes there are things that have no value, but then society finds value in them, and fatwas (legally binding decrees made by Islamic religious leaders) change and evolve to suit the times."

He explained further, "Chess used to be haram because it involved gambling. But chess itself is not gambling but a socially valuable game of math and strategy, so the mullahs made a new fatwa, and while gambling is still haram, chess is not."

Such changes in the law are quite natural in all cultures, said the ayatollah, and a similar evolution happened with how Iranian society views kidney sales. "Once thought valueless, now kidneys have become full of value. We have learned that many of the organs of the body have a value we hadn't seen before." Therefore, it became acceptable to sell kidneys, particularly because, like blood, they have a use outside the body that does no long-term harm to the seller.

But, he pointed out, there were complicating factors that Iranian jurists still needed to work out. First, how do you place a price on the gift of life? Some suggested using the value of a kidney applied in tort judgments (the *diye* that must be paid when a person is injured), but a kidney donated is not the same as a kidney lost secondary to a crime or accident. To put a tort value on a kidney undervalues the sacrifice of donation and neglects the distinction society rightfully makes between intentionally saving a life and incidental harm to an organ.

The solution according to the ayatollah was not to consider the money received by the donor as a payment but as a token of appreciation. "We have many similar examples in Islamic law. You cannot sell the Qur'an, because it is the word of God. This is something that is invaluable. Similarly, we have come to understand blood and kidneys as invaluable because of their usefulness to others—because of the life-giving nature of donation." In short, you can't put a value on saving a life, so no matter how much money is given a kidney donor, it can never be enough to be more than a token—a gift, not a payment, because as payment it could never suffice.

In addition, Sharia law prohibits exploitation of those in need—there is an explicit interdiction against profiteering. "It is acceptable to sell bread if no one is starving, but to the poor starving man, one should give bread away for free." That doesn't mean one can't pay the person who gives one bread; it just means the donor cannot demand payment in the strictest sense of the word "payment."

Iranians are conflicted about kidney selling because often both parties to the relationship are in desperate need: one at risk of dying, the other at risk of financial ruin. To avoid either the donor or recipient from running afoul of the prohibition against exploitation, Mohaghegh Damad explained, the relationship is framed in terms of exchanging gifts, rather than a commercial transaction. Donors give a part of their body to save a kidney recipient's life, and the recipient (with the help of society) gives the donor the monetary assistance needed to avert financial ruin. Both acts in and of themselves are good deeds, worthy of praise. The ayatollah repeated something we had heard from both donors and recipients: "The Qur'an looks favorably on those who help themselves by helping others."

This quote from the Qur'an reminded me of something the Dalai Lama had said. In *The Art of Happiness in a Troubled World*, the Dalai Lama criticizes Western culture for assuming compassion requires a form of self-sacrifice where all the good achieved is solely directed toward the recipient. The Dalai Lama writes in his concluding chapter: "[T]here is a sense [in the West] that if one has any thought for one's own welfare when showing another kindness [that] it 'doesn't count' as an act of altruism or pure compassion." Both Ayatollah Damad and the Dalai Lama suggest that we should not dismiss altruistic actions as less valuable to society simply because they are also motivated by self-interest.

The final issue the ayatollah addressed was that it is one thing to allow gifts of thanks for an altruistic act, but it is quite another to require them. The reciprocal gifting of money in exchange for a kidney, Mohaghegh Damad said, must be legally enforceable. The donor must either give back the money or donate. And the recipient, who can't give back a kidney, must be legally forced to pay the monetary gift promised the donor. This point was made by several of the donors we interviewed. For example, Sasan, whom we interviewed later at Alzahra Hospital in Isfahan, said he had heard rumors that donors could get 15 or even 20 million tomans for a kidney if they did it illegally without the *Anjoman's* assistance, but he had looked into it and didn't see how he could be sure to get his money without the *Anjoman*. With the *Anjoman's* oversight, Sasan would get the six million he was promised, and he knew the deal included the recipient paying for his lab work and other benefits, none of which could be guaranteed outside the legally sanctioned system.

While the notion of a gift in Western thought implies an absence of legal obligation (like the notion of altruism implies a lack of self-interest), under Sharia law a promise of reciprocal gifting is legally enforceable. Under Sharia law the result is not a commercial contract but a binding decision to provide each other with a gift—in the one instance a kidney, in the other a predetermined amount of money or another gift. There is no commercial contract in the Western sense but an implied promise which, as with gifting a Qur'an, Iranian law has decided to enforce: "I donate my kidney to you unconditionally, and you donate a predetermined amount of money to me unconditionally, and if I don't receive the promised payment, I can take you to court." This may seem like a commercial transaction to Westerners, but the Iranian attitude toward this type of reciprocal gifting is clearly something more than a mere buying and selling—such transactions entail an altruistic element not required in the usual course of business.

Another reason to make a promised gift to donors a matter of law is to prevent indefinite indebtedness. Some gifts, like the gift of a kidney, are so great that they can never be repaid. So to mediate the fear that acceptance of a kidney will cause an unbearable burden on the recipient, the law creates a system whereby the donor can agree to a finite reward for his or her gift, thereby relieving the recipient of any further obligation. Thus, if the parties wish, payment can be the full extent of their relationship.

In the United States the concept of immeasurable debt is described as "tyranny of the gift." Interestingly, we often heard Iranian recipients tell us the reason they used a paid donor instead of an altruistic relative or friend was to avoid the potential burden of feeling permanently indebted. Asad, a recipient we interviewed at Labafinejad Clinic, received his first kidney from his brother, but he said he would never get a kidney from a relative or friend again.

> My brother has done a saving and kind act for me. But every time I see him—there's a psychological and spiritual issue involved. I have to be appreciative of my brother for donating his kidney, right? Yes, it is true that his donation has worked to my benefit, but I will be indebted to him indefinitely: always appreciative, always saying thank you. If a person gets paid five or ten million, then the relationship is over. In that situation, I would be grateful but my debt is paid, and I could move on with my life.

We spent almost two hours at the ayatollah's house. I could have easily spent two more, but he had another engagement. I was reminded of a radio interview where I once heard Sandra Day O'Connor (the first woman to serve as a justice on the U.S. Supreme Court) answer a question about whether she felt she should be replaced by a woman once she retired from the Court. In essence she said, "It doesn't matter. Women and men focus on different issues, but a wise man and a wise women will always, after due consideration, come to the same conclusion." There is no doubt that Iranian society and Western society are different, perhaps even incompatible, but could we both, like Justice O'Connor's wise men and wise women, eventually come to the same conclusion regarding compensated kidney donation?

While I was impressed with the ayatollah's pedagogy and clarity of thought, I couldn't help but think interpretation is everything. He made such a well-reasoned argument for why Sharia law accepts and even condones both cadaver and living kidney donation; yet I couldn't help but also remember other things Sharia law condones, depending on how one reads it — the cutting off of hands for theft, stoning people to death for adultery, debtors' prison, and many other atrocities, all in the name of God's will. I realize similar punishments are not alien to Anglo-American legal history, but they were abolished centuries ago.

I had an inkling that Ayatollah Mohaghegh Damad was hoping the Iranian interpretation of Sharia law would evolve in a similar direction. But how many in the Iranian clerical hierarchy agreed with his vision? How long will it take, if such modernization materializes at all? *How much human suffering must be tolerated in the meantime?* "All law evolves," the Ayatollah Mohaghegh Damad said, and when it comes to solving the organ shortage, he might ask me the same type of question: How long will it take for Western jurisprudence to evolve to the point where kidney disease patients aren't dying needlessly because donation isn't incentivized properly?

The Grand Ayatollah's Granddaughter

On our last day in Tehran, I was privileged to have lunch at the home of Dr. Mohammad Reza Khatami, the brother of the president of Iran before Mahmoud Ahmadinejad. Dr. Khatami is a nephrologist who has served in the Iranian parliament. He spoke eloquently and confirmed many of the things we learned from Dr. Ghods, Dr. Broumand, and others. Dr. Khatami and Dr. Bastani spent much of their time in an intense conversation about the upcoming presidential election: What changes, if any, could they expect? While I was fascinated to later hear from Dr. Bastani what they had discussed, I spent most of my time conversing with Mrs. Mohammad Reza Khatami, the grand-daughter of the Grand Ayatollah Khomeini.

A photo prominently displayed in the living room framed a bearded man in a white robe and a black turban holding a baby in his arms. He cradled the baby gingerly and smiled with pride as any grandfather would.

"Is that who I think it is?"

Mrs. Khatami picked up a glass of tea, taking the time to put a sugar cube in her mouth, and sipped some tea before answering. "Yes, the Grand Ayatol-lah was my grandfather. And that is me as a baby."

Mrs. Khatami reminded me of the woman-of-the-house of the Parisian family I lived with when I studied in France. She was wearing a silk blouse with gilded buttons and fine gold jewelry. She had a French manicure, and her above-shoulder-length hair was coiffed in the manner of a Western profes-sional. She didn't wear a headscarf—headscarves are optional in one's own home—and she spoke in perfect British English. Mrs. Khatami is an activist for women's rights in Iran and is rightfully proud of her successes, which, among other accomplishments, include helping convince the *Majilis* to reform laws that disadvantage divorced women. She was eager to explain how in Iran "sometimes big strides come in small steps" and that there was still much for her to do.

At a lull in the conversation, she looked pensively at me and then seemed to make up her mind about something. She walked elegantly, gliding across the room, and removed a gilded 8-by-10 frame from a cabinet, and returning to where I sat, handed it to me. I held it gingerly, trying to avoid getting fingerprints on the glass. The photo was of a young woman who stood majestically in a long white wedding gown with a lacy, beaded train spread out in an arc before her.

"Is this you?"

"No, no," she said, blushing. "From my daughter's wedding in Paris."

"Ohhh. She is beautiful!"

"The dress is Dior."

At first I thought I may have misheard her, but all I had to do was look at the intricate lace and beadwork to know I had not misheard. She had said "Dior."

I handed back the photo, "Yes, very beautiful indeed." But I couldn't help but wonder what her grandfather, who had lead the Iranian people in a revolt against "Western decadence," would have thought.

The order in which we visited cities in Iran was fortunate. Shiraz was the most like the United States because of its well-developed cadaver procurement program and its policies against organ selling. Tehran used the Iranian model most familiar to foreigners who know anything about the Iranian organ market. But as I would spend the next month learning, my most interesting discoveries were still to come.

𝄆 (6)

The Poor and the "Lucky"

On the flight to Isfahan, Dr. Bastani told me a parable about how the three Abrahamic religions view justice. Moses teaches his people to see with their right eye: "Give my people strength and self-confidence in themselves and their God." The people of Moses know how to fight for their place in the world. Jesus teaches his people to see with their left eye: "Turn the other cheek when someone transgresses against you." The people of Jesus try to make peace in the world. Mohammad teaches his people to keep both eyes open: "Tell my people to mete out mercy when possible but justice when necessary." Dr. Bastani continued by explaining that a good Muslim knows that sometimes justice requires punishment and that demanding proportionate punishment is just, but only forgiveness and mercy can make a just and good man morally great.

At the time, I wasn't sure why Dr. Bastani was sharing this parable since I didn't think of Iran as a place of religious tolerance. And it isn't, at least not by Western standards. But Dr. Bastani was using the parable to explain how Iranian Muslims see themselves as part of the Abrahamic tradition—as having evolved from and, in Muslims' eyes, evolved beyond Judaism and Christianity. I already knew that Iranians revere their cultural heritage, but in Isfahan I learned that this reverence extended beyond art and literature to religion. In the Persian mindset, it is acceptable to disagree with, but not to disrespect, your forefathers. As a result, Iran is one of the most religiously tolerant and diverse countries in the Middle East.

A Dream City Sleeps

Shiraz was tropical and enchanting, but Isfahan was like a warm embrace. There is no doubt that Isfahan is my favorite city in Iran and one of my favorite cities in the world. Parks line both sides of the fecund Zayandeh River, encouraging a leisurely pace. Ancient, arched, multilevel bridges traverse the Zayandeh, a perfect place to sit and watch the ducks swim by. The people of Isfahan refer to their city as "the pearl of Persia" or "half the world"; both appellations fit the city well. Isfahan was the capital of the sixteenth and seventeenth century Safavid Dynasty, and it reminds me of European cities like Prague that charm through a blend of ancient and modern.

When we first drove into Isfahn from the airport, there were people everywhere, busily on their way to work or running errands, but I immediately sensed that the city was designed for more. I could imagine street performers, painters at their easels, cafés, food vendors, merchants hocking their wares, children playing, and tourists—oh, Western tourists would flock here if they were only given the chance. Instead, I found the city all but devoid of street culture: I saw one couple strolling along the river; one young man sitting on the edge of Chubi Bridge, swinging his legs and watching the ducks below; and one vendor under Khaju Bridge selling tea and dried-out cakes from a makeshift cart. According to Dr. Bastani, Isfahan used to be much like what I imagined, but things changed when the morality police shut down the teahouses. Now it is considered immoral to have too much fun in public, particularly if it involves talking to or, God forbid, laughing with someone of the opposite sex.

Greece but Not

Only a month after leaving Iran, I went back to Greece for the first time in 40 years. I couldn't help but marvel at how many tourists there were. Every café sold lattés and cappuccinos, not just the black Turkish coffee I remembered. Some even sold crêpes with Nutella, which, like lattés and cappuccinos, are not a traditional Greek food—none of these treats were available the last time I was there. Street vendors sold jewelry, pottery, and other souvenirs. And, as I remembered, men sat at tables in the park and in cafés playing backgammon. Iran, particularly Isfahan, reminded me of what I knew of Greece from my childhood: people wearing severe colorless clothing, women in black headscarves, men drinking in cafés where women weren't welcome. But now, Greece has transformed into a modern European country, and Isfahan doesn't even have cafés anymore.

Greece has come far since I lived there in 1968. It is facing an unfortunate economic crisis, but it is still more modern, more colorful, and more fun than it was. Towns and cities are filled with men and women experiencing the best of street culture together. And tourists still flock there, albeit in lower numbers than just a few years ago. Even in these economically depressed times, the Acropolis in Athens is always crowded, as are the ruins at Delphi and the Palace of Knossos on Crete. With all its Persian and Islamic architectural treasures, natural beauty, and fascinating history, Iran could easily be a major tourist destination, like Greece. *What a shame to deprive the world of Iran's treasures. What a shame to deprive Iranians of the pride in sharing their cultural heritage and of the income a vibrant tourist trade could generate.*

Dr. Shiva Seyrafian of the Isfahan Kidney Disease Research Center arranged rooms for us at the Azadi Persian Hotel, just a few paces from the Si-o-se Pol Bridge. The Azadi was nothing like the Alborz Hotel in Tehran. It had all the amenities of home. I even spied an espresso machine behind the bar—yes, they had a bar, but no liquor was served. I love tea, and I have no problem doing without alcohol, but I did miss good coffee. The first few times I ordered coffee in Iran, I was served instant coffee—usually Nescafé—so I stopped asking and stuck to tea. But here, hopeful, I tried again. I pointed at the espresso maker. "Café."

The man behind the bar nodded. Steam hissed, and the dark scent of coffee reached my nostrils as the machine hummed and frothed. With great expectation, I sat down at a table decked in white linen with my pastry and coffee. I was poised to enjoy, but my longing had made me susceptible to deception: I hadn't smelled anything fresh-brewed. The light brown swirls with brown flecks gave away my coffee's powdered origin. What a disappointment! More Nescafé, only this time made with frothed milk. My pistachio-filled baklava-like pastry, however, was beyond reproach.

Testing the Waters

I couldn't wait to get out and explore the banks of the Zayandeh River. Dr. Bastani sensed my enthusiasm and offered to take a walk with me after dinner. It was beautiful, but I didn't take in as much of the scenery as I would have liked. As soon as we started walking, Dr. Bastani began telling me a story about a professor he knew who had an affair with a graduate student. *Usually Dr. Bastani's stories are from Persian mythology or Islamic theology. Why is he telling me this?* He went on to explain that the young graduate student had become pregnant, and the professor divorced his wife to marry his lover. But something went terribly wrong during the delivery, and his young wife suffered a ruptured brain aneurysm. The baby survived and so did the mother, but the mother was paralyzed.

Dr. Bastani stopped walking and turned to me. "Maybe it was God punishing them for the affair?"

I said, "Oh, no. No one deserves to have something like that happen to them."

Dr. Bastani turned to point out some ducks in the water, and in so doing brushed up against me. I was flustered and tried to quickly think of some way to modify my response. Maybe, *"Not that what they did was right, but ..."* Instead I just started walking again.

Dr. Bastani told me that he knew the professor's first wife and knew she was lonely and had little to do now that her own children were grown and out of the house. He wondered whether I thought she should help raise the baby.

"That's too much to ask," I said as I quickened my pace.

"But if she ever really loved him—"

I cut him off. "It doesn't matter. He has done something unforgivable."

Dr. Bastani looked quizzically at me. "You mean if Bob had even the smallest meaningless fling, you would leave him?"

Because of all the bobbing up and down with the differences in our strides, I had to stop to meet his eyes so he would know I was serious. "Yes, and I've told him as much."

"Huh, Sigrid, I'm not sure I believe you."

I turned around and started walking back toward the hotel. "Bahar, it's not you I need to convince. And besides, I trust Bob loves me enough not to take the chance that I might be true to my word."

He took an extra long stride to catch up with me. "But why would you leave someone you love and have spent almost 25 years of your life with over a relatively minor moment of weakness?"

"Because I couldn't live with someone I didn't trust. Nor could I maintain my own sense of dignity and self-worth if I knew he had cheated on me."

I didn't look up, but I could feel him smile. "That's the key, isn't it? If you knew. Or rather, if other people were aware that you knew. The professor in my story was known for his indiscretions. I'm sure his wife just pretended not to notice to save face."

"Bahar," I said, my voice starting to echo the faster pace of my breathing, "there isn't much difference between doing and knowing."

"What do you mean?"

"I mean it would hurt the relationship Bob and I have even if I didn't know because he would know."

"You mean Bob would act differently because he felt guilty?"

"Yes, I guess that's it." Actually there was much more to what I was saying— how can one lose oneself in love while worrying that one's lover might sense something amiss? Even a slight unease or a misplaced word can cause tension if not give away that someone has been untrue.

When we arrived at the Azadi, Dr. Bastani suggested we sit and have a cup of tea before going up to our rooms. It was still early, but I was weary and out of sorts. It didn't bother me that Dr. Bastani thought a wife should forgive her husband if he strayed; I assumed Bahar was modern enough in his thinking to also feel a husband should forgive his wife if she had an affair. That such transgressions weren't as grievous as I made them out to be was an opinion I'd heard expressed before by many of my friends. What bothered me was that having this conversation could mark the end of our genial relationship. I didn't dare complicate things any further by voicing my thoughts. Instead, fully aware of the inanity of my statement, I responded, "I think I'll turn in. Tomorrow is going to be a busy day."

The History That Defines Us

On our way to give talks at Al-Zahra Hospital, Dr. Atapour, professor of nephrology at Isfahan School of Medicine, told us of two patients he had seen that morning. One was a female donor who needed money to pay for her daughter's education. Her husband earned enough to send their daughter to college but didn't want to "waste" his savings on a girl, so the mother sold a kidney to pay for her daughter's education herself. The other patient was a father who sold his kidney to pay for his son's leukemia medications. Dr. Atapour said he would mention our intention to visit these patients to the head nurse of the recovery ward.

Al-Zahra Hospital was a huge glass-and-concrete structure nestled in the foothills of the Zagros mountain range. The hospital's boxlike shape was softened by arches over each set of windows and twin curved staircases leading up to the second floor. The building lay above the city but beneath the pre-Islamic Zoroastrian fire temple of Atashkadeh as if the hospital watched over the people of Isfahan, and in turn, the Zoroastrian fire temple watched over the hospital.

There aren't many practicing Zoroastrians in Iran anymore—estimates are anywhere from 30,000 to 100,000—but many Iranians speak fondly of Zoroastrianism as part of their Persian heritage. Zoroastrianism is the first religion known to have postulated an invisible, omnipotent, supreme being and is believed to date back to 1,500 B.C. A fire temple at Yazd, a town about 260 miles south of Isfahan, claims to nurture a flame that has burned continuously for over 4,000 years. One physician at Al-Zahra Hospital proudly announced to me that he wasn't an Arab or a Muslim but an Iranian of purely Persian decent and a practicing Zoroastrian.

If there was a chance for the conversation to drift in that direction, most of the Iranians I met boasted about their heritage, often about their relatedness to one or the other Shi'ite imam. Dr. Bastani is proud to be a descendant of the Fourth Imam. He is of both Arabic and Persian descent, but oddly, Dr. Bastani's father looks so much like my own father that I did a double take when I first met him—they could be brothers. Dr. Bastani's father must have some Indo-European features from his Persian forefathers that caught my eye; otherwise, how could he look so much like my half Norwegian, half English father?

Until this trip, I didn't think of Iran as a melting pot of cultures and ethnicities, not in the American sense, anyway. But you can see it in people's faces and hear it in the stories they tell about their ancestors. Many Iranians proudly describe their Persian heritage in the same way I proudly share my American Revolutionary heritage and my husband's American Indian heritage. My many-greats-grandfather Joshua Fry was best friends with Thomas Jefferson's father, Peter Jefferson, and the two men mapped the state of Virginia together. As a colonel of the Virginia Militia, Joshua Fry gave the young George Washington his first command. When Joshua Fry died at the beginning of the French and Indian War in 1754, George Washington carved an epitaph into a tree near Fort Cumberland, Maryland. A historic plaque still marks the spot today.

On my husband's side of the family, the American roots run even deeper: Bob is part Blackfoot Indian. Both his parents can trace their heritage back to Native American ancestors from the Great Plains; on his father's side, they know the tribe was Blackfoot. Because my husband's surname "Corn" is French, I imagine somewhere on his father's side there must have been a French trapper who married a beautiful Blackfoot squaw. Everywhere in the world, people share their roots with pride and as a means of finding common ground. Iran was no different, and this type of talk, like talk about sports or music, was a language I knew how to speak.

Once inside Al-Zahra Hospital, I was conscious of the stark contrast between its concrete-and-glass exterior and the plush, moss green velvet curtains and gold tasseled pulls that hung in its conference rooms. How unusual for a hospital, but how Iranian—an austere Muslim exterior, but inside, a touch of the ornate Persian heart. I took one of my favorite photos from the trip in such an embellished conference room: Dr. Shahidi, a nephrologist at the hospital, sitting at the conference table in her midnight-blue hijab, adjusting a slide under the microscope, with regal green and gold velvet curtains framing her profile.

Unfortunately, by the time we arrived at the transplant ward, we could not speak to the patients Dr. Atapour had suggested: The woman who sold her kidney to fund her daughter's education was in surgery, and the father whose son had leukemia had already checked out of the hospital. But there were plenty of other patients to talk to, and we did some worthwhile interviews.

The most interesting person we spoke to at Al-Zahra Hospital was Sasan. Several bad checks were about to land Sasan's wife in debtors' prison. She offered to sell her kidney to pay off her debts, but Sasan wouldn't hear of it. "I told her we couldn't risk her not being able to care for our child." He joked that it would be much easier on the family if he were temporarily laid up rather than her. It bothered me when Sasan confided in us that he needed only 2.5 million tomans to pay off his wife's debts, but he had told the *Anjoman* that he needed six million. The *Anjoman* found him a recipient who could pay five million toman, and with the one million toman *issar* from the national government, the *Anjoman* was satisfied that Sasan would receive enough to solve his financial crisis. But then Sasan went on to say, while he didn't need that much money originally, circumstances developed that made the extra financial cushion fortunate. All the time he was required to take off work for the pre-transplant testing caused him to lose his job. "You know, I kept leaving to go to the medical lab, but I didn't want to tell anyone why I was leaving." Sasan didn't seem all that upset about being unemployed. He said he hadn't been happy at work anyway, and now he had an incentive to make a long-needed change.

The majority of stories we heard at Al-Zahra Hospital were a variation on this same theme (getting out of debt), but that doesn't mean the donors' actions were self-serving and nothing else. The testimonials we collected revealed mixed motives, all of which were, at least in part, altruistic. Every donor mentioned the satisfaction of helping recipients overcome their illness, but beyond that, they also usually needed the money for selfless reasons. The money from kidney sales was rarely used to help just the donor. Ten percent of the donors we interviewed claimed to have purely altruistic motives. (Shiraz data was not included because of its unreliability on this point.) Of those who admitted to having financial motives, 58 percent indicated that the sale was not intended to benefit them directly but to help their families—usually their children but sometimes the donor's sibling or spouse. Another 15 percent said they needed money to get married and start a family. And yet in other cases, where donors admitted the money helped them decide to donate, monetary gain was a secondary consideration, like for Ebrahim, the donor we met at the Isfahan branch of the Tehran *Anjoman*, whose story I'll tell below.

A Disappointment

Isfahan has two *Anjomans*. The first *Anjoman* we visited was a branch of the Iranian National Kidney Foundation. The setup was quite different from what we had seen in Tehran: no computer terminals, no shiny laminate countertop, no smiling intake clerks handing out photo IDs to donors. This *Anjoman* was located in a desolate part of town. The sand-blasted concrete and asphalt reminded me of housing complexes I'd seen in Bulgaria during the communist era: devoid of greenery, stark, and inhospitable.

We entered one of the multiple identical entrances to find an interior courtyard lined with unadorned, mustard-yellow railings—still no plants and no people. But there were a few signs of life: a ball left abandoned on the ground, laundry strung on a line, a trash can outside someone's back door. The *Anjoman* was housed in an apartment on the second floor. A mustard-yellow gate that matched the stair rails was slightly open, but the door to the *Anjoman* was shut. Next to the door on the wall, an unremarkable small brown sign read: "The Society for the Protection of Kidney Disease Patients. Closed on Thursdays."

Dr. Bastani knocked and entered without waiting for a response. I briefly considered taking off my shoes, as is the custom when entering someone's home, but reminded myself that this was a place of business. A short, heavy-set, lethargic, slightly paunch-bellied man greeted us. He was barely more than five feet tall. He wore grey pants, grey shoes, and a white shirt that protruded a good two inches beyond his ill-fitting grey jacket. He had more of a beard than most; it matched his overdue-for-a-trim hair. He hurried us into a small room and left, saying he would be right back, as if we had interrupted something— maybe his morning toilette.

The room was tiny, no more than a large closet with a desk and two chairs. The only other piece of furniture was a lopsided file cabinet. The industrial-style furniture was the same dappled-grey metal common in U.S. schools in the 1950s and '60s.

"What are those?" I pointed to the colorful marbled folders in pink, orange, light green, and baby blue, stacked so high on the desk they were in danger of toppling over.

Dr. Bastani took a peek. "It looks like donor and recipient files, grouped by blood type."

"This is their matching process?"

Dr. Bastani shrugged and took a seat next to me. The grey-clad gentleman shuffled in, tray in one hand, pulling a wheeled office chair with the other. He offered us tea, setting the tray down beside him on the beige, possibly once-white linoleum. *Where is everybody?* There were no staff, no donors, and no recipients making inquiries. Isfahan is a city of over a million and a half people, almost half as large as Shiraz. *How can there be no one here?*

Once we finished tea, we began interviewing our host, Mr. Mohammad Ismael Khani, but were interrupted by a knock on the door. A rectangular face with a meticulously coiffed Elvis-like hairdo peered through a crack in the doorway and asked if there was anyone who could help him. We decided Mr. Khani's interview could wait and shifted our attention to Ebrahim.

Ebrahim wore a double-breasted olive-green suit with a slight pin stripe, a zinc-colored button-down shirt, and a cream sweater vest. He spoke at first with reticence but then opened up: "In the beginning, when I still lived in Tehran, to tell you the truth, there was a financial problem, but after a while, thank God, my financial problem was solved." Ebrahim told us he had lost his job in Tehran and had run out of money. He had looked into selling a kidney to help make ends meet. Then a friend found him a job as a sewing machine mechanic in a textile factory in Isfahan. He told us proudly that he had a rare blood type and that the Tehran *Anjoman* wanted him to stay and donate— but taking the job in Isfahan was clearly the best option.

Not before long though, the Isfahan branch of the Tehran *Anjoman*, having heard about Ebrahim from the main office, was calling to ask if he would still consider donating. After some consideration, Ebrahim thought to himself, "Why not? It couldn't hurt to look into it." Then he met the recipient, and there was no turning back. "This recipient and I shared a rare negative blood type, and this servant of God had found hope in me. The money didn't matter. I wanted to help him."

Ebrahim felt an affinity for his recipient. "He is young, about my age. He has a daughter, 8 or 9 years old—the same age as my son. He has a lifestyle like mine, no more, no less. ... We have become friends."

"As far as the payment, what kind of gift are you being paid?"

"The price is five million—they gave me three from the recipient, one from the *Anjoman* through charity, and one in *issar* from the government. ... I was offered a much higher price in Tehran ... but because I met this patient and I got to know him, I just wanted to donate my kidney to him at any cost or circumstance." Ebrahim said he didn't need the money anymore because he now had a job, but he realized he only had one kidney to give and the five million tomans would make a nice nest egg should he fall on hard times again.

When we mentioned to Dr. Shahidi how moribund the *Anjoman* was, she chuckled and said that in Isfahan there is little going on at the Tehran-affiliated *Anjoman*. Instead we should visit the independent *Anjoman*, run by the Charity Institute of Abulfazl—the "Bazaaree charity" as Dr. Bastani called it—namely, the charity that receives its funding primarily through a fraternity of local merchants. But before we headed there, Dr. Bastani wanted to visit his childhood nanny, Nobar, who lived in a village outside of Isfahan. *What a wonderful opportunity*, I thought, *to see the countryside and learn about rural life in Iran.*

For the Love of Nannies

We traveled by car for more than an hour beyond the city to the neighboring village of Sedeh. The town square was deserted, and what must have once been a village green was now just clay—*Thank God, no whipping post*, flashed through my mind. Nobar's son-in-law appeared on a moped and guided us through the cramped back roads. At one point, the way became so narrow we had to park the car and proceed on foot. The mud-brown walls were 10 to 12 feet high with dull, unmarked doors that flanked us on both sides. The last time I had been on a village road this narrow was in the Greek islands, but I must admit, white plaster with brightly colored flowerboxes and doors with lion-headed knockers had a totally different feel than these dusky walls and weather-beaten doors with rusty, nondescript hardware. It would have been impossible to find Nobar's house without help.

Once through the main door from the street, there was a small courtyard, maybe a hundred square feet, with an ancient quince tree, a walled-off Iranian-style outhouse, and a door to the inner dwelling. Leaving our shoes in the courtyard, we entered a front room with shelves molded into dune-colored walls and a low, arched, white plaster ceiling. A bed rested against a half wall that divided the kitchen from the rest of the room. Off the kitchen was another room, which is where I supposed the nanny's daughter and son-in-law lived.

Nobar was overwhelmed with joy to see Dr. Bastani. He bent down to hug her, and she took his head into both her gnarled hands and kissed him on the cheek. She was dressed in brown, baggy pants that curved awkwardly to accommodate her extremely bowed legs. Her top was more of a smock than an Iranian-style tunic; it had a European pattern: cream, light blue, and grey rectangles of various sizes with one intermittently spaced square, which after repeated examination, I confirmed was a depiction of an octopus smiling from a plate. Over her smock she wore a grey cardigan with a strip of flowers winding their way up along the buttonholes. She wore a black headscarf that revealed reddish-grey hair at the edges and carried a bamboo cane. Her whole countenance was round, from her bowed legs and chubby hands and face to her slow, rocking cadence. She enunciated slowly and deliberately for my sake, not realizing that doing so would not improve my comprehension.

Nobar bade us sit down on an intricately patterned Persian rug that took up most of the room. I was amazed to see such an old woman sit herself down on the floor and wondered if she would need help getting up. Her adopted daughter brought tea and flat, lemon-flavored cookies. The whole conversation was in Farsi, but I saw her gesture repeatedly at the photo of her husband hanging on the wall, nodding to me as if the tale she told was for my benefit. Dr. Bastani later explained that her husband had left her while she was still employed by the Bastani family because she couldn't have children. He married a younger woman and had a daughter. Later both her husband and his new wife died, leaving Nobar to care for their daughter, who lives with her now and is the joy of her life.

Sitting in Nobar's small but comfortable house, I began to sense the frailty of the human condition, and how we all are prone to loneliness and vulnerability. The way people back home were dying for lack of kidneys seemed to epitomize a failure in the social net of interdependence that we ultimately all rely on. Leaving Nobar's house, I was struck by how different her life turned out from the life of my own nanny Lella.

Lella had been my mother's nanny and, in turn, mine. She had raised my mother, just as Nobar had raised Dr. Bastani. Lella spoke no English, so she taught me German. Unfortunately, one day my little sister ate some of Lella's blood pressure pills and had to get her stomach pumped. Ingrid was fine, but Lella took the incident as a sign that her days as a professional caregiver were over. Lella returned to Berlin to retire near her sister. Many years later, when I was a student at the University of Geneva, Switzerland, I visited Lella. She had a lovely little apartment and a government-provided aide who visited twice a week to make sure Lella was taking her medications, to bring her groceries, and even to clean her apartment; but Lella was lonely. "There used to be a lady from church who took me to Mass, but my legs are too weak now. I'm afraid I'll fall." Lella complained bitterly that she had come to Berlin to be near her sister and her children, but they never visit. "You, Sisi, come see me more than they do, and they only live a few blocks away!"

I couldn't help but compare the lives of Nobar and my Lella. Was Lella, despite her access to excellent social and medical services, any better off? She lived in a society much like ours in the United States, where her relatives were busy professionals who probably rationalized not visiting her by saying they knew the government was taking good care of her. But I know for a fact that Lella would have gladly exchanged a few government services for a visit or two from her nieces and nephews and their children.

In Iran, there is a deep sense of familial responsibility, like what I know from living in Argentina and Greece. Family simply comes first, and even careers often take a backseat to the needs of children or elderly family members. I was interested to hear from my son Nathan, who lived in Japan for a year, that nursing homes are all but unheard of there—the elderly are esteemed and play a prominent role in family life. Iran was more like Japan, Argentina, and Greece than the United States or Germany in this respect. I never visited a nursing home in Iran, but the dialysis centers I visited exhibited a very different approach to old age and infirmity from what I knew of dialysis centers in the United States.

In the United States, dialysis centers look much the same as they do in Iran, but by comparison they are devoid of life. U.S. dialysis centers are empty except for the patients and the health professionals caring for them. Some patients are dropped off and picked up by family members, and the occasional physician or social worker does rounds, but many patients are delivered by van, and in very few cases does a family member or friend stay while a patient is dialyzed. In one dialysis center I visited, relatives and friends had a waiting room and were not allowed into the area where patients were dialyzed. I noticed right away in Iran how full of activity the dialysis centers were, not just with healthcare professionals but with patients' relatives: spouses, children, cousins, and others who sat chatting, arranging patients' blankets and pillows, bringing them tea and food, and reading to them. At first when I saw this in Sadra City (near Shiraz), I thought this might be an anomaly, but every dialysis center I visited in Iran had a significant number of relatives and friends who stayed with patients while they were dialyzed.

There may be more at play than a general cultural ethos that family members should personally look after the elderly and the infirm. U.S. dialysis centers are, by their very nature, more dismal. Most people on dialysis in Iran are waiting for a kidney that they can expect within a few months. In the United States people often wait for years and can't realistically expect to get a transplant at all. Even if they do, the operation is more likely to fail because we prioritize sicker patients who have been on dialysis longer. Furthermore, in the United States we use lower quality cadaver organs instead of the living donor kidneys most commonly used in Iran. So it is understandable that the general mood in dialysis centers in Iran is more hopeful and upbeat than in the United States.

Also, unlike in Iran, in the United States I was struck by how almost all the dialysis patients I spoke to overestimated their prospects of survival. Were they lying to themselves or were they being lied to? It's probably a little of both. An American dialysis social worker told me people are in denial about the effects of dialysis and their chances of receiving a transplant because that is how they survive. "It would be cruel to remind them of the realities of life on dialysis. They already know all they want to know." Giving people hope or letting them harbor unrealistic expectations helps them make it through the daily misery of dialysis. There is nothing to be gained by bludgeoning them with a sobering assessment of their chances. "If dialysis is all you have, you accept it and deal with it as best you can." It would be rude for those lucky enough to get a transplant to go on and on about how much better a transplant is than dialysis, knowing how most of the people they befriended at the dialysis center don't have a choice but to remain on dialysis.

In Iran, where pretty much anyone who medically qualifies to receive a transplant gets one, there is less reason to mince words about the horrors of dialysis. Akbar, one of the recipients we interviewed, told us, "There is no life on dialysis. Dialysis is death. I would have killed myself if I couldn't buy a kidney." Another recipient Hamidreza remarked:

> The living conditions of a dialysis patient resembles the life of a vegetable. … First, you have to be on three to four hours of dialysis. Then you have to return to dialysis every other day. It just doesn't work with anyone's lifestyle. Even after my blood was purified, I would almost pass out. I couldn't do normal things until the next day. I could not carry out my responsibilities as a father, as a husband. … This disease made me a useless, worthless person. Everyone used to hold me up by my arms and help me. Now that I have a transplant, I've become a productive man again.

Then Mehdi told us, "Once I realized what dialysis was all about.… I don't know how to say this because I don't want to scare anyone. But dialysis is a living hell, a real living hell." Asad, who had just had a few dialysis treatments before getting his transplant, said, "It was like night and day. I would never be satisfied with dialysis. I prayed to God, telling him if you want to keep putting those big needles into me, then just go ahead and kill me now."

We heard comments like these over and over again in Iran, but the only person out of the dozens of dialysis patients and transplant recipients I interviewed in the United States who openly expressed similar feelings was my friend Steve. Everyone else downplayed the difficulties of life on dialysis, and one dialysis social worker even spent more than half an hour explaining to me that the medical regimen required to maintain a transplant "can be" just as arduous as life on dialysis. Her diplomatically chosen words—"can be"—may be technically true, but the evidence is clear that, for the majority of transplant recipients, there is no comparison. Life with a transplant is ten times preferable to life on dialysis, particularly if the patient was still relatively healthy at the time of the transplant and the kidney came from a healthy living donor.

I had confusing thoughts running through my mind. *How could my Lella be more alone in an advanced country like Germany than Dr. Bastani's nanny in Iran? How could dialysis patients in the United States suffer so, alone in their misery, while dialysis patients in Iran were full of life and hope?* There was so much to figure out, so much that didn't make sense to me.

The Real *Anjoman*

The next day we headed out to visit the Abulfazl *Anjoman*, hoping to find more opportunities to interview donors and recipients than what we found at Isfahan's Tehran-affiliated *Anjoman*. The Abulfazl *Anjoman* building was on the outskirts of town, but it was a whole building, not just a single apartment like the Tehran-affiliated *Anjoman*. Several mopeds and small motorcycles were parked in the shade of an elm tree in the courtyard. Even though it was within the safety of a high exterior wall, the whole front of the building was covered with security bars. These bars, however, were not discouraging like those we'd seen at the other *Anjoman*. They were white and freshly painted, which made the atmosphere sunny, even if cautiously so, and more inviting than the somber, beeswax-colored railings we'd experienced earlier that week.

After exiting the car, I turned my face to the sun and closed my eyes, basking for a few seconds like a cat in a sunny window. I took a deep breath and noticed the sweet scent of something flowering. When I opened my eyes and turned to look for the source, I saw instead a large green wooden sign on the outside wall of the compound. The logo was a white oval with a long-stemmed rose and a large green leaf with two buds—one an opening red rose, the other a kidney. How tenderly sentimental compared to the Tehran *Anjoman's* symbol of stylized, cupped hands holding a kidney. The sign in front of me read, "Abulfazl Institute Charity, Heart and Kidney Health Services of Isfahan. Established 1990."

We started our visit in the customary fashion of a get-to-know-you session where we ate cucumbers and oranges and drank Chay E Bahareh Lahijan (the spring season tea of the Lahijan region) or some similarly fragrant Iranian tea. I patiently waited, knowing that the preliminary interviews with *Anjoman* staff, while mostly untaped, were a necessary prelude to our being allowed to interview donors. Dr. Bastani and I sat on a sofa against the wall farthest away from the entrance, and three *Anjoman* directors sat on chairs arranged in a semi-circle across the coffee table. Two desks stood at the other end of the room near the front door, and an animated young woman sat at the first desk, asking people their business as they came in.

We learned a great deal about the Abulfazl Institute: its founding, its history, and all about its wide-reaching charitable activities. It struck me how late kidney disease treatments had come to Isfahan. Dr. Azani, the chairman of the board of directors, was the first nephrologist to come to Isfahan in 1975, and he brought the first dialysis machine in 1988. In the United States, dialysis machines were introduced in the 1960s and widely available by the 1970s, close to 20 years earlier than they became available in Isfahan.

Unlike the Tehran-affiliated *Anjoman*, this place was bustling with activity. A woman in her 20s, dressed in full hijab and carrying a motorcycle helmet, entered and spoke to the bright-eyed clerk. I couldn't help but wonder if her flowing black robes got in the way when she drove her moped. A young man, after a brief inquiry, was handed a clipboard and sat down on a chair along the wall. He balanced the clipboard on his lap as he filled out paperwork. An older man spoke so softly that the intake clerk had to lean forward over her desk to hear him. After a brief back and forth, she looked through the drawer of the neighboring desk and handed him some papers. He left, seemingly satisfied.

The *Anjoman* directors were beaming with pride as they described, for close to an hour, the Abulfazl Institute's many achievements, which in addition to providing services for kidney disease patients, included, among other things, funding surgeries for infants and children with congenital heart anomalies.

It is hard to feign interest when one doesn't understand the language, and the director sitting to my left noticed that I was struggling to pay attention. He leaned over, took the orange from my plate, and with his paring knife, carved back the peel in strips of varying lengths, tucking some into each other. I watched with delight, as after just a few moments, he transformed the orange into a blossoming fruit, dressed in the petals of its own peel, and placed it back onto my plate. I held his creation on my lap admiringly. He motioned, knife in hand, encouraging me to partake. I picked up the orange, plucked out a section, and began to eat. He nodded with approval.

One of the administrators noticed a woman entering and waved her over. She moved toward us with hesitation. "You must meet Somayeh," he told us. Chairs were re-arranged and now all eyes, including mine, were on Somayeh, who sat clutching her chador around her chin in a white-knuckled fist. She was 55 but appeared 70—like an aged version of Edvard Munch's "The Scream." *What kind of life would cause vertical wrinkles?*

After introductions, Somayeh agreed to give a videotaped interview. At first she didn't relax and, despite the pleasantries exchanged, she answered Dr. Bastani's preliminary questions looking down at the coffee table and speaking in a voice so low everyone had to strain to hear her.

Seventeen years ago, she, her husband, and their daughter lived as squatters in a mosque. One day when she was feeling unbearably ill and drained of energy, she came to the Abulfazl *Anjoman*, which has a reputation for helping the sick and homeless.

It turned out Somayeh had kidney disease. The *Anjoman* took her to the hospital and arranged for dialysis. Abulfazl staff found a donor, paid his fee, and did the paperwork to arrange for Somayeh's transplant. The institute covered all the medical costs associated with her transplant that were not covered by government insurance and stood by her when her transplant failed. After a heart attack, Somayeh didn't medically qualify for another transplant, so now the *Anjoman* was helping her with dialysis-related expenses.

Once Somayeh's anxiety subsided, it took little encouragement to get her to tell her story in intimate detail.

"How did the charity organization help you in these 17 years?"

> In every way—my medications, my everyday expenditures. ... We didn't have anything. Because my husband wasn't working, we didn't have insurance. He's still not working; we don't have anything. Everything we have is from charity. We didn't have a home; we'd been living in the mosque. We lived in the kitchen, and my husband got sick. God bless the Abulfazl Charity, they came and bought us a house. They even added a room to it. I feel bad to come and ask them for money. I'm embarrassed to come. ... But if I ask, I know they will provide.

One of the directors added that they have also helped Somayeh find treatment for her mentally ill daughter, but their assistance didn't end there. They also regularly provided Somayeh's family with food, clothing, and other basic necessities.

My thoughts wandered back to the generally bleak experiences of the donors and recipients we interviewed in Tehran. How different things are in the big city as compared with this provincial town! It was easy to get lost and forgotten in a city like Tehran, but here in Isfahan it was somehow different. People seemed to take a more personal interest in the well-being of others. The words of Farid, one of the lucky ones in Tehran, came to mind. He had been visibly shaken when he told me he had heard another donor at the *Anjoman* counter in Tehran pleading, "Please, please, just take my kidney; I'm bankrupt."

An angry voice coming from the entrance caught my attention. I briefly looked out from behind my camera to see the young intake clerk literally chase a man out the door. I desperately wanted to find out what was going on, but we needed to finish our interview with Somayeh. She concluded, "Thank God I don't have all those problems anymore; everything I need I get from charity. So now we have some peace in our lives; it's not like the time when we were living in the mosque." One of the administrators got up and showed Somayeh to the door, promising he would not forget to schedule her next dialysis appointment.

We moved to the other side of the room and prepared to interview the spirited young lady at the front desk. One of the administrators took over dealing with walk-ins at the next desk over as we spoke to Miss Mohammadi. Miss Mohammadi was a vibrant young woman in her 20s. She wore a chador, but it hung partially open at the neckline where a mossy-green, Iranian-style manteau peeked through. She wore a *maghnae*, the tight-fitting head covering like what I wore, so I couldn't tell her hair color. But what was most notable about her was her bubbly personality and how she tackled everything with zeal.

Miss Mohammadi turned out to be an excellent source of information. As the gatekeeper, everyone—whether they were a potential recipient, donor, or someone else—needed to start with her. If someone came to inquire about kidney donation, she initiated the questioning and made the preliminary assessment of whether that person was in the right place. If yes, she continued the interview, taking down both medical and social background information. If not, she steered him or her to another organization for further inquiries.

Every donor (and recipient for that matter) would eventually have to speak to a social worker or psychologist, but Miss Mohammadi was the one who got the ball rolling.

"What kind of forms do they have to fill out? Like what is that form there?"

"This is the form for consultation."

"So this is a form that every donor must have, where a lady with a masters in psychology has to approve the donor. What does the psychologist check for?"

"The first thing she asks is why does the donor even want to donate? Then, what are their problems? For instance, a man wants to divorce his wife, and he is donating the kidney to get money." (In Iran men legally have to give their wives money at the time of divorce; the amount is predetermined at the time of marriage.) "So the psychologist talks to these people and discusses other options and tries to help them reconcile so he doesn't need money to divorce, and therefore doesn't have to donate his kidney."

Miss Mohammadi went on to explain that the psychologist "has to follow up on every aspect of the process." In Iran the distinction between psychologist and social worker is blurred, so this person may be the U.S. equivalent of a licensed social worker. Miss Mohammadi described a recent case where "the psychologist referred the donor and his family to a social service committee and their mortgage problem was solved, so no one needed to donate a kidney."

"So what is this other form?"

"We try to pay the 400–500 thousand tomans for the donor's labs to help recipients, so it's not a burden on them. This form is in case the donor gets second thoughts and leaves, and so we get a promise and a check from the donor just in case." (This *Anjoman*, like most, asks the donor for some form of collateral to pay for tests should the donor pull out without legitimate reason.)

At every step of the way, although the recipients are the *Anjoman*'s priority, the whole staff works to make sure donors' needs are met as well. There is no shortage of donors, so the *Anjoman* feels obligated to assess that each donor has exhausted all other avenues for getting help before deciding to donate a kidney. Otherwise, there may be problems that come back to haunt the *Anjoman*, like unhappy donors who harass recipients or come to the *Anjoman* demanding more money. "Since we sit here from the beginning with the donor and recipient, we talk to them and explain the conditions, and they accept those conditions. Thank God we haven't had any problems—at least, not during the five years that I've been here."

I wondered why Miss Mohammadi chased away that young man who came in earlier. I tried to communicate my question through Dr. Bastani, but she just said, "That was nothing," and continued instead to talk about how it is in everyone's interest to keep donors happy—an opinion that echoed what Nurse Sharareh Fadaee had told us at Al-Zahra Hospital: "We don't want trouble. The *Anjoman* is not doing its job if we end up with an addict who cries for more pain medication, or an angry father who comes storming into the hospital demanding to know why we have taken his son's kidney."

The staff, at least at this *Anjoman*, clearly did everything in its power to solve donors' financial problems and to make sure donors and their families were fully informed of what a kidney donation involved and the conditions of payment. The *Anjoman* had more than enough potential donors, so excluding probable troublemakers and making the extra effort to prevent complaints down the line was worth their while.

Miss Mohammadi also mentioned something not immediately evident but obviously considered by the most conscientious of *Anjoman* staff. She said it was her job to find donors for whom selling a kidney is truly the only solution. "It would be sad if a potential donor for whom selling a kidney was the last resort had to be turned away because another potential donor who had other options was allowed to sell a kidney instead." I was deeply impressed by this young woman's compassion and profound understanding of her role in trying to make sure the *Anjoman* helped as many people in the greatest need as possible, whether they were recipients or donors.

After we finished talking to Miss Mohammadi, we interviewed Farzan who, unlike the supposedly altruistic donors we met in Shiraz, seemed sincere. Farzan was 30, divorced, and living at home. He was articulate with a ready smile, a deep-cleft chin, and an eye-catching unibrow. He explained his motivations:

> The major reason for my donating is to please God, and the recipient is someone I know. Also, the recipient and his family are not financially secure enough to buy a kidney. I found some potential donors and introduced them. But for one, the blood group didn't match, and the other one didn't have a healthy kidney. So then I saw there is no one better than myself. I am thankful to God that the results for all my tests are good. Ten days from now we have an appointment for the operation.

Farzan said he was willing to do the donation for free, but the *Anjoman* convinced him to apply for the one million from Tehran and also accept one million tomans in cash and five years of health insurance through the Abulfazl Institute. He felt this was more than fair and expressed great satisfaction at being able to help a friend.

I left the Abusfazl *Anjoman* with a renewed faith in humanity. How different my impressions would have been if all I knew of kidney donation in Isfahan were what I'd experienced at the Isfahan branch of the Tehran *Anjoman*.

Facing the Crowd

Time flew by too quickly. Friday, my last day in Isfahan, was the Muslim day of rest and prayer, so we had no interviews. Dr. Bastani wanted to visit with family, and I was glad for the opportunity to spend some time alone. The Zayandeh River beckoned, and despite Dr. Bastani's advice to the contrary, I headed down to the water for an early sunrise walk. I tucked my money purse and camera under my tunic and took my tripod with me in case I needed it for self-defense. I joked, "I have a tripod and am not afraid to use it." While perhaps humorous, I did carry my two-foot-long metal tripod everywhere I went, swinging it deliberately for everyone to see. I never felt the need to actually strike anyone, but it did give me a sense of security. (I missed my tripod when I was in Athens a month later and got lost in a bad part of town.)

There were double takes as I passed people on Isfahan's Aeeneh Khaneh Boulevard: maybe because I was a woman out alone, maybe because I was a foreigner, or maybe because I was merrily brandishing a tripod. If someone thought a Western woman out on her own might make an easy target for a mugging or a kidnapping, I was hoping they would think twice before choosing the one carrying a metal club. Most people just gave me a wide berth, and I was fine with that. This outing wasn't for meeting people; it was to explore the river as the city on its banks yawned to welcome a new day.

There was practically no one down by the Zayandeh. The mallards were zigzagging and circling, dipping their heads in the shallow water looking for food, twitching their tail feathers, hoping someone would throw a morsel their way. I wished I had some bread. I stood and watched a solitary man, more prepared than I, feeding the ducks. I moved on, past the unused exercise stations neatly interspersed between stretches of lawn, flower beds, and benches. Two middle-aged women in full black regalia passed as I stopped to admire a type of flowering bush I'd never seen before. I watched them disappear down the path; both wearing white running shoes. I wondered, *Is this as close as Iranians get to jogging?*

After a hotel breakfast of naan, dates, walnuts, and goat cheese, Dr. Bastani headed off to visit with relatives, and Nooshin Mirkheshti, a female physician who worked as a researcher, took me sightseeing in Jolfa, the Armenian quarter. Today, we know Iran as an oppressive, intolerant regime, but for centuries, if not millennia, Iran was a haven for oppressed minorities. Cyrus the Great is credited with the first declaration of human rights. His cuneiform cylinder, dating back to the sixth century B.C., reads in part that Cyrus "strove for peace in Babylon and all of the god Marduk's sacred sites [in all the world]" and that he "abolished forced labor," with specific reference to the Jews who had been enslaved in Babylon.

Despite all the Iranian government's anti-Israel rhetoric, it is more tolerant of its Jewish population than most other Islamic Middle Eastern countries. The Iranian Jewish community has shrunk from 75,000 to 25,000 since the Revolution, but Iran still has the largest Jewish population in the Middle East after Israel, and many Iranian Jews claim their Iranian heritage dates back hundreds of years.

Christians, Jews, and Zoroastrians are protected by the constitution of the Islamic Republic and are legally allowed to practice their religions; they are exempt from military service and have guaranteed seats in the *Majilis*. When I was in Iran there were three Christian, one Jewish, and one Zoroastrian representatives in the *Majilis*. Iranians are proud of their religious tolerance, but it has its limits. It is against the law for Baha'is to practice their religion, in public or otherwise, and they are discriminated against openly when it comes to jobs and education. Also, while someone born into one of the tolerated faiths is protected, and conversion to Islam is accepted or even encouraged, a public conversion from Islam to another faith is punishable by death.

The largest religious minority in Iran today is Christian. Most Iranian Christians belong to the Armenian Apostolic Orthodox Church and can trace their lineage in Iran back to one of several Armenian migrations, starting with the Armenian flight from Ottoman oppression in the sixteenth century. While the Armenian "Golden Age" in Iran ended with the 1979 Revolution, Armenians are still allowed to indulge in certain Western forms of "debauchery." Mixed-gender gatherings, dances, and the consumption of alcohol are tolerated as long as they are done in private and do not involve Muslims. They even have non-segregated sports facilities where Christian women exercise without wearing hijab.

The Armenian quarter was established by the Safavid Shah Abbas the Great in the late sixteenth century when he transported a whole colony of Armenians from Jolfa in northern Iran to the then capital city of Isfahan and called their colony "New Jolfa." Shah Abbas brought the Armenians to Isfahan because he was building a new city, and the Armenians were known for their architectural prowess and masterful craftsmanship. Now the Jolfa district in Isfahan, with its grand cathedral, is the center of Armenian culture in Iran.

The Armenian grand cathedral complex that Dr. Mirkheshti took me to see emphasized the Turkish genocides from which the ancestors of the Armenians now living in Iran had escaped. The infamous systematic extermination and forced marches carried out by the Ottoman Empire post-WWI are considered by many historians to be the first modern-day genocide. By that time, however, ethnic cleansing policies had already been an Ottoman/Turkish policy for over three centuries. Vank Cathedral's museum is dominated by exhibits describing the massacre of Armenians by Turks, but the cathedral itself also includes the more general Orthodox Christian themes of pain and suffering, damnation, and redemption.

A mix of Christian and Muslim elements is evident throughout the Vank Cathedral complex. While unmistakably Christian-gothic in style, its buildings are also trimmed with Iranian-style mosaics. After seeing so many mosques with their pleasing, intricate geometric patterns and absolutely no depictions of scenery or living beings, I viewed the Vank Cathedral's frescoes with an embarrassing lack of enthusiasm.

Dr. Mirkheshti had brought me to the cathedral thinking it would interest me, and it did, but I also found it morbid and depressing. One fresco showed a lion-like beast tearing at the breast of a woman with a demon looking on, reveling in the scene. Others showed martyrs suffering intolerable injustices at the hands of their tormenters.

I felt compassion for the Armenians, but I was getting sick to my stomach and wanted to leave. I was reminded of my daughter's reaction the first time she saw a life-size crucifix. Lauren, then age four, having been affected by the statue's gruesomeness, turned to me and said, "Mommy, I don't think children should be allowed to see things like that!" I wondered if non-Armenian Iranians ever come to see Vank Cathedral and what they thought of the frescos.

Around mid-afternoon, Dr. Mirkheshti needed to meet up with her family, so we rendezvoused with Dr. Bastani, and he and I headed out to do some sightseeing on our own. We started walking toward Imam Square, one of the largest and most majestic city squares in the world. On our way there, we came across a parade of prancing Arab horses, their bridles jingling with bells and their riders dressed in colorful, traditional Iranian folk costumes: replete with sashes, sabers, and feathered or tasseled hats. We followed the parade and found ourselves at Imam Square.

The square is over a mile long and lined with arched bazaar porticoes, interspersed with architectural treasures like the Ali Qapu Palace and the Sheikh Lutfollah Mosque built for the use of the Shah's wives. But on this day the square was overrun by a gathering throng. *What is going on?*

People organized themselves by affiliation. One group of men wore Shriner-type fezzes; another wore baseball caps with a logo I didn't recognize. Then there was a group of children, perhaps a boys' club like the Cub Scouts, and a group of women, probably the Ladies Auxiliary for the Red Crescent, judging from the insignia on a flag one woman was holding up to help others find the group.

We were swept into the square by a wave of people entering through one of the porticoes, but we didn't know where to go from there. Dr. Bastani thought maybe if we wove our way over to a stage we saw off in the distance, we could find out what the gathering was celebrating. Dr. Bastani led the way, and I took shelter in his wake. He maneuvered through the crowd like Moses parting the Red Sea but then stopped. We stepped up on a small curb that lined the inner square and surveyed which way to go.

Dr. Bastani pointed. "The stage is over there."

"OK, let's go."

"We can't."

"Why not?"

Dr. Bastani bent down and whispered, "All the ladies."

It took me a few seconds to understand, but then I teased. "Oh ... of course, all the laaadies. ... Let me go first."

The taboo in Islamic culture against touching someone of the opposite sex who is not related, or at least a family acquaintance, is extremely strong. Even an accidental touching is offensive. On one of our flights to Tehran, Dr. Bastani had taken the middle seat so I could have the window seat, but we had to switch because the woman who had the aisle didn't want to sit next to a man she didn't know. And so it was now my turn to lead the way, flanked by two groups of women and children with Dr. Bastani in my wake. He looked a little ridiculous as he walked sideways, trying to make his impressive frame as thin as possible to avoid accidentally touching anyone.

We never found out what all the commotion was about, but once we reached the stage, it was easy to sneak out through the portico behind it. My only regret is that I had to forego seeing the inside of Imam Mosque, but my experience later at the Gohar Shad Mosque in Mashhad more than made up for it.

It was hard to leave Isfahan. What an inviting city with so much potential! There would always be a fond place in my memory for the wonderful people I met there. In Tehran I had my doubts about compensated kidney donation, but, when I saw how hard the Abulfazl *Anjoman* staff worked to meet the needs of both recipients and donors, I couldn't help but wonder: *Immoral exploitation of the poor? Honestly, can anything I saw at the Abulfazl Anjoman qualify as either immoral or exploitive?* It was becoming ever clearer that there were no simple answers. I have no doubt that much of the kidney selling going on around the world, particularly on the black market, is exploitive and immoral, but neither of those terms, by any stretch of the imagination, applied to what I observed in Isfahan.

Ⅴ (7)

The Rich and the Holy

Our arrival in Mashhad was uneventful. A driver bearing a sign with Dr. Bastani's name was waiting for us at the airport. He greeted Dr. Bastani warmly but didn't even acknowledge me. Dr. Bastani began making calls to ensure we had a place to stay. I trudged along after them, carrying my own suitcase and camera equipment. Usually, I didn't mind being treated as if invisible, but this time I was tired and really could have used the help.

A Woman's Place

Most of the medical professionals I met during my trip didn't ignore me. As a matter of fact, they were curious and excited to speak with me. The average Iranian, however, tended to act as if I weren't there, particularly when I was with Dr. Bastani. Normally, this was convenient. After all, I could do a better job of observing our subjects and running my camera if I blended into the background. Nonetheless, I couldn't avoid thinking how hard it would be to live in a culture where women were generally treated so dismissively.

When I mentioned this, Dr. Bastani didn't try to defend the draconian practices of most Muslim countries. Instead, he was quick to point out that being treated differently isn't the same as being treated badly. He emphasized that the Qur'an says women should be respected. I never responded, yet I couldn't help but be reminded of how African-Americans were treated as "separate but equal" under American law and how hypocritical that was. I'm sure Dr. Bastani would assert that the "separate but equal" treatment the Qur'an requires is not the same, but why not? Because men and women, unlike blacks and whites, really *are* different and, therefore, are rightly treated differently by the law?

As I struggled with my bags outside the airport, I became officially annoyed. I dropped one of my cases on the way to the car, and the driver, Mahmud, just watched. Once I made it to the car, Mahmud opened the trunk but then stood idly by while I wrestled my luggage and equipment into the trunk. I opened my own door and got into the car. Ordinarily, being treated like Dr. Bastani's porter didn't rattle me, but my tolerance was worn thin after spending much of the night transferring my camera footage to multiple hard drives so we could leave copies behind with friends for safekeeping—a precaution in case I was robbed or the authorities confiscated my equipment.

Once we were all inside the car, Mahmud proceeded in silence. Dr. Bastani was still preoccupied with making phone calls, so I let my mind wander, remembering a time when I was a child in Istanbul with my parents. We were walking down the street on our way to the Hagia Sophia when the entourage in front of us stopped abruptly, causing a traffic jam on the sidewalk. Three women in line behind a man all came to a halt, and we watched as the man turned, put out his foot, and pulled up his trouser leg. The last woman came forward, knelt with one knee to the ground, tied his shoe, got up without looking up, and returned to her place in line. I glanced at my mother in bewilderment. She winked at me and said, "Not so bad if you're wife number one." My father shot her a glare as if to say, *Are you sure she's old enough for a joke like that?*

My mother ignored him and continued, "When your father and I were in Morocco after the War, we saw men walking with their wives and the order was reversed: woman, woman, woman," she paused for emphasis, "*horse*, and *then* the man."

"Why?"

Without looking at me, she answered, "Land mines."

A chill ran down my spine, and I could feel my father gape at my mother in disbelief. *The child is only eight; why are you telling her such things?*

But my mother was wise in her own way. She smiled at me, and then, as she turned and smiled at my father, said, "So Sisi, when the time comes, make sure you marry the right man." She looked pensive for a moment. "Not all Muslim men disrespect their wives any more than all Christian men are drunkards who beat theirs."

Her words made quite an impression, which I'm sure was her intention, but she hadn't been totally forthcoming. I learned later, while volunteering at a battered women's shelter in Alaska, that abusive relationships exist in all countries and cultures, but in some it is definitely easier for the woman to escape than in others.

Several times when I was in Iran, I was told a joke that goes something like this: In Iran, the man always has the last word … and that is, "Yes, ma'am!" You don't have to be Iranian to appreciate this quip: In Iran, as in many cultures, women often decide everyday household matters. But joking aside, it was clear that in anything of real significance—or even in trivial household concerns if the man chose to make them his business—it was the man and not the woman who had the final say. No matter how irrational or cruel his decision, society in general, and the law in particular, was likely to side with him, not her.

A Sacred Place of Wonder and Mixed Emotions

Mashhad is a holy city. Some Shi'ite Muslims consider it the most sacred city after Mecca in Saudi Arabia and Najaf in Iraq, thus making it, for many, the holiest city in Iran. Mashhad is also the second-largest city after Tehran. Mashhad is exotic and mysterious, and the people I met were kind and generous. However, out of all the places I visited in Iran, Mashhad was also the most alien to me. Capital cities have things in common: pollution, crime, bureaucracies. Economically depressed cities, like Kermashah, where we were yet to visit, have many things in common as well: lackluster streets, fatalism, joyless hearts. But a holy city like Mashhad was something new to me.

We were in Mashhad during Muharram, a time of mourning in remembrance of the murder of the Prophet Mohammad's grandson and his close relatives by Yazid, the self-proclaimed king of Syria and the whole Muslim world. There was a palpable anguish in the air but also a sense of expectation. Mashhad is a city where couples come to marry, sinners come for absolution, and parents come to pray for sick children. I felt more out of place than I have ever felt before. I have nothing against prayer and spiritual healing as a supplement to science-based medicine, but in Mashhad, I feared an abandonment of rationality. I had a sense that the people here spoke not only a different mother tongue, but a different emotional language as well. I feared that I might not be able to communicate, even to the extent I had elsewhere in Iran. But by the end of my stay in Mashhad, I realized I couldn't have been more wrong.

The hotel where we stayed did little to lift my spirits. My room reminded me of the hospital housing in Shiraz, but this time there were no doilies or plastic flowers, and the barred window of my first-floor room looked out into an alley, not a lawn with orange trees and magpies. All day long and periodically during the night, there was activity in the alleyway, making it hard to concentrate or sleep. And, every morning around 4:00 A.M., a tanker truck stopped on the street outside my window, motor revving. *Varoom, varoom*, then a loud sucking and gurgling sound and an unmistakable, offensive odor—outhouse—the kind without chemicals.

G. Clotaire Rapaille, the anthropologist who coined the term "culture code," says Americans take their bathrooms very seriously compared with the rest of the world, and that may be so. But for people who like to wash their feet several times a day, Iranian bathrooms are surprisingly lacking. This time, my bathroom had neither commode nor shower curtain, but most distressing was the lack of a damper on the stoop toilet's drainage pipe. The truck in the alley started to rumble, a motor whirred, and within seconds my whole room smelled like an open sewer. I tried a trick I'd read in a novel about the eighteenth century French aristocracy: I doused the collar of my nightgown with the jasmine water I'd purchased as a gift for my daughter. That helped, but not until I dabbed some directly on my upper lip could I escape the smell long enough to fall asleep.

"Living" Cadaver Donors?

I was ill-rested the next day and, at first, had trouble keeping my eyes open at our meeting with Drs. Sharifi Pour, Nazemian, and Naghibi. However, as Dr. Bastani began to translate for me, I became energized and wanted to learn more. Imam Reza Hospital did things differently—far differently from anything we experienced in Shiraz, Tehran, or Isfahan.

Mashhad had an active cadaver organ procurement program, and two hospitals did deceased donor kidney transplants on a regular basis. But unlike Shiraz, no one forced anyone to accept a cadaver organ. Rather, doctors and the *Anjoman* encouraged patients to get on the cadaver organ waiting list, suggesting there is no harm being on the list while simultaneously making arrangements for a living donor.

Unfortunately, all Iranian deceased donor programs suffer from a lack of PR. Outside Shiraz, fewer than a quarter of the people we interviewed, including the people we interviewed in Mashhad, had heard of the free cadaver kidney option. The majority of transplant recipients we told about the option said they would have preferred a free kidney if they had known about it, but few thought it was worth waiting for a free kidney if it would take longer than paying a living donor. Even recipients who acknowledged that the living donor fee was a financial burden quickly added, if the cadaver alternative meant staying on dialysis longer, they would find a way to bear the cost of paying for a living donor.

Everyone we interviewed in Mashhad who was on the cadaver organ waiting list said they planned to take the first available kidney, regardless of its source or whether they would have to pay for it. This being said, it was clear that sometimes which option materialized first depended on how fast a patient could raise money or arrange for charity. Almost half of the recipients we interviewed in Iran received some financial assistance beyond family contributions, usually through the *Anjoman*, other charity organizations, the recipient's town, or neighbors and friends. But arranging for charity funds is not instantaneous, and two kidney transplant recipients we interviewed admitted that they were in the process of arranging for charity when their families became impatient and found their own sources of funding—they probably gathered contributions from extended family and/or took out loans.*

In addition to their reluctance to wait longer for a kidney, Iranians have more general concerns about the use of cadaver organs—some justified and others not. Most Iranian's believe living donor kidneys are "fresher" than cadaver kidneys. In one sense this belief is justified. It is well documented that cold-ischemia time, the time an organ is outside a body on ice, has a significant correlation with transplant failure. This is true for the initial success of the transplant operation and also for the longevity of the transplanted organ. In the United States, efforts are made to reduce cold-ischemia time by using organs as soon as possible after harvesting them from the deceased. But even in the United States, kidney disease patients are encouraged to improve their transplant outcomes by trying to find a living donor.

But the general dislike in Iran for kidneys from deceased donors is often exaggerated beyond what is justified by the risks of cold-ischemia because of a linguistic ambiguity. Farsi does not distinguish between the words "corpse" and "cadaver," using *"jasad"* to mean either. So without this distinction, *"jasad"* is as likely to conjure up images of decaying flesh (like the English word "corpse") as it is to refer to medical procedures performed on preserved dead bodies (like the English word "cadaver"). In Mashhad, the medical community and the *Anjoman* deal with this semantic difficulty by not using the word *"jasad"* at all.

---

* Data for Shiraz are not included in the percentages given for people who receive charity contribution to help pay for kidneys because of that city's ban on recipients paying donors. In Shiraz, as on the black market, there are no legitimate avenues for charity to help purchase a kidney. In Shiraz, even if recipients received charity from neighbors or friends to help pay a living donor, they would probably not admit it because doing so would be incriminating.

Instead they use the English "cadaver" and explain to potential recipients and their families that "cadaver kidneys" come from patients who are brain-dead, but not fully physically dead. In other words, the kidney is still functioning, not decaying, because medical technology is keeping the organ "alive" even though the donor is dead.

Finally, Islamic culture historically had a religious objection to removing organs from the deceased: The Qur'an prohibits the desecration or "mutilation" of dead bodies. It took much considered deliberation among Iranian mullahs before it was accepted that the Qur'anic prohibition didn't apply to the use of body parts to save someone's life. Not until the year 2000 did the *Majilis* pass a law condoning the use of cadaver organs for transplantation. There is now little dissent among clerics and politicians, but residual feelings still linger among the general public that the use of cadaver organs is somehow wrong.

Despite some concerted efforts, like in Mashhad (and Shiraz), to modernize and expand the scope of Iran's organ procurement system by encouraging cadaver donation, there is little impetus in places such as Tehran to change the status quo. When we were in Tehran, it was evident, at least at the hospitals we visited, that a lack of established protocols for procuring, storing, and using cadaver organs meant organs from deceased donors were regularly left un-harvested, or worse, were harvested and then discarded for failure to prep a potential recipient in time for a transplant operation.

In my mind, particularly after what we saw in Mashhad, the Tehran medical establishment had no good excuse for not moving forward with the creation of a more efficient city-wide deceased donor program.* Other cities, like Isfahan, Kermanshah, and maybe even Tabriz, had more legitimate excuses because those cities had fewer medical resources in terms of infrastructure, supplies, and staff to create an effective cadaver procurement program. As one physician in Kermanshah told us, "You can't expect the only surgeon in town trained to do kidney transplants to get up in the middle of the night to do a cadaver transplant when he already has a full schedule doing living donor transplants during the day."

---

* An anonymous reviewer of my book who was clearly from Iran said that I misrepresented the cadaver organ program in Tehran. He said that the system was up and running and just as active, if not more active, than in other parts of Iran. That review was done in 2013 and perhaps Tehran has improved its deceased organ procurement system since I was there at the end of 2008. Nevertheless, I stand by my description as being what I witnessed in 2008 when several physicians, at different transplant centers in Tehran, told me their staff didn't do cadaver kidney transplants for the reasons I describe here and elsewhere in this book.

In Mashhad, they are well on their way to overcoming the obstacles we saw elsewhere. As Iran's second-largest city, it has the staff and supplies to establish a functional cadaver organ retrieval program. The university had an enthusiastic and devoted organ procurement coordinator. It was his job to stay in contact with area hospitals to ensure the Mashhad Transplant Center was notified of potentially brain-dead patients. Mashhad also had two physicians dedicated to organ retrieval and a rotating on-call schedule for staff surgeons to handle cadaver kidney transplants when the opportunity arose.

Finally, Mashhad had found a creative way to overcome the cold-ischemia problem: Surgeons didn't harvest kidneys and dispatch them across the region, across town, or even from hospital to hospital in coolers, as is common in the United States. Instead, they transported the brain-dead patient on life support by ambulance to the transplant center. Then, the donor was placed in an operating room adjacent to the recipient's, and the kidney was transferred directly from one patient to the other in the same manner used for living donor transplants. The remaining organs were then put on ice and shipped to other transplant centers as needed.

Studies at Imam Reza Hospital show only a slight (and statistically insignificant) difference in the success rate of kidney transplants done as described above compared to transplants using living donors. This is not surprising since we know from studies carried out in the United States and elsewhere that living donor organ donations are medically superior to transplants from deceased donors. In the United States, 95 percent of kidneys transplanted from living donors are still functioning a year later, compared with 89 percent for cadaver kidneys; five years later, 80 percent of kidneys transplanted from living donors are still functioning but only 66.5 percent of those received from deceased donors are still functioning.

Dr. Nazemian suggested that the ever-so-slight discrepancy they saw between the success rates of transplants done with living donors and cadaver donors using their unique technique was probably due to the fact that death itself stresses organs. A kidney that survives a trauma that kills the patient might itself be traumatized from the experience, making it minimally less viable than a kidney from a healthy, living donor. But the stress experienced by such kidneys is nothing compared to the stresses experienced by cadaver kidneys in the United States and Europe, where they might suffer up to 30 hours of cold-ischemia time before being transplanted. Such organs sometimes take several days to start functioning again. Not to mention the fact that cadaver kidneys are in such short supply in the United States that they are regularly harvested from ever older deceased patients (sometimes 70 or older) or even from less optimal patients who have died from stroke or have a history of high blood pressure or cancer. These conditions can take quite a toll on an organ separate from any damage caused by cold-ischemia. All this adds up to kidneys that are less viable once transplanted.

The high success rate of Mashhad's cadaver organ program underscored another irony of the U.S. system: More cadaver kidneys are harvested and transplanted in the United States, but the average organ is of poorer quality than in Mashhad. Because Mashhad has a reliable living donor source of kidneys to fall back on, it can afford to pick the best cadaver organs and transplant them under the best conditions possible. We don't have that luxury in the United States. So unfortunately, even though the United States arguably has the most efficient deceased donor organ procurement system in the world, the quality and long-term functioning of the cadaver kidneys retrieved is lower than in Mashhad.

A Different Kind of Land Mine

After our meeting with the transplant team at Imam Reza Hospital,* Dr. Bastani left to give a lecture, and I accompanied Dr. Sharifi Pour to the doctors' lounge. A long wooden table with eight chairs, a kitchenette-style counter with cabinets, a sink, fridge, and electric kettle graced the room as they might in any American or European hospital lounge. Dr. Sharifi Pour ordered food, and by the time we had made ourselves tea, an orderly was at the door with rice, kabobs, yogurt, and fresh herbs, neatly packed in styrofoam take-out boxes. I was pleased to notice men and women sitting at the same table, chatting amicably.

A young doctor—so young he must have just finished medical school—sat down beside me. As we exchanged mundane pleasantries, he innocently commented, "Your hijab suits you. You look like you could get used to it." All the warnings my sister Ingrid gave me about keeping my feminist streak in check came flooding back. The room went silent—without wanting one, I had an audience. I couldn't resist. I paused, took a breath, and allowed myself a brief lapse in etiquette. "No," I said calmly, "I'm afraid there is no chance of that." He frowned. The other physicians at the table quickly looked away and resumed their conversations, pretending nothing had happened. I finished my meal in silence.

Sometimes it is hard not to react emotionally. I know I shouldn't have been so blunt with that young physician. I'm sure he meant no harm. But the discrimination against women in Iran is blatant, and the implication that I might actually like wearing a hijab was too much for me to bear in silence. Nonetheless, I stand by the tagline I have below my signature on emails: "True intel-

---

* Note that "Imam Reza" is a popular name for hospitals in Iran. Several hospitals we visited in different cities had that name. They are not part of a hospital chain.

lectuals have the fortitude to change their minds when faced with new evidence."

I adopted my tagline based on something the magician Penn Jillette once told me. We had been discussing how hard it can be to admit a mistake and change one's political position, particularly if those beliefs are a long-held tradition among family and friends. At the time it struck me how wise Penn was to recognize that changing one's stance takes courage. Penn's aphorism is true in all contexts, not just politics, and I take his point seriously. However, it is similarly wrong to assume that new evidence necessitates a 180-degree change in opinion. When it came to women's rights in Iran, I didn't switch from assuming Iran was intolerably misogynistic to saying it was fair and just. Rather, I started to see things more as they were: a nuanced grey, instead of an emotionally driven black or white.

Iran's treatment of women is undoubtedly somewhere in between my stereotyped expectation that women would be treated rudely, patronized, and abused, and the reality I experienced of generally being treated with polite respect. I learned from Dr. Bastani and others that Iran is more advanced when it comes to women's rights than most Muslim countries. Iran is not the Taliban-terrorized Afghanistan, nor is it like Saudi Arabia where women aren't allowed to drive, have limited access to education, and are denied the right to vote. But still, Iran is not the United States, Europe, or even Turkey. I'm sure that as a foreign professional I was afforded more deference than most women in Iran. As a result, I felt obligated to try to parse the truth from fiction, particularly when it came to Iran's treatment of female kidney sellers.

A short time after my return from Iran, I gave a talk at an American Society for Bioethics and Humanities conference. Having just returned with information about kidney selling in Iran never before collected by a Westerner, I volunteered to discuss my preliminary findings. I spoke to a room packed with medical professionals, professors, and others interested in the field of medical ethics.

At the close of my presentation, a woman asked, "Did your research find that more women donate than men? I've heard that in Iran men force their wives to sell their kidneys—for example, to support a husband's drug habit."

I wasn't surprised to get such a question because I had heard similar rumors before my trip. But that was not what I found when I observed the system firsthand. I started to answer, "I wouldn't rule out that a husband might pressure his wife into donating, but that isn't what I saw. In Iran male donors far outnumber female donors, and none of the women I spoke to—"

But my questioner cut me off before I could finish my answer. "Well that can't be," she said indignantly. "Everyone knows women are exploited in Iran." She paused for dramatic effect and then huffed, "You don't know what you're talking about."

I couldn't believe the number of heads in the audience that nodded in agreement despite the fact that neither they nor my questioner had the slightest factual basis to support their assumptions. After all, I was the only Westerner with firsthand knowledge on the subject. I wanted to ask the woman the source of her claim for what "everyone knows," but the session ended and she left before I had a chance to ask. This woman's visceral reaction reminded me of a similar encounter I experienced only a few days after returning from Iran.

The mother of one of my daughter's friends was from Iran, so I called her naively thinking she might be interested in helping me translate my interviews. She listened politely as I described the research I had done and then said she was sorry but she couldn't help. In essence she said there is no way I could have done such extensive research unless I were in cahoots with the government.

When I explained that I had done all my research without government approval or supervision, she remarked, "You made it out alive, didn't you?" She told me she would never forget seeing one of her friends being thrown off the top of a building during the Revolution; she had fled Iran that very day and never looked back. Clearly her hatred for the post-Shah regime was understandable in light of what she had witnessed. Perhaps the woman at the ASBH conference who asked me about female kidney donors had also been through a personal trauma that clouded her judgment.

I was learning quickly that when it comes to Iran, and particularly Iran and women's issues, emotions run blindingly high. As a result, my motivation to get my interviews translated, my data tabulated, and this book written took on new meaning—I had to find a way to share what I had learned, the good and the bad, as quickly as I could.

What Money Can and Can't Buy

From Imam Reza Hospital we headed over to the *Anjoman*. What an unexpected pleasure: a sweeping marble entranceway, stone counters, light rose-colored walls, and white columns with crown molding. I wondered what this building had been before it became the *Anjoman*—probably a small upscale hotel. There was even a framed painting of a pastoral scene on the wall, something quite out of place for an *Anjoman*. In every other *Anjoman*, the walls were hung with informational posters, portraits of *Anjoman* founders, or photos of one or both of Iran's supreme leaders, Khomeini and Khamenei. I later spotted the missing Khamenei portrait; it was leaning against the wall on top of a file cabinet. It was as if someone had said, "We better put it up somewhere, but where? How about here for now?" and then never got around to hanging it.

We were introduced to Dr. Jawad Afzali who, per his father's request, donated the building to the *Anjoman* when his father died. More modestly dressed than pretty much everyone else I'd met so far, he was thin, fit, slightly balding, and sported a fine but graying mustache.

Dr. Afzali was soft-spoken and focused his comments on efforts to create a balance between cadaver and living organ donation. With 25,000–30,000 fatal car accidents every year—Iran has one of the highest rates of automobile-related deaths in the world—"Efforts should be made," he told us, "to reduce the automobile fatality rate, but, in the meantime, it is also a waste not to find a way to use the organs that are so readily available."

Dr. Afzali also spoke of a need to "even out the heads of society," a Farsi expression for working to diminish socioeconomic inequalities. He suggested that instead of a one-time payment, kidney donors should receive lifetime health insurance, employment, or even "shares in government organizations or larger companies" to give them more permanent assistance and stability in their lives.

His words echoed views we'd heard from Dr. Ebrahim Khadeghi from the University of Mashhad. Dr. Khadeghi had described how the Organ Transplant Center and its affiliated hospitals (Imam Reza and Ghaem) were working to arrange "permanent" insurance for donors to come to their clinics indefinitely for follow-up care, whether that care was directly related to their kidney donation or not.

Dr. Khadeghi also elaborated on the work being done to encourage deceased organ donation. Even more effective than donor-card drives, he explained, are the efforts made to show society's appreciation to donor families.

> The family must be treated with great respect. This means we pay the deceased's hospital bills, funeral costs, and the cost of transporting the deceased back to his home village. We even provide a headstone: "Here lies in peace the soul of one who has given a new life to a person in need."

Such gestures of gratitude are important because they serve to educate the public. People see the funeral procession and the physician who comes to speak at the memorial service, or they see and read the tombstone and become curious. The more questions people ask, the more they will understand the importance of cadaver donation. "The goal of all of this is to help build support and a culture of awareness." In the six years that Dr. Khadeghi had served as transplant coordinator, the rate of family consent for cadaver organ donation increased from 10 to nearly 50 percent.

While waiting in a large antechamber for an opportunity to interview donors, we heard Mrs. Jalal Kazemi, the *Anjoman's* nurse/social worker, arguing with a woman at her desk. After the woman left, we went over to ask Mrs. Kazemi what the commotion was all about.

Unlike the Abulfazl *Anjoman* where we had witnessed the intake clerk argue with a young man and were told, "That was nothing," Mrs. Kazemi did not hesitate to share her frustration. The woman wanted to donate her kidney, but Mrs. Kazemi felt she was not a good candidate because her predicament might be compounded rather than alleviated by the donation. The woman was in her early 30s and still living at home with parents she deemed unbearably restrictive. She wanted to donate her kidney so she could get a place of her own. Mrs. Kazemi was obviously exasperated, telling us the woman couldn't understand that she must first get a job, then come back and talk to the *Anjoman* if she still needed the money to buy or rent a home. Mrs. Kazemi posed the obvious question: "How will it help to anger your parents by leaving if a few months later you have no choice but to move back in with them?"

I silently wondered if this woman had a different problem than the one she was claiming. Maybe she needed the money for an abortion—but then I realized if that were the case, her pregnancy would be detected during pre-donation testing, and she would be excluded. Abortion is illegal in Iran. The only time I suspected that money from a kidney sale might have been used to pay for an abortion was when one recipient, Amir, told us that the *Anjoman* let a donor sell Amir his kidney without requiring the usual parental permission because the donor was "doing it for his sister." Amir's donor didn't provide any further details other than to say his sister was "in trouble" and his parents could under no circumstance learn what that trouble was.

Another potential donor, a woman with her 3-year-old daughter, approached, so we retreated to a table at the other end of the room to allow Mrs. Kazemi to do her job. The little girl cocked her head curiously at us and then wandered over. Her multi-colored, striped poncho and headscarf with large yellow and blue flowers were a bright splash of color that seemed to cry out in defiance of her inevitable dark-clad future. I drew a rabbit eating a flower on a piece of paper and handed it to her. She grinned, sat down at the table, and started coloring in the petals with my blue fountain pen. Her mother asked over her shoulder whether Mia was bothering us.

"No, not at all."

A few minutes later, Sara joined us. Mia climbed onto her mother's lap and snuggled into her shoulder, wiggling and adjusting herself like a puppy circling in its bedding before taking a nap. Sara was 27 and married. She wore a full chador, but a black and white striped lapel peeked out when she let go of her outer robe to tend to Mia. I never saw Sara's hair, but I marveled at her perfectly sculpted eyebrows and straight teeth. By contrast, her lips were chapped and peeling, and her nails were short, cracked, and unlacquered. Sara wasn't wearing makeup though I caught a faint whiff of jasmine perfume. Maybe it was Mashhad's religious character or perhaps because it was the month of Muharram, but the women here were more conservatively dressed than what I'd seen elsewhere in Iran—more chadors, even on younger women, and far less makeup.

Sara was quite chatty. She seemed irritated and wanted to talk, but her thoughts were scattered. "I feel if I do this, at least I can get a house … where I can be comfortable, or where I have given a down payment so I can pay rent— even if it's in the lower end of the city, or in a village outside of Mashhad."

But purchasing a home wouldn't be enough to solve Sara's problems: "If my husband doesn't find work, all will be lost." Then she mused, "He is a great photographer. If there was this money, he could go with as little as one or two million tomans and become a partner somewhere in a studio—to do photography and teach, or maybe he can find a small job." She told us that he had already tried to make a living as a photographer, but it hadn't gone well. Instead, he had recently turned to eking out a living as a carpenter, but even in that line of work, he'd been out of a job for more than a month.

Sara admitted that Mrs. Kazemi was not sure Sara was a good candidate for selling her kidney. She had told Sara as much several times. At their meeting that day, Mrs. Kazemi gave Sara contact information for several charities she should visit, but Sara said she had already tried everything else and felt Mrs. Kazemi was being unreasonable. Sara already had a 200,000-toman loan she couldn't repay; Sara had told Mrs. Kazemi that it didn't make sense to try for yet another loan, but Mrs. Kazemi refused Sara for the fourth time, and said she should not return to the *Anjoman* until she had exhausted absolutely every other option.

Sara's prospects were bleak. Staying with in-laws wasn't an option because her husband was an orphan. And moving back in with her own parents, although an option, would be too disgraceful for her husband, so she would have to go alone—They might have to divorce. "But I could never do that to Mia," she whispered, gazing down at the child asleep in her arms, blissfully oblivious to her mother's plight.

Sara and her husband had agreed that it would be better for her to donate rather than him so that he could continue looking for a job. She felt she could take care of Mia while she was recovering, but as a family they couldn't afford to have him out of work. On the other hand, even if they got enough money to pay off their loan, the back rent, and to purchase a small house, her husband still needed to find a studio where he could buy in as a partner. "Hopefully," she said, her manner less confident than her words, "there would be enough for that too." She wavered. "Well, if nothing else, we could pay our rent for a while."

I understood why Mrs. Kazemi hesitated to agree to let Sara donate—her plan was too undefined. If Sara's husband had a specific studio he was ready to buy into, the situation would be different, but Sara was speaking hypothetically. After the interview, Dr. Bastani and I gave Sara some money, enough to pay her back rent and the next month's rent as well. We hoped we had bought Sara and her husband some time to come up with a more concise plan, something better than using the money to temporarily stave off an inevitable financial collapse.

Another donor we met at the Mashhad *Anjoman* had a typical donor story of a different kind. Iran has some of the most advanced medical facilities in the Middle East, but it still falls short of what is available in Europe or the United States. Hamed was at the *Anjoman* to sell his kidney to pay for an operation for his wife that could be performed only abroad and which neither the government nor his private insurance would agree to cover.

Hamed was 28 but looked more the age of my own boys who are in their early 20s. His tight, dark-brown curls and large doe eyes with thick lashes projected an innocence that defied the severity of his grief. He never smiled; he kept repeating that he had to do right by his wife.

Two months earlier, Hamed's wife had lost her sight in an accident while riding on the back of his motorcycle. I thought of the many couples I'd seen weaving in and out of traffic on their mopeds and motorcycles, often with a child wedged between them and none of them wearing helmets. Once I saw a man driving with an infant on his lap, holding the baby in place with one hand and steering with the other. An involuntary shudder shook my frame. "Dr. Bastani, was anyone else hurt? There wasn't a child, was there?"

"No," was the reply, and I let out a sigh of relief.

To try to repair his wife's vision, Hamed had already spent eight million tomans beyond what his insurance would cover. His wife's doctors suggested that taking her to Germany was their only hope.

"So now you would like to donate. How much do you think you can get from the sale of your kidney?

"Well, I don't really know, but the more I can get the better. I've three million in loans, but I'm still about nine million short."

Dr. Bastani pointed out that the going rate for a kidney is only five million tomans.

"Well, then I will still need to think of a way to get the remaining four million."

Dr. Bastani inquired what Hamed would do if selling kidneys were illegal in Iran as it is in other countries. Hamed's face went ashen, and in a soft, defeated tone he said, "Well … I don't know. I would have to sell my successful spice shop, which is my only source of income. There would be no other way." Dr. Bastani told him not to give up hope. There were charities that might be able to help, or maybe he could ask his family for more money.

Later, Dr. Bastani explained to me that Hamed's wife lost her vision due to a brain hemorrhage caused by the accident. Dr. Bastani wasn't optimistic that the German doctors could help recover her vision after so much time had elapsed, but we both understood Hamed's determination to do everything he possibly could to help his wife, even if her chances of recovery were slim. What else could he do? Most likely he would be selling his kidney and spending money on a futile trip to Germany, but his conscience demanded it.

Mashhad is a city that brings out the best in people, and the Mashhad *Anjoman* is lacking in neither funds nor initiative. I hoped that, in one way or another, the staff could help both Sara and Hamed overcome their financial difficulties, perhaps by working in conjunction with other charities or government services. That night I dreamt of Hamed leaning over his wife in a hospital bed in Germany. She blinked and strained to see him through vision blurred by tears. I could see the relief creep over his face: Muscles tired of frowning slowly released their tension as he smiled tentatively, leaning over to kiss his wife, afraid to believe what he was seeing was true.

I held my breath when I heard back about follow-up interviews. Was Hamed among them? No—the phone number we had for him, like most of the numbers of our interviewees, was no longer valid.

The Face of Death

I tried to check my email regularly while in Iran, but most of the time I couldn't get through to my Yahoo account, even on hospital computers. Finally, after a week's hiatus, I got into my email and smiled to see a message from Bob. But it was not the usual "I miss you" or "The kids are up to this or that." Today's note started, "I received a call late this afternoon from the Loudoun County Sheriff's Office. They told me that Lais was involved in an accident and that I should come home right away." Lais was our au pair from Brazil, whom I had hired to help Bob with the kids while I was away. We have had a few au pairs in our time, and they almost always became close friends of the family. Lais, 21, vivacious and excited to be in America, had been with us for only a few months. I knew she was a responsible young woman, but that December morning brought home to us all just how fragile life can be.

Lais had dropped my daughter Lauren off at the bus stop and was on her way home. She had stopped the car to open the gate across our driveway, but she must have accidently missed "Park" and slipped the car into "Reverse." She turned to see the car rolling away, backwards down our long driveway, but instead of letting it go, she chased the car and tried to get back into the driver's seat. The door swung open and struck her, pinning her to a tree. The mailman found her there, hours later, the car engine still running. I was in shock and wanted to be home with my family.

When I mentioned what had happened to Dr. Bastani and Dr. Hekmat, they wanted to know if Lais had been our family nanny for long. I said no—she just joined us a few months earlier. I was expecting a sympathetic response, but instead Dr. Hekmat said something odd, even crass: "People die every day. She was just the hired help, right?" While this was true, it left me wondering if his insensitivity was due to his being a physician, or if it had more to do with his being a physician in a developing country where death is more a part of everyday life than in the United States.

Yes, death does happen every day, and America has its share of Auroras and Columbines, traffic accidents, and work related accidents, but in the United States most of the everyday death of old age and illness is sanitized and choreographed. When most Americans experience death firsthand, it is usually someone dying in a hospital bed or at home on hospice, nothing as shocking or as lonely as what happened to Lais—a body found hours after she died, no medical attention, no rush to the hospital.

Once when I was in Rio de Janeiro, I saw a body in an alley. I'd grown accustomed to seeing drunks and beggars sleeping in doorways, but this body caught my eye as somehow different. No, actually, it caught my nose. When I turned to look, the body was lying face up with a shoeless leg jutting out at an unnatural angle. Rats were scurrying around. One stopped and stood up on its haunches to give me a "What's it to you? Mind your own business!" look. I swayed, took a step back, and covered my nose and mouth as I tried to see without entering the alley. Maybe he was just drunk? People walked by, glancing at me and down the dark corridor without breaking their stride. Whose business was this? Why hadn't anyone called the Brazilian equivalent of 911? I moved on. I didn't call anyone.

My grandfather was a doctor in Argentina. His formal training was in infectious diseases. This was before HIV and AIDS, so there were no epidemics the year I lived with him, but he nonetheless kept track of deaths in our area. My grandmother would report, "Walter, I heard a farmhand at the Salazar hacienda died. No evidence of violence; they say he died in his sleep." Sometimes my grandfather would rush out to go see if he could examine the body before it was buried, but often he was too late. No hospital, no doctors, no coroner, just straight from deathbed to grave—usually a grave on the property.

I never witnessed anything like either one of these stories in Iran, but I do know the poor often take care of their own when it comes to death and burial. Dr. Malakoutian said people in villages often die and are buried without ever seeing a doctor, and seeing a doctor is such an expense that many people wait too long. No physician means no death certificate and no known cause of death.

At Ghaem Hospital I witnessed a burden of death no one experiences in the West. I was waiting outside the hospital for Dr. Bastani to catch up after someone stopped him to ask a question when a man, probably in his late 70s, caught my attention. He was struggling to push a hospital gurney across the parking lot. The frail old gentleman barely kept the gurney under control as it jolted down from the curb. The dingy maroon blanket covering his cargo slipped, and the man's bony arm jutted out to save the blanket from touching the ground, but he was too late: The gurney tipped, one wheel spinning wildly, and his burden was revealed. He took a deep breath, steadying his footing, and glanced at the figure for a split second before gently tucking in the blanket as if tucking a child into bed. I caught only a glimpse—a silhouette of a face and shoulder wrapped in a white sheet under the blanket—but it was unmistakably a corpse.

His passenger secured, he jerked the gurney back into motion, weaving his way back and forth across the parking lot, avoiding the most egregious breaks in the pavement. He positioned the gurney against a beat-up Renault hatchback. He opened the hatch, stared at the body, looked around—His eyes, strangely dull, noticed me. He hesitated for the briefest instant. *Does he need help? Should I offer? What's the proper etiquette in a situation like this? I don't even know the Farsi words for "May I help you?"*

He pulled his load off the gurney, setting it down feet-first, holding it in one arm as if they were about to take a stroll. He opened the back of the car, bent down, and hoisted his companion into the vehicle with such a groan that I wondered if his pain were more emotional than physical. I cringed as he slammed the car hatch shut, the body shifting inside. He plodded back to the hospital with a lighter, much more manageable gurney, like someone returning an empty shopping cart to a store. I stared at the car and its contents, remembering what Dr. Khadeghi had told me about the ambulance ride back to the village being the most expensive part of an Iranian funeral. I wondered if this old gentleman, maybe with the help of neighbors, would dig the grave himself.

What a contrast! In the United States, it is against the law for relatives to dispose of a body. In every case authorities must be notified, whether the police, the coroner, hospice, or the mortuary, and someone must declare and document the death. Most bodies, whether there is a family or not, are released to mortuaries. In the United States the cheapest option, outside of illegally burying a body oneself, is to donate the body to science — not organ donation, but donating the whole body to be used for medical education or scientific research, such as dissection in anatomy classes or forensic studies on body decomposition. The point is that in the United States bodies are supposed to be examined by medical personnel before they are disposed of, and the law requires documentation of the cause of death and a death certificate. Family members never, at least not legally, dig a hole in the back yard or local cemetery themselves.

My own father had died only a few months before I left for Iran. How different his death and burial might have been if we were poor and living in Argentina or Iran. I held my father's hand while he died, lying in his own bedroom, in a hospital bed provided by hospice. Once I knew he had taken his last breath, I called June, my father's hospice nurse. Three people showed up: June and two men I hadn't met. June asked me for the leftover morphine drops and flushed them down the toilet. The men set a gurney up next to my father's bed, and transferred him to a body bag. They let me say one more goodbye before they zipped up the bag and rolled the gurney out of the house and into an ambulance. Then, they drove my father to the mortuary where he was cremated. I never had to do a thing: Everything was done for me as I stood in a daze, realizing I would never hug or speak to my father again. I have no idea what it cost to transport my father from his house to the mortuary.

I wasn't at Lais' funeral; we weren't immediate family and we weren't invited. Her American relatives, who lived in Ohio, arranged for her body to be shipped to her parents in Brazil. I can only imagine how much that might have cost. I had considered going home to be with my husband and children, but I would have had to return to Tehran and try to get an earlier flight. It would take at least two or three days to get out of Mashhad, maybe longer depending on the availability of flights, and after that it would probably take another week before I could be scheduled to fly home from Tehran. Bob said I should stay and finish my research; there wasn't much I would accomplish by coming home early. I knew he was right, but at the time I was ready to drop everything and go.

Forbidden Fruit

Several times during our stay in Mashhad we met up with Dr. Hekmat and, despite his insensitive comment about Lais' death, spending time with him was a treat. Dr. Hekmat was a middle-aged man of average height and build with a full mustache, receding hairline, and thick glasses. He dressed more casually than most of the physicians I met in Iran, often in just a polo shirt and khakis under his lab coat instead of a suit. Dr. Hekmat liked to court danger by dabbling in Western thought, and he found in me a willing accomplice. Our conversations ranged from Goethe, Shakespeare, Marx, and Husserl to Kierkegaard and the existence of God. Dr. Hekmat seemed starved for an intellectual challenge, and I was happy to oblige.

Ironically, one of our conversations took place while we were out to dinner with Dr. Bastani and an older woman who was there to introduce her daughter, a beautiful girl in her 20s, to the bachelor Dr. Hekmat. They exchanged pleasantries, and I noticed Dr. Hekmat glancing furtively at the young woman, but the opportunity to discuss the forbidden intellectual fruits of philosophy won him over. The other ladies at the table didn't seem incensed or upset about the intensity of our conversation or at my willingness to debate, although Dr. Bastani did ask us to lower our voices a couple of times; the women just seemed bored and excused themselves as soon as it was polite to do so. I had a feeling they weren't surprised at my forward behavior because I was a Western woman. But I was also pretty sure Dr. Hekmat was taking liberties with me, getting into heated philosophical discussions in a way he never would with an Iranian woman.

Interestingly, I found that Iranians often took liberties with me that I'm quite sure they wouldn't take with others, particularly not Iranian women. I don't mean sexual liberties like inappropriate touching: There is a different type of liberty that Iranian men and women both seem to reserve for their Western visitors. For example, there is little doubt in my mind that the topics Dr. Hekmat and I covered were generally not acceptable conversation for polite company in Iran. To acknowledge an interest in non-Islamic thought is to acknowledge that such ideas might have credence, and to do so barely falls short of blasphemy.

Both women and men also took advantage of my so-called Western sensibilities about female dress and behavior. Three different nurses showed me photos on their cell phones of themselves dressed in exercise clothes, doing karate kicks, yoga, and boxing. They obviously loved these activities but felt uneasy sharing their pastimes with other Iranians without knowing how they might react. However, because I was from the West, they assumed I would approve. And twice, without any prompting on my part, male guides showed me photos of their half-clad wives—nothing too revealing by Western standards, but clearly risqué by Iranian standards. All I could think was that they kept these photos on their phones for their own pleasure, and because I was a Westerner, they assumed there was little chance that I would sic the morality police on them.

Even cab drivers took similar liberties. Some drivers would play music by forbidden female vocalists when I was in the car. Our driver Ali in Tabriz even showed me a cartoon video on his phone of two cell phones meeting, embracing, and having sex. It was such a ridiculous vignette that I had to laugh, but why on earth he thought it would be a good idea to share it with me, I never figured out. Perhaps because I was a Westerner, he thought it would be acceptable to do so, not realizing that even in the West such conduct would generally be frowned upon. When he drove us around after that, Ali would sometimes point to his cell phone and chuckle. In response, I would shake my head or roll my eyes; he loved it.

But in Mashhad, it was mostly Dr. Hekmat who challenged my conventional views of Iranian culture and provided me with a familiar form of company in what was otherwise an extremely interesting, but lonely, experience. I was beginning to see that loneliness wasn't always about isolation from the world but also estrangement in the world: Dr. Hekmat was an oppressed thinker. He wanted to explore things he'd read and share his insights with someone, but he was generally dismissed as somewhat odd, just short of being subversive. And I, a Western woman in town for only a few days, was that rare person in his life he could trust to take his endeavor seriously. When we parted company, he gave me a great compliment: "So where can I find a woman like you?"

I smiled and encouraged him, "Keep looking. You will find her!" But I wondered silently, *How many female philosophy Ph.D.s are there in Iran, and of those, how many have ever studied anything other than Islamic or Persian ideologies?*

Make Way for the Pilgrim from Afar

Mashhad is Iran's holiest city, the burial place of the Eighth Imam. Imam Reza was the seventh of Prophet Mohammad's descendants and the 8th of 12 imams, according to Shi'ite Islam. His shrine, the Imam Reza Shrine Complex, is both the spiritual and physical center of Mashhad. Around 20 million pilgrims visit Imam Reza's mausoleum every year. The complex is huge: It includes museums, prayer halls, seminary buildings, a dining hall, and a cemetery, in addition to numerous fountain-adorned courtyards and mausoleums. The complex is the largest mosque in the world, measuring in at over six million square feet, but the third largest in its capacity to accommodate worshippers. Only the Sacred Mosque in Mecca, where the Kaaba is located, and the Mosque of the Prophet in Medina, originally built by Mohammad, can accommodate more of the pious in prayer.

The Imam Reza Shrine Complex was nothing like other mosques I'd visited. In those other mosques, I was struck by the homey atmosphere. Women were there with their children, some praying, but some speaking softly to their children and their neighbors. Almost always, someone helped me put on a chador and showed me where to sit. They would offer me trail mix, blessed by the mosque's imam, and point me in the proper direction for prayer.

I entered the Imam Reza Shrine Complex shortly after midnight with our driver Mahmud's wife and daughter as my guides. They were kind and understanding hostesses, helping me straighten my chador when it fell from my head, and giggling when I tripped trying to hold it up while walking. Right before the men and the women were about to part ways, I turned to Mahmud, "Please tell Bita and Nooshim that I thank them from the bottom of my heart for the kindness they show me."

He translated and answered back, "They are glad to help. My wife says she likes you. She senses your visit is important."

Nooshim suggested I put one end of the chador between my teeth to hold it in place without using my hands, but I kept forgetting to keep my teeth clenched. They just shook their heads and smiled.

To say the Imam Reza Shrine Complex was awe-inspiring is an understatement. I had seen people on the streets in Mashhad, crying or praying, but here it seemed as though every tenth person entering the complex prostrated him- or herself in supplication. And *everyone* stopped, spellbound, before moving on.

The amount of gold was bedazzling—the domes, the towers, inside the arches, and most of the mosaic writings were in gold. The fountains were lit to make the water dance, and strings of lights guided my gaze up to the top of the minarets. I can't even begin to describe how many arches or people there were, but the main square was full of worshippers, even in the middle of the night, and there was precious little room to maneuver. As we made our way through the crowd, I was grateful to have my two new lady friends by my side. They offered to show me the Imam's tomb. I knew it was forbidden to non-Muslims, but my guides didn't seem concerned, and no one questioned us as we entered the inner sanctuary. It was standing room only. I swayed with the current of bodies, mesmerized by the mirrored mosaics reflecting back on themselves, a never-ending loop of sparkling light.

In most mosques I had visited, there was at least one women who monitored the goings-on and kept things neat. One such woman, carrying a feather duster on a long stick, approached, took me by the hand, and urged me to follow. I felt a pang of anxiety, not wanting to be separated from my companions, but they waved me on.

"From?"

"America." By now I knew not to answer "U.S."

She started speaking loudly in Farsi, pulling me along through the crowd. She kept repeating something. I recognized "*Haaj Khanoom*," the Farsi expression for pilgrim, and the word "America," and put two and two together. She was saying something like, "Make way for this lady. She is a pilgrim from faraway America."

The woman pressed on, tapping away right and left with her feather duster as we went, glancing back frequently to make sure she still had the right person by the hand. She continued on her quest to get me as close to the sarcophagus as she could, tapping away—"Make way. Make way. This lady is a pilgrim all the way from America." She tapped some of the women quite hard—*Oh no*, I winced, *Please don't hit the wailing ladies!*—Sincere pilgrims, many of them crying, moved out of our way as I muttered apologies under my breath. Once we were about five feet from Imam Reza's tomb, my escort smiled a self-satisfied smile, nodded to indicate her job was done, and disappeared into the crowd.

I admired the gilded cage that surrounded the tomb but didn't resist as mourners pushed their way past me with outstretched arms forcing notes or money through the tomb's screen. The swelling crowd forced me ever farther back, away from the inner shrine. Ten or so minutes later, I turned and started working my way back toward the entrance where I was relieved to find Bita and Nooshim waiting for me. They flanked me once again as we proceeded from the Imam Reza Shrine through a courtyard, under a portico, and into another chamber with yet another tomb. And there were Dr. Bastani and Mahmud; they must have prearranged to meet us there.

Dr. Bastani explained we were at the shrine of the famed sixteenth-century cleric-philosopher-poet Sheikh Bahai—not in any way related to the Baha'i religion. I was moved that he thought to bring me here. Dr. Bastani and I exchanged meaningful glances. Earlier that day, the *Anjoman* staff had presented me with a framed poem by Sheikh Bahai. Dr. Bastani had translated it for me:

> Every day to be fasting; every night to be praying;
>   and every year to do pilgrimage on bare feet to Mecca.
> Constantly murmuring that I am answering Your call
>   and accepting Your invitation.
> Take refuge from worldly pleasures, staying in the mosques
>   or in temples, avoiding all sins and all wrong doing.
> Friday nights not sleeping. Whispering to God all night,
>   asking His Eminence for all one's needs.
> I swear to God that none of these are on par with opening
>   the door for a person in need.

In other words, the *Anjoman* staff was acknowledging me even as a non-Muslim, telling me they knew there is more to being a good person than adhering to religious rites. It is a testament to the Persian heart—so integral to the Iranian character—that the author of this poem is enshrined in the same complex with the Eighth Imam. Dr. Bastani explained to our companions what had happened earlier that day, and they nodded at me in recognition. I felt honored and beamed, taken in by the profundity of feeling in the air. Like other pilgrims, I touched the carved marble sarcophagus for good luck. Maybe I understood Mashhad after all.

Is caring for the less fortunate a personal or a governmental responsibility? My feeling is that it must be both, but how does one decide which responsibilities lie in which sphere? Government welfare can create a sense of entitlement on the part of recipients and a sense of apathy on the part of taxpayers. But too much personal involvement can create an entangling web of obligation, shame, and indebtedness potentially causing resentment in both donors and recipients. The *Anjomans* in Iran work as a safety valve: They allow government regulation and community support of the living donor matching process while simultaneously allowing donors and recipients a certain degree of anonymity if they so choose. But the system is far from perfect. At this point in my research, I had no sense of what could be done to improve the situation. Striking the right balance is hard. And now it was on to Tabriz where I would learn a different lesson—namely that efficiency sometimes comes at the expense of individualized care.

∧ (8)

Organs for Opium

Tabriz is a city of skyscrapers, industry, and business located in the northern-most corner of Iran between Turkey and the Republic of Azerbaijan. The city is a place of convergence, a stop on the Silk Road where business has always been king. Our driver, Ali, worked for the University of Tabriz's International Business Liaison Office—a telling title given the city's view of itself as the business capital of Iran, at least after Tehran. Tabriz is Iran's fourth-largest city with a population of almost 1.5 million, but it didn't feel like Iran.

One major difference was the climate: It was nothing like the tropical warmth of Shiraz or the temperate breezes of Isfahan. Snow fell while we were in Tabriz, but it wasn't just the weather that marked a change. The cultural climate was also different. Tabriz had been a Mongolian and a Turkmen capital long before it was a Persian capital, and unlike other Iranian cities I'd visited, the Persian influence was muted; Tabriz seemed more like Turkey. Even Dr. Bastani was out of his element: When we interviewed donors and recipients, half the time *he* needed a translator.

Not Persians

As I learned from Ali, who spoke English fluently (yes, the one with the boink-ing cell phone video!), Tabriz is the center of the Azerbaijani part of Iran. A fourth of Iran's population is Azeri, yet these Turkish-dialect-speaking Shi'ites are not second-class citizens, and they would never dream of leaving Iran to join their brethren in Azerbaijan. As a matter of fact, more Azerbaijanis live in Iran than in Azerbaijan, and the current Supreme Leader of Iran, Ayatollah Khamenei, is himself an Azeri.

The Azerbaijani roots in this part of Iran run deep. All the Tabrizies I spoke to were proud to be part of Iranian society. My guess is the Azeris of Iran are thankful for the relative stability of their region. Perhaps there is a conscious rejection, albeit one I can't comprehend, of Azerbaijan's secular Muslim society in favor of the Iranian Shi'ite theocracy. Also, Tabriz's economy was thriving. The city seemed more alive, vibrant, and "on the move" than any other Iranian city I'd visited, even more so than Tehran. I could tell, even before we reached the impressive El-Goli Pars Hotel, that I would enjoy my stay.

Back in the Swing of Things

Ahhh! A Western-style bathroom and all the other wonderful amenities that come with a four-star hotel. By now, I was ready to be pampered, and the Tabriz El-Goli Pars Hotel was the perfect place for me: a spacious, 20-story hotel with a fragrant flower arrangement in the entrance hall, a panoramic view of the city, and a restaurant with linen tablecloths and real Turkish coffee. And best of all, no alley or sewer anywhere in sight.

I was getting a bit trip-weary, and after what had happened to Lais, I wanted to be with my family. I was haunted, not knowing how long Lais had been pinned to the tree before she was found, or whether she had lingered or died instantly. Perhaps the autopsy could provide some answers, but because we weren't related to Lais, we were left in the dark. I decided I needed to focus my energies elsewhere. Instead of dwelling on the horror of what had happened to Lais, I needed to concentrate on getting back to work.

Tabriz University's organ transplant program was well established but, for the most part, not innovative. It seemed much like a small-scale version of what we had seen in Tehran. Tabriz University had most of the resources needed to run a more progressive program like Mashhad's, but instead it focused on volume rather than innovation. All the members of the transplant team were extremely hard-working and devoted to getting as many transplants done as efficiently as possible, but none seemed interested in questioning the status quo. At the time we were there, their cadaver kidney donation program was floundering, and there was little impetus for change.

Everything was so imbued with a business ethos that when transplant ethics came up, the physicians I spoke with didn't ask about resource allocation, donor rights, exploitation, or informed consent: They wanted to discuss medical tourism. The discussion wasn't about selling kidneys to foreigners; they wanted to market their transplant services to foreign patients who could bring their own donors. Some members of the team were uncomfortable with the idea. Medical tourism could create an incentive to favor high-paying foreign patients over Iranians whose treatment was paid for at a lower government rate.

These are important inquiries, but I was there to try and answer a different set of questions.

My Daughter for Your Kidney

The Tabriz *Anjoman* was not wealthy or showy like the Mashhad *Anjoman*. It was well run and well maintained, but its staff, like the Tabriz University transplant team, seemed more focused on the number of people helped than on assuring that each individual's specific needs were met. Like in Tehran, donors and recipients had to protect their own interests. I saw no conscious mistreatment or neglect of donors or recipients, but the individualized interactions so prevalent in Isfahan and Mashhad were missing.

That said, Mr. Adel Firoozi, head of the Tabriz *Anjoman*, readily shared stories of just the opposite. His anecdotes, both heartening and shocking, were not borne out by our observations. He told us that recipients who worked in factories had given donors jobs and shares in their companies. Mr. Firoozi added with pride, "All of this is so the donor is taken care of and they do not feel alone.... This is for gratitude and appreciation. Especially in our province, it has become part of the culture."

I cringed when Mr. Firoozi told us that recipients are sometimes so grateful that they tell donors, "You can have my daughter," and sometimes the donor really marries into the family. He said this breezily, not hesitating to speak of women as chattel while praising recipients' generosity. Mr. Firoozi brought this up twice without having the faintest idea how disconcerting such a suggestion might sound. Mr. Firoozi's comments confirmed that while some Iranians have more enlightened views about the role of women, others, like Mr. Firoozi, feel secure enough in the legitimacy of such backward practices as daughter-gifting to speak of them as praiseworthy.*

I felt more comfortable with Mr. Firoozi's discussion of other types of donor benefits: He mentioned that Tabriz University offered donors reduced college

---

* Dr. Bastani disagrees with my interpretation of this part of Mr. Firoozi's interview. Dr. Bastani says the Persian expression "give my daughter in thanks" is an idiomatic hyperbole. Generally, I defer to Dr. Bastani when it comes to questions of cultural interpretation, but in this case, I beg to differ. The second time Mr. Firoozi brings up the topic of daughter-gifting, he actually says, and I quote directly from the video transcript of his interview, "At least once what happened was that the donor married the recipient. The family of the recipient was so pleased with him that as a thank you they gave him the daughter as an appreciation."

tuition. This seemed in principle like a good idea, both for encouraging students to donate and to give uneducated donors a chance to improve their life by pursuing higher education. But it didn't seem as though many donors took advantage of this program. Poor donors who need money to get out of debt and/or to support their families usually can't afford to go to school, even if offered full tuition. From what we heard of such programs in other cities, the degree of tuition remittance is supposed to be need-based, but none of the donors (or potential donors) we interviewed in Tabriz or elsewhere mentioned getting reduced tuition, or looking forward to getting reduced tuition, as part of their benefits package.

Mr. Firoozi also mentioned that donors "basically get health insurance for life." This seemed to be the practice in wealthier regions like Mashhad, but as we were to discover later, it even occasionally occurs in less well-off regions like Kermanshah. The national government only guarantees one year of health insurance for donors. That seems to be the norm in Tehran, but in other provinces the booklet of health vouchers given to donors is renewed at the *Anjoman's* discretion (if it has the resources to do so).

The donor benefits Mr. Firoozi described were fascinating but clearly not the norm. By the end of our trip, we had collected over 200 firsthand donor and recipient stories from six different regions, and no one had mentioned daughter-gifting or educational benefits as part of the deal, not even aspirationally so. Twice, *Anjoman* staff told stories of donors and recipients marrying each other, and in three instances staff mentioned vocational training or educational benefits being available. None of the donors or recipients we interviewed, however, had firsthand knowledge of such benefits even though many donors mentioned that what they really needed was a job. Only one donor mentioned a situation where a recipient helped a donor find work, but that was a second-hand account, not a story from the donor's own experience.

Most donors mentioned at least some health insurance as being an important part of the deal. Several donors we spoke to had negotiated and received extended benefits for themselves or their families. However, most of the assistance donors received (beyond financial or basic healthcare benefits) were things like clothing, housing, household goods, food, eyeglasses, dental care, and other material goods for themselves and their families. These are valuable benefits, but the benefits we documented never included an education, a wife, or shares in the recipient's business. Of course, it is possible that these types of gifts are sometimes exchanged, but none of the donors and recipients we spoke to were involved in such transactions.

It was also clear that the *Anjomans* were more or less involved in donors' lives depending on how the staff defined its role. The more staff saw themselves as members of a charity institute that helped people in general, the more likely it would be that they worked equally to meet both donors' and recipients' needs. On the other hand, if *Anjoman* staff saw their main purpose as providing services to kidney disease patients, then helping donors was of secondary importance, and potential benefits beyond the bare minimum were rarely considered. This said, it was also clear that what interested donors most was not education credits, goods, or most services, but rather money, health insurance, and in some instances, exemption from military service. None of the other potential benefits mattered much unless donors could also receive enough remuneration to solve their immediate financial concerns.

What Donors Actually Want

Money was clearly the greatest motivator for donors, and the Iranian system, while heavily regulated, is still a market. That market has evolved in two significant ways since it first began more than a quarter of a century ago. First, as the backlog of people needing kidneys diminished and the system developed a surplus of potential donors, *Anjomans* and medical staff became more selective about the people they chose as donors. Their selectivity was not limited to medical factors, such as eliminating drug users, but expanded to include social factors, such as picking donors whose lives could be changed in positive ways, financially or otherwise.

The second significant change was that as a surplus of donors developed, the price dropped, creating an atmosphere in conjunction with the aforementioned selectivity where helping individual donors with financial and psychological counseling began to take on a new significance. For some medical and *Anjoman* staff, but not by any means all, meeting the needs of desperate donors became as important as meeting the needs of kidney disease patients—in part because happier, less troublesome donors are easier to work with, but also because it improved the morale and social ethos of the whole transplant community.

Smoking Ages the Skin; Opium Ages the Soul

There is some evidence that early in the development of its living donor program, the Iranian transplant community should have been more careful in how it chose donors, particularly when it came to letting drug addicts donate. There has always been agreement that IV drug users should be excluded. But there is still some disagreement about opium and hashish users. Several physicians told us that neither opium nor hashish use negatively impacts kidneys.

One of the things the Iranian transplant community has learned is that, regardless of whether there is a medical reason to distinguish among different types of addicts for kidney donation, there are without a doubt practical and societal reasons for excluding all of them. One serious repercussion of not excluding addicts from the program has been the damage done to the reputation of kidney donation in general. The belief still lingers, both at home and abroad, that most kidney donors in Iran are drug addicts.

The number 80 percent kept coming up when we asked how many kidney donors were addicts. But some transplant personnel were more nuanced in their responses. We quickly learned that we needed to be aware of whether our interviewee was speaking of past, present, or aspirational practices, and how he or she defined drug use.

More self-aware medical and *Anjoman* staff mentioned the ethical discomfort they felt about enabling addicts and expressed relief that Iran's policies with respect to the use of addicted donors had changed or were changing. Rules and guidelines regarding the testing of donors and elimination of drug users from the donor pool exist, both at national and provincial levels of administration, but their implementation is inconsistent, with considerable variation from region to region and even from institution to institution. The more recent the transplant, the more likely the donor and/or recipient was to say that drug testing was part of the screening process, but there was still evidence that not all current potential donors were being screened.

The Tehran *Anjoman* had a policy of testing all donors: Every donor was given both urine and blood tests to rule out as many forms of drug use as possible. In other provinces, however, routine drug testing was not uniformly practiced—probably as a cost-saving measure. Some of the *Anjomans* and transplant teams in cities other than Tehran told us that donors were screened for drugs only if drug use was suspected, and they determined which tests were appropriate on a case-by-case basis.

Several nurses, and a few of the *Anjoman* staff we spoke to, mentioned a practical reason for excluding drug users (or at least addicts) from donating: Simply put, addicts are fickle, untrustworthy, and make bad patients. They miss appointments, lie about their medical histories, are often unhappy with the amount of money or benefits they receive, and tend to be needy patients on the recovery ward. Nurse Sharareh Fadaee told us, "I can point out the addicts; it's easy. They're the ones crying out, complaining that we haven't given them enough pain medication. Who needs it? I wish the *Anjoman* did a better job of not sending us such troublemakers."

Also important was how people defined "addiction." Some medical or *Anjoman* staff said if someone had withdrawal symptoms when he or she stopped using, then that person was an addict—which is as true for IV drug users and opium or hashish smokers as it is for tobacco smokers and coffee drinkers. By such criteria, most of the population in both Iran and the Unites States are addicts.

A second common definition of addiction was to call anyone who used illegal substances an addict. In Iran, this puts IV drug users and those who drink alcohol in the same category. Both are illegal substances, and anyone who uses them is considered an addict who should be disqualified from donating a kidney. By such criteria, half the population of the United States, where much of the adult population drinks alcoholic beverages regularly, would be considered addicts and thus ineligible to donate a kidney.

For some of the Iranians we spoke to, it was clear that any kind of smoking, whether cigarettes, hashish, or opium, was a sign that the person was of a lower class: a likely drifter or a person of little use to society. This judgmental approach was prevalent, but these Iranians are probably not alone in making such generalizations about drug users (although most of the world, including most Iranians, don't judge cigarette smokers quite so harshly). Nonetheless, by such criteria anyone who smokes anything is suspect, potentially a lowlife and an addict, and not an ideal candidate for kidney donation.

I asked two of Dr. Bastani's college-age nephews about drug use at Tehran University. They said all the students from rural areas and Afghanistan or Iraq smoked one thing or another, but that among the Iranian youth from Tehran alcohol was the drug of choice. It is the forbidden fruit from the West and available at most "high-class"—their words—parties. When I asked about heroin use, they said, "Yes, it exists, but a heroin user doesn't last long in school."

Alcohol use may be on the rise among Iran's college youth, but it is an insignificant problem among potential kidney donors because alcohol use is not prevalent in the general population. *Anjoman* and medical staff told us they would, nonetheless, automatically exclude from the donor pool anyone they suspected of regular alcohol use.

One nurse told me she doesn't need to wait for the results of a drug test to recognize an addict, and she methodically listed the telltale signs. First, a general neglect of hygiene: Addicts usually have smelly feet, dirty fingernails, unkempt hair, and old or torn clothes. Second, most have a split in the lower lip caused by habitual use of a hookah. When I ask her if that couldn't also signify a tobacco smoker, she said yes, but if one or more of the other types of signs are also present, it is an indication that the person smokes opium or hashish.

Third, addicts exhibit lethargy or a general fatalistic attitude toward life. Finally, addicts show signs of premature aging, like crows' feet around the eyes or graying hair on someone in his 20s. I thought to myself, *Smoking tobacco ages the skin; opium ages the soul.*

When I went through our videotaped interviews specifically looking for these signs, I found a dozen or so people who met at least one of her criteria—most notably the split lower lip and, in a few cases, premature aging. However, no one exhibited all the signs. For example, no one seemed particularly lethargic, but a few donors were definitely fatalistic. I couldn't do the hygiene test other than to see if their clothes or hair looked particularly shabby, but none did. I couldn't check their hands and feet because, in most cases, I hadn't filmed them. Finally, I couldn't do a smell test based on a taped interview, but I did double-check my notes, and nowhere had I mentioned that anyone was particularly pungent.

The tradeoff that took place in the fledgling Iranian living donor program was obvious. At first, the *Anjomans* and medical staff tended to look the other way when addicts wanted to sell their kidneys. As the donor pool grew, transplant staff could afford to be more selective and did so in part for moral reasons, but mostly for convenience: Non-addicts make better patients and are less likely to cause problems both before and after the transplant operation. Also, as time passed, the transplant community began to realize that using addicts as donors reflected badly on the medical community and its organ procurement program. Some hospital and *Anjoman* staff we spoke to acknowledged how difficult it will be to reverse the stigma created by originally having allowed drug users to donate. They hoped the new stricter screening requirements would eventually rectify the damage done by the lax practices of the past.

The question of drug-addicted donors clearly made many of the people we spoke with uncomfortable. Some joked about it: One doctor told me he had heard that there once was an addict who wanted to donate his second kidney. When the *Anjoman* staff explained that a person can't live without at least one kidney, the addict said, "Yes, they can. I'll go on dialysis."

Others told horror stories that hardened them toward addicts. One such account was shared by Dr. Safai, whom I'd spoken to in another city. He told a story about an IV drug user he'd treated. "He was barely human anymore. He had deteriorated to such an extent that he had maggots in his injection tracks."

I was horrified, but morbidly fascinated. "People like that, they might as well be kidney donors," he said. "They're never going to be good for anything else." At the time I was shocked into silence and didn't ask him the follow-up questions I should have: *What about rehab? Could the hospital, the Anjoman, or the government make successful completion of a rehab program a prerequisite to letting someone like this donate? Do they even have rehab in Iran? Maybe not—if they did, they would have to admit to having a drug problem, and that doesn't seem like something the Iranian government would want to do.* As shocked as I was, I can attest that no one else I spoke to in Iran openly shared such sentiments.

Food for Thought

In a lighter moment, Dr. Safai told me a story from when he studied in Germany. He said of the Germans, "The people are nice enough, but the food is terrible." He complained that every time he ordered yogurt with his meal, his food was inedible. He couldn't tell me what exactly was wrong with it, but after a while I figured out what must have happened: a cultural culinary misunderstanding. In Iran, it is common practice to eat yogurt with almost every meal. It is a lovely sensation of taste and texture to eat plain yogurt with meat, rice, or curried dishes. But in Germany, as in America, yogurt is most commonly eaten as a sweetened snack or dessert. This poor soul must have poured sweetened yogurt over his *Wienerschnitzel* or *Sauerbraten*—not likely a gourmet experience.

Dr. Safai's culinary mishap and addict story jogged my memory of an event I had long forgotten, or more likely intentionally sublimated. My sister Ingrid and I had just spent a week with German friends in Borkum, an island in the North Sea. We helped pack up their car with clothes, seashells, and leftover food for the long trip back to their house in Düsseldorf. Even after driving at 100 miles an hour most of the way, it was late by the time we got home, and we were hungry. As we unpacked the car, the lady of the house made sandwiches that she proudly announced were roast beef sandwiches in the American style, meaning they weren't the open-faced sandwiches Germans usually eat. In hindsight, I wish they had been.

Anyway, we sat down to eat, and I hungrily took a bite, chewed, and swallowed, but when I looked at the half-moon bite in my sandwich, well.... "Dear Madam," I said (I'm often accused of being overly formal when I speak German), "I suggest you forgo partaking. I sincerely regret to inform you." I looked around the room. "Actually, none of you probably should eat just yet," I said as I showed her my sandwich. She squinted, put on her glasses, and then jumped up from the table, mortified. I don't think I've ever seen anyone clear a table quite so quickly or with such determination. She snatched the sandwiches out of our hands and off our plates and took them to the kitchen. "We are going out," she proclaimed as she pushed the sandwiches from the platter into the trash with a napkin, "We'll finish unpacking later." I didn't have much of an appetite left, and my sister asked if a person could die from eating maggots. I told her, "No, maybe get a stomachache." But to our surprise, the rest of the evening and the next day were gastronomically uneventful.

Unlike every time I go to South America, I never once got sick in Iran, not even a single instance of traveler's trot. But Dr. Safai's story of the addict with maggots in his arm still turns my stomach.

"A Man Must Find His Own Way"

The first donor we interviewed at the Tabriz *Anjoman* was facing a situation we encountered many times before, but his story is worth telling because he was one of the donors we were able to contact for a follow-up interview. Iman was 32 at the time of our initial interview. He was in financial straits because his work, doing odd construction jobs, was sporadic. He was also about to get married and needed money for his wedding. When Dr. Bastani asked Iman if his father could help, Iman said his father had his own troubles. "Brother to brother, a man must work to earn his own money. This is natural. A man must solve his own problems and find his own way." Then remembering that I was in the room, he quickly added, "Or females. I do not mean to discriminate; they too must solve their own problems. That is better, too."

At the time of our first interview, Iman had met the recipient and gone through most of the testing. Three years later we learned that the five million tomans he received for his kidney solved his financial problems. He is now married with children and works regularly as a bricklayer. He told us he wished he had received more for his kidney, and he would like to be more financially secure, but all in all, things are fine. At least at present, he was making ends meet without going back into debt. It was good to hear that Iman was doing well and that the money he received selling his kidney helped him overcome what turned out to be a temporary financial crisis. At the time of our first interview with Iman, he was only a few million tomans in debt, but in this next story, the donor's problem could not be solved so easily.

Another predicament commonly facing donors is the burden of a tort judgment. Pejmani was a 22-year-old ambulance driver who worked at Ali Nasab Hospital. He had expressionless, hollow eyes. His pea coat was thin and worse for wear. Pejmani had gotten into an accident with his ambulance, the result of which was a 15-million-toman tort judgment entered against him by an Iranian court. He and Yasaman, his wife of four years, were making inquiries about his application at the Tabriz *Anjoman*. He was eager to move the process along so he could make headway paying off his judgment and avoid debtors' prison.

His story also provided yet another insight into the discrimination women experience in Iranian culture: I learned that the *diye* ("blood money," tort payment) for taking the life of a woman in Iran is only half the *diye* for taking the life of a man. But interestingly, Iran's kidney market served as a counterexample to such discriminatory practices. A woman's kidney usually brings the same price as a man's, and sometimes even more if she is petite. Small adult kidneys are in high demand for children who need transplants.

It is incredibly hard for me to understand how someone could be working as a professional driver and not have insurance, but supposedly this is not uncommon in Iran. Car insurance is mandatory, but several people told me the law is not enforced, and many drivers are underinsured or have lapsed policies. Pejmani was one of those people. It is also curious that when Dr. Bastani asked how Pejmani's employer felt about his predicament, Pejmani replied he was still working at the same hospital and still driving an ambulance.

The price Pejmani negotiated for his kidney was the going rate of five million tomans, one from the national government and four from his recipient.

"You have 15 million in *diye*. If you sell your kidney for five million, what will you do for the remaining ten?"

"Well, we have four million, we've borrowed two million, and we'll see what else we can do."

"Have you bargained for any more?"

"The recipient himself has financial problems.... No, I wouldn't want to ask him."

"But that still isn't enough.... What will you do?"

"There would be nothing that I could do. I would have to declare bankruptcy... and probably go to jail."

Then his wife Yasaman chimed in, "Well, I can contribute too."

"You have money?"

"No, I can donate my kidney."

Neither Dr. Bastani nor I had the heart to point out to them that a 15-year-old (yes, Yasaman was only 11 when they married) is too young to donate. *What will happen to them? These kids are way too young—at least she is—to be dealing with such problems.*

I hoped we would get a follow-up interview with Pejmani and Yasaman, but like so many of the donors we'd interviewed (and most of the recipients), we were unable to reach them three years later.

Demographics Don't Lie

We never encountered any other donors, or potential donors, who were child brides—at least not that we knew of—however, some of the *recipients* we interviewed probably were. Several recipients told us they had dropped out of school in their early teens, and it can probably be assumed they did so to get married. But these were all recipients, not donors, and the same was true of those we interviewed who were illiterate; they too were all recipients, not donors.

Out of the 93 donors and recipients for whom information on their level of education was collected, three male and nine female interviewees were illiterate. (They signed their interview consent forms with a squiggle, an X, an inked thumbprint, or a carved wooden seal). I don't think the fact that the interviewees who had married young or were illiterate were all recipients bears any significance as far as the Iranian organ procurement program is concerned.

These results probably just reflect a changing attitude in Iran towards education and marriage. Recipients tend to be from 2 to 4 decades older than their donors. Women, and even men, born in the 1950s or '60s, especially those from rural areas, were more likely to marry young and be illiterate than Iranians born in the last 20 to 40 years. Almost all the donors we interviewed were in their 20s. The recipients we interviewed who dropped out of school, married young, or were illiterate, with one exception, were all over 50.

Another issue regarding rural patients, which I find to be more important to understanding Iran's organ procurement system than child-marriages or illiteracy, has to do with access to health care. Iran does fewer kidney transplants per capita than the United States. Some people have suggested this implies Iran has a "hidden" waiting list for kidneys. They say this disparity in the number of transplants is proof that some people stay on dialysis instead of getting a kidney because they can't afford to get on the waiting list, and thus, the claim that there is no kidney shortage in Iran is a sham. But we found nothing to support this conclusion.

Most of the Iranian citizens we met at dialysis centers were actively engaged in arranging for a transplant or were waiting for their health to improve so they would qualify for a transplant. Those who said they were not trying for a transplant fell into a few distinct categories. The first and largest group was made up of people with heath conditions that made it impossible for them to qualify for a transplant. Examples included patients with heart conditions or other comorbidities that made a transplant operation unacceptably risky.

The second group consisted of people who had a psychological reason for not wanting a transplant. One woman said, "I could never swallow all those pills transplant patients have to take." A lawyer we met said, "I don't want someone else's organ inside me." A third dialysis patient said, "I lost my transplant; I won't go through all that stress again. Every day, worrying if my kidney is OK."

The final group was Afghan refugees who wanted transplants but didn't think they could raise enough money to pay for a transplant operation, even with the help of charity. So this group technically does fit the category of people who stay on dialysis because they can't afford a transplant. These patients, however, are not Iranian, and their biggest impediment is not the cost of a kidney, but the 10 to 20 million tomans they would need to pay for the transplant itself. Note that I'm not aware of any country, not even the United States, where non-citizens have the same right to publicly funded transplants as citizens.*

Still, transplants aren't arranged instantaneously, not even for Iranian citizens. For all dialysis patients, whether they live in Iran or the United States, time is of the essence. Statistics from the United States indicate that the chances of a transplant succeeding drops significantly the longer a patient is on dialysis and that most patients die within four years of going on dialysis. So taking the time to raise funds for a kidney donor disadvantages Iranians who do not have the money readily available. On the other hand, kidney disease is progressive, and most people learn they have kidney problems long before they go into renal failure and need dialysis. Consequently, most Iranian patients have time—maybe even years—to come up with the money needed to purchase a kidney. But for those Iranians who can't save enough, or whose kidney disease is discovered later, the medical consequences of having to spend time on dialysis has a significant impact on their long-term prognoses. But these difficulties need to be kept in perspective.

---

* According to the National Immigration Law Center, one subclass of non-citizens, namely legal immigrants who have been permanent residents of the United States for at least five years, are eligible for Medicare. Once eligible for Medicare they become eligible for listing on the UNOS organ waiting list.

Even with the time it might take to raise funds to pay a donor, the potential suffering and risk of dying on dialysis in Iran is small compared to what it is in the United States. U.S. dialysis patients on average wait five years for a kidney transplant. In Iran we found that on average it takes one to three months to find a donor and do the pre-operative tests if all goes as planned. But as a practical matter, many recipients wait longer than that because they have medical complications, need to find a source of funding to pay their donor, or one or more potential donors are excluded, usually for medical reasons.

Taking these common hold-ups into consideration, the average time the recipients we interviewed waited for a transplant was 16.5 months. This number includes waiting times for all recipients, whether they received a kidney from a living or deceased donor. The average waiting time for a cadaver organ was at least three times as long as the waiting time for a living donor, but still not anywhere as long as the five-year average in the United States.

I don't doubt that there are Iranians who die on dialysis because they can't afford a transplant, but like the stories of recipients who offer their daughters in marriage in exchange for a kidney, such instances are probably rare. Aref told us his sister had waited eight years for a cadaver kidney because his family couldn't afford to pay a living donor, but we don't know how hard the family tried to arrange for charity, if at all. The reason we know of this case is that Aref, who was preparing to donate to a stranger, told us he felt guilty that he hadn't offered his kidney to save his sister when he had the chance. On the other hand, our data includes six patients from Mashhad and Tabriz who were initially only on the cadaver waiting list for financial reasons, but then scraped together the funds they needed to start the living donor process because the cadaver route was taking too long.

Despite the claims of some U.S. academics who have not seen the Iranian system firsthand, we found no evidence of any conspiracy to underestimate the number of people waiting for kidneys in Iran. Like in the transplant wards, at dialysis centers we went from patient to patient without anyone telling us whom we could ask for an interview. If there were large numbers of people who couldn't afford a transplant being warehoused in dialysis centers, we didn't see them.

The more likely explanation for why Iran has fewer transplants per capita than the United States has nothing to do with a conspiracy to underestimate the need for kidney transplants. The answer probably lies in the fact that Iran is a developing country with poor medical services outside its large metropolitan areas. Dr. Malakoutian told us that in rural areas people don't get regular checkups—many don't go to the doctor unless they're at death's door. She doubted that Iran has less kidney disease than other countries. I brought up the obesity epidemic in the United States and that Iran doesn't seem to have a similar problem. Dr. Malakoutian responded that Iran has other causes of kidney disease that are less prevalent in the United States, such as untreated infections that damage the kidneys.

The statistical discrepancies, she said, were more likely due to the fact that in Iran many people with kidney disease die without ever being diagnosed, or they go without specialized medical care long enough to no longer qualify for a transplant. This point brought to mind Morad, the donor in Tehran who was devastated when his 48-year-old adoptive father died from a heart attack during surgery. If Morad's father's kidney disease had been discovered earlier, perhaps he could have survived the transplant operation.

Heart disease is common in kidney disease patients all over the world, and in the United States it is the number one reason people get dropped from the transplant waiting list. In Iran, Dr. Malakoutian explained, many patients have already developed serious comorbidities like heart disease, hypertension, and strokes before they even get on dialysis and that is why the per capita transplant rate in Iran is lower than in the United States.

So Iran's claim to have solved its kidney shortage is accurate for two reasons: First, Iran has in fact solved the supply side of its kidney shortage; and second, a significant number of Iranians die of complications associated with kidney disease before even getting on the transplant waiting list. The need to diagnose kidney disease earlier is a serious public health concern that needs to be addressed by the Iranian government, but it also provides the most logical explanation for why there are fewer per capita kidney transplants in Iran than in the United States.

Christmas in Iran

By this point in my journey, I had learned a great deal of valuable information about the Iranian system of kidney procurement, and I was dedicated to learning more, but as the winter holidays grew near, my thoughts kept drifting toward home. I've never been away from my family on Christmas, and it was hard for me to focus on my work.

I kept thinking of all the preparations Bob must be doing with the children: cutting a fresh tree in the woods, decorating, and baking. In our home Christmas is a mélange of New and Old World traditions. On Christmas Eve we light the Christmas tree with live candles as has been the tradition on the European side of my family for hundreds of years—60 burning wax candles on a 12-foot, open-branched spruce. The glow from the tree is entrancing as the tinsel and ornaments sway, ever so slightly, in the dancing candlelight.

One by one, we open our presents. To begin, the youngest family member picks a gift for someone other than herself. We watch with anticipation as the gift is opened, then that person picks a present for someone else, and the process repeats itself until all have been opened. With six people opening their gifts one at a time, this process lasts as long as the candles—about two hours.

The next morning, Christmas Day, we follow a tradition from my husband's side of the family and check the stockings hung over the fireplace for whatever goodies might be waiting. Then, we start cooking: goose, homemade mashed potatoes, green beans with almond slivers, crescent rolls with lingonberry jam, and of course, home-baked pumpkin pie with real whipped cream. I promised myself, that day in Tabriz, that I would never spend another Christmas away from home.

Holiday homesickness aside, the Tabriz University transplant team was a lively group, and it was a joy to spend time with them. The Tabrizies have *a joie de vivre* that seems more relaxed than what I had experienced elsewhere in Iran, and being with them made it easier to be so far away from home.

It also helped that our Christmas interviews were more uplifting than some. Several donors in a row claimed that once they met their recipients, they were all the more eager to help. Several also offered a story typical of Tabriz: They were not selling a kidney in a desperate attempt to avert financial ruin, but rather to make an investment in their future—starting a new business, expanding an existing business, or modernizing an old one.

Rahim was a 30-year-old metal worker, married but with no children. He looked like a picture-book blacksmith: a stout man, balding, with shining, friendly eyes, thick-knit eyebrows that crept up his forehead when he smiled, and an impressive mustache. He wore a double-layered boiled wool coat, heavy with age and dust. He looked like he could swing a five-pound hammer all day with ease.

I noticed Rahim's coat was torn at the pocket. I remembered how my son had been teased by his elementary school classmates with "poor boy" because I had patched his soccer jersey instead of purchasing a new one. Nathan had asked, "Are we poor?" And I had reassured him, "No, far from it. We just have different priorities. Why waste a perfectly good shirt? Besides, it would take me longer to go buy a new one than to mend the one you have." I hoped my explanation would help Nathan learn an important lesson. I wondered if Rahim had his priorities in order. He claimed to be financially secure, that he was only donating his kidney so he could afford to start his own business, but I suspected his coat gave away the true state of affairs. As it turned out I was wrong.

"I donated a kidney because of the frailness of the girl, and to please God. … I saw a chance to help with my future."

Dr. Bastani probed, "How is your emotional health right now?"

"My emotional health is excellent because in the presence of such an opportunity one feels humbled."

Before the donation, Rahim was an apprentice. Now, two weeks after his kidney donation, he looked forward to getting the money he needed to open his own shop. The final deal he struck was one million tomans from the national government and five million from the *Anjoman*. The recipient's family was too poor to contribute.

Rahim was one of the donors whose contact information was still valid when we did follow-up interviews. He told us the money from selling his kidney went to improve the house where he lived with his wife and parents, presumably to build a metalwork shop. Rahim said that because of the kidney sale his family was financially secure and "living much more comfortably."

For three years Rahim went to the *Anjoman* to get his free health insurance renewed, but recently he let it fall by the wayside. He never speaks with the recipient, who was only 15 at the time of the transplant, but does speak to her mother regularly. He reported that "the girl has regained her health and that her life has changed completely. Everyone owes something to God for this life we have.... Now when I die, I can face God without shame." Rahim said he thinks about the girl every day, and the fact that he was able to do this for her brings him joy. "If I had another kidney to donate, I would!"

Most donors we came across in Tabriz, like elsewhere in Iran, needed money to get out of debt, but we also came across several donors like Rahim who were looking toward the future. Iman was saving up money to get married, Ghafoor wanted to expand his shoe shop, and Ata wanted to start a business providing logoed merchandise, such as bags, pens, and T-shirts.

One such story I found particularly befitting of Christmas Eve. Aref was giving the money from selling his kidney to his oldest nephew to help him strike out on his own. Aref started caring for his nephews and nieces four years earlier when his sister died, but he had since married and now had one child of his own and another on the way. The money Aref would make selling his kidney would give his oldest nephew the capital he needed to invest in his own business and help support his three younger siblings.

Dr. Bastani asked, "Doesn't their father take care of your sister's children?"

"Well, after my sister's death, he went and remarried...." Aref looked down and didn't finish his sentence—he didn't need to. We understood that he didn't want to say anything negative about his former brother-in-law. Aref had taken over responsibility for the children; no more needed to be said.

I couldn't help but wonder, was the dream these donors had a mirage? Some opponents of the Iranian system argue that whatever financial relief donors achieve will be short-lived, and they will eventually regret having sold their kidneys. But by what right would these critics deny donors like Rahim, Iman, Ghafoor, Ata, Aref, or any other potential donor a chance at improving their lives, however fleeting that hope may be? And besides, at least for some, the realization of a dream fueled by the money from donating a kidney was not imaginary. On this Christmas Eve my sentiments shifted from not wanting to stand in the way of donors' dreams to actively wanting to share their stories so others could learn from their experiences.

On Christmas Day, five members of the Tabriz transplant team treated me to a meal at a Turkish restaurant with lively conversation and sumptuous food. At the restaurant I watched with amusement as two doctors, after ordering sparkling cider, couldn't figure out how to open the bottle. Finally one of them took out a pocketknife and cut off both the foil and the wire cage before popping the cork. I guessed these two must not be in the habit of violating the government ban on alcoholic beverages, at least not by drinking champagne, or they would have known how to open a beverage fermented under pressure.

The next day, seven faculty members from Tabriz University and their families took us to an almost Disneyesque Persian restaurant. It had brightly colored walls and a walkway lined with blazing torchères. What I remember most vividly is the dozen or so faculty children running back and forth between the tables, whispering and giggling as I wiggled my fingers at them in a secret greeting under the table.

More Ancient than Persian

Our final day in Tabriz was spent sightseeing. Dr. Ardalan, who impressed me with his linguistic acumen and his wealth of knowledge in the field of medical history, took us to the Azerbaijan Museum. There we saw exquisite Iron Age artifacts, like a 3,000-year-old copper helmet and stone "handbags" from the third millennium B.C., believed to be symbols of wealth. Then Mr. Fallah from the International Office took us to the Blue Mosque, known for its intricate sky colored majolica tiles. Sadly, the mosque and its tiles still showed signs of damage sustained after a 1779 earthquake.

While the mosque and its history were fascinating, I was most intrigued by what we went to see near the mosque. Behind a parking garage was a recently completed archeological dig with graves dating back 4,500 years. We could only speculate as to why the dead were all laid facing the same direction and why the skeletons were tall—one of them clearly over six feet—belying the common belief that ancient *Homo sapiens* were smaller than we are.

I was loath to leave the comfort of the Tabriz El-Goli Pars Hotel. I knew Kermanshah was economically depressed, and Dr. Bastani warned that I would not like it there.

"Does it have a kidney transplant program?"

"Yes," Dr. Bastani answered.

"Well, then we have to go."

We did indeed have to go, particularly since Dr. Zargooshi, the most vocal opponent of the Iranian kidney procurement system, lived in Kermanshah. I'd been corresponding with him for months, and he said he would speak with me if I came to Iran. So reluctantly, we boarded the plane for Kermanshah, the last city on our research tour. Ironically, Kermanshah would also be the city where I heard my most surprising donor story.

٩ (9)

Too Poor to Pay

Dr. Bastani was right: I didn't like Kermanshah. Kermanshah has impressive Persian and Islamic historic sites like most major cities in Iran, and the mountains are majestic, but for the first time on my trip, I felt as if I were in a Third World country. We had traveled through villages where people were poor, but Kermanshah wasn't a small village where farmers eked out a living. It was a moribund city of over 800,000 inhabitants with a stagnant economy.

According to several travel guides, Kermanshah is Iran's western agricultural core for grain, rice, vegetables, and oilseeds. Guidebooks also tout the city as an important industrial center with a petrochemical refinery, textile manufacturing, and food processing. Yet, if Kermanshah is a breadbasket, the basket was empty when I was there. And if it is a manufacturing hub, none of what it manufactured was openly for sale.

Perhaps because it was winter, the place was desolate, and whatever economic activity there was didn't compare in the least with the hustle and bustle of Tabriz. What was most prevalent, which was not even mentioned in any of the travel entries I'd read about the city, was the military. Kermanshah lies a little more than 100 miles from the Iraqi border, and the military presence was stronger than in any other city we'd visited. Every time we went out we saw young men in camouflage, often carrying submachine guns.

I was tempted to take a photo of a huge sign on a high razor-wire-topped chain-linked fence that showed a camera with a red circle and slash through it. But my mind conjured up images of an alarm going off and SUVs careening around the corner, tires screeching, with men hanging out of the top of cars shooting at everything that moved. Then, I remembered that the Iranian government had banned cars with sunroofs, specifically to reduce the chances of such a scenario. Nonetheless, I chose not to tempt fate and kept my camera safely stashed under my tunic.

A Non Sequitur

Our driver Mohammed seemed like a nice enough young man, but he complained that he was still living with his parents because his only income came from the occasional driving gig. The rest of the time he sat at home doing nothing. When Dr. Bastani inquired why he didn't try to find a second, or better job, he told us he failed his military physical so there was nothing else left for him to do. Dr. Bastani suggested he get an education or move. Mohammed nodded politely but obviously wasn't interested in pursuing the conversation further.

I was surprised not to see more homeless people or beggars in Kermanshah, or anywhere else in Iran for that matter. My experience from other developing countries, and some supposedly developed ones as well, was that there were always panhandlers and beggars; back alley city streets all had the occasional person sleeping in a doorway. But I didn't experience anything like that in Iran. Once I started actively looking, I noticed a few people: a blind man sitting near the entrance to the Tomb of Ferdowsi (the famous Iranian author of an epic poem of pre-Islamic mythology) in Tus just a few miles from Mashhad and a woman with her two children subtly begging at the bazaar in Tehran. But no one reached out to grab my pant-leg as I'd experienced in Italy, Argentina, and even France. And there were none of the murmurings of "I'm homeless," or "Help a jobless veteran, won't you?" that I'm used to hearing in Washington, D.C. This was Kermanshah, a military city: Where were the wounded veterans? Where were the homeless and infirm?

In Tehran there were groups of "street urchins," children who ran up to people and tried to sell them strips of paper on which someone had written out lines of verse. Dr. Bastani explained that Iranians sometimes go to the Qur'an or a book of Sadi's or Hafez's poetry and randomly open a page and read, hoping to be inspired or gain insight. The children we saw in Tehran were Afghan refugees trying to cash in on this custom, but I didn't see any such children in Kermanshah.

The refugee children in Tehran brought back fond memories of the street urchins I played with in Naples, Italy when I was 9. We drew with sticks in the dirt, climbed trees, and played tag. I gave one a macramé bracelet I'd made, and when I told my mother they were begging, she gave me a box of Cap'n Crunch Cereal and a loaf of bread. The children and I shared the Cap'n Crunch (I can't believe my mother let us eat such sugar bombs), but I brought the bread back home. "Mommy, why will their father beat them if they come home with bread?"

My mother in her ever so matter-of-fact way said, "He wants them to bring home money for drink or drugs, not food."

The street urchins of Naples were poor, as were the beggars my mother would allow us to give coins to at the market, but I remember one time she hesitated. I had pointed out a man with stumps for legs, half an arm, and a face wrapped in rags.

"Can I have a coin?"

"Oh, how tragic," my mother whispered as she took me by the hand and held me behind her with a grip so tight my hand ached. She leaned over from several feet away and tossed coins into his bowl, with me straining to get a better look around the handbag dangling in my face. As we got closer, the smell was like rotting flesh, the same smell I'd noticed when I had watched my grandfather change the bandages on a burn victim's arms in Argentina—both times, I struggled to control my gag reflex.

"Leprosy. He has leprosy." My mother looked gravely at the half a man sitting before her.

"Leprosy, like in *Ben-Hur*?" We had just watched *Ben-Hur*, the 1959 film starring Charlton Heston. "In these days? I thought that was from Roman times."

"No, unfortunately, it still exists. Doctors can control it, but not everyone can get the care and treatment they need."

"What about the leper colony, like in *Ben-Hur*? Is there still such a colony near Rome?" I asked, remembering the heart-wrenching scene when Ben-Hur visits his mother and sister at the leper colony.

"I don't think so, but I know there is one in Hawaii."

"Is that where the American lepers go?" *There are American lepers?*

"Yes, dear! But they are cared for—they don't live like this."

Sadly, that was not the only time in my life that I saw someone with leprosy, or "Hansen's Disease" as it is now called, begging on the street. But, after more than seven weeks in Iran and having visited six major cities, I looked around Kermanshah and wondered, *Where are the Iranian lepers?* I looked for them: no beggars, no homeless or mentally ill, not even a handicapped veteran.

All Dolled Up

The hotel was nice, nothing as impressive as the El-Goli Pars Hotel in Tabriz, but certainly much more pleasant than the hospital housing in Shiraz or Mashhad. It was probably on par with the Alborz Hotel in Tehran, with one major, welcomed difference: Things seemed to work, and the water coming out of the faucet was clear. So in general, I didn't have any complaints. That being said, I really didn't seem to have much luck with Iranian plumbing, and my room in Kermanshah was no exception. I took a shower the first night we were there—this time I had a shower curtain—but, to my dismay, I discovered after my shower that the water had not flowed toward the toilet drain as it was supposed to but instead into the bedroom, where it had soaked a good three feet of the wall-to-wall carpet. I didn't dare take another shower the whole time I was in Kermanshah, and, luckily, the desert air was on my side: Most of the dampness had evaporated by the time we left.

One night while we were at the hotel, I was fortunate to witness a party. It amazed me to see so many teenagers primly dressed. There were fifty or more faces bright with anticipation. Most were wearing Western-looking evening attire—except of course that the girls also wore head coverings. But how exactly this party was going to be fun was a mystery; the young women and young men were relegated to opposite sides of the hotel. The trick, Dr. Bastani volunteered, was that they could catch glimpses of each other here and there as they moved through the common entryway. Well, it still didn't seem like much fun to me, but given the excited voices and laughter I heard, they obviously had no sense of what they were missing.

A Limited Perspective

My main reason for coming to Kermanshah was to interview Dr. Zargooshi. We had spoken with Dr. Ghods, the major proponent for the Iranian organ-procurement system, so I wanted to speak with Dr. Zargooshi, its major detractor. Dr. Zargooshi had agreed to speak with me if I came to Kermanshah, and I was eager to meet him—but when we called, Dr. Zargooshi seemed surprised that I had come. Dr. Bastani tried to convince him to meet with us, but Dr. Zargooshi was opposed to the idea. I tried to encourage him to give us an audience, but he responded that his articles spoke for themselves and that he would rather not have something on tape that might be taken out of context. Eventually, Dr. Zargooshi agreed to be interviewed, but regrettably, he made us promise not to share the details. So what I relate here are general observations bolstered by what I learned from his published works.

Dr. Zargooshi is a bitter man, and from what I can tell, justifiably so. Any potential career he may have had as a nephrologist or transplant surgeon was nipped in the bud when his original findings on kidney donors were shared with the Iranian Ministry of Health more than 20 years ago. He became a pariah, shut out by the transplant community, and turned to urology instead. Ever since, he has had no direct involvement in the Iranian organ procurement system.

Four of Dr. Zargooshi's articles on kidney selling are available in English. Two are research articles he published in 2001 in *The Journal of Urology*, and two others were published as part of a book based on a 2007 international organ-transplantation conference held in the Netherlands.

Dr. Zargooshi's articles in *The Journal of Urology* have dire conclusions about the socioeconomic and psychological state of compensated kidney donors:

> The majority of vendors stated that what they obtained from vending did not compensate them for what they lost. *None* were able to remove themselves from poverty and debt or change their lives radically. Quality of life was impaired in *all* aspects. Rejection by family and friends and attempts to remain unidentified indicate the disapproval of organ sales by the Iranian society. [Emphasis added.]

His two articles in *Organ Transplantation: Ethical, Legal and Psychosocial Aspects Towards a Common European Policy* (2008) are equally critical. His main conclusion in the first is that the relationships between donors and recipients is "purely commercial" and in the second, that 69 out of 71 patients on the waiting list had "no hope" of receiving a kidney because they were too poor to afford one.

All four articles rely primarily on research Dr. Zargooshi did more than 20 years ago as a medical student, with follow-up interviews that were only as recent as the year 2000. The two most recent articles are supplemented with slightly more up-to-date data collected at a recipients' clinic and dialysis center but include no new donor interviews.

Most of Dr. Zargooshi's interviews were carried out in the early 1990s when the Iranian government's regulation of compensated kidney donation was in its infancy. Some of his interviewees had donated before the system was regulated at all; many had donated before the medical community issued guidelines for donor selection or the government started providing the one-million-toman *issar*.

The policies and laws that now make up the organ procurement program in Iran were still being developed and weren't fully enforced in the 1990s and, truth be told, were still being tweaked well into the twenty-first century. It took time to redirect transactions customarily arranged privately into regulated channels. It was during this formative time that Dr. Zargooshi did his research.

In addition to the obvious limitations of his older data, Dr. Zargooshi also mistakenly generalizes what he found in Kermanshah to all of Iran. Perhaps Dr.

Zargooshi wasn't aware of how compensated kidney donation was being implemented in other parts of the country, or perhaps the divergences are new, but by the time I did my research, it was wrong to assume that Kermanshah's experience was the same as that of Shiraz, Tehran, Isfahan, Tabriz, or Mashhad. So Dr. Zargooshi's findings, while helpful for understanding the history of kidney selling in Kermanshah, are not evidence of what was going in the rest of Iran, or even Kermanshah at the time of my visit.

Finally, Dr. Zargooshi makes some sweeping conclusions that need considerably more explanation than he provides in any of his articles. He concludes that *none* of the donors he interviewed were able to free themselves from poverty and that their quality of life was negatively impacted in *all* aspects by the donation. (See my emphasis in the Zargooshi quotes above.) And with respect to recipients, he concludes 97 percent of them have "*no* hope" of receiving a kidney. In addition to these being categorical conclusions that are hard to quantify, they are not borne out by my more recent observations.

I don't question Dr. Zargooshi's sincerity or in any way condone what the medical community or Iranian government might have done to try to silence a dissenter, but Dr. Zargooshi's findings are limited and need to be kept in perspective. His work is primarily based on old data in a system that is evolving, and it is limited to data collected from an extremely economically depressed part of Iran—arguably the most underdeveloped kidney procurement program in the country. So even if Dr. Zargooshi's conclusions are representative of Kermanshah's experience for the historic period covered by his data, they probably never were applicable to the rest of Iran. It would be like making conclusions about the whole U.S. medical system based on healthcare in Mississippi, or more aptly, Mississippi 20 years ago.

The limitations of Dr. Zargooshi's research aside, I was greatly disappointed by what I found in Kermanshah. After what I had seen elsewhere in Iran, I was dismayed by the appalling donor-vetting practices I witnessed at Kermanshah's Imam Reza Hospital.

The Human Meat Market

Some of my greatest fears about the alleged backwardness of organ procurement in Iran were confirmed when we arrived at Kermanshah's Imam Reza Hospital. We were escorted into a conference room to witness the evaluation of potential kidney donors. In Shiraz we had watched a review session for recipients, but I had not experienced such a session for donors, so I was eager to observe.

In Shiraz, a nurse had ushered in potential recipients one at a time, seating them in a chair facing a panel of half a dozen doctors. Each recipient looked worried, forlorn, and intimidated, but all left looking relieved. They were informed that they were in fact candidates for a transplant and that unless they could find relatives or friends to donate, they would have to be patient and wait at least six months for a cadaver kidney before they would be allowed to ask the *Anjoman* for help in finding a living, paid donor.

The donor evaluation I witnessed in Kermanshah was shockingly different. The physicians sat around a conference table discussing potential donor files, then requested that a donor be brought in and told him to stand in front of the room and take off his shirt.

I whispered to the physician next to me, "Should I leave?" After all, I was the only woman in the room, and they had just asked the donor to partially undress.

He said, "Oh, no. He knows this is a medical exam."

I watched one of the doctors get up and literally poke the donor—I guess he technically was palpating his abdomen, but it sure looked like poking. The donor flinched a little and never stopped staring at the floor. Then the doctor returned to his seat, and the physicians continued their discussion while the donor just stood there, staring at his feet. He looked up to answer a question, and our eyes met. I sensed his humiliation and felt horrible. I tried to show him some respect by giving him a slight smile, then making a deliberate show of turning to the papers in front of me—I wrote the words "meat market." I did not look up again until I was sure he had left the room.

I thought to myself, *How degrading!* then asked, "What about female donors?" Several physicians chimed in at once: "They are different." "We don't do their exams this way." "We don't like using female donors, anyway—so there are few."

That last statement piqued my interest. "You don't use women?"

Then one physician volunteered, "We don't like to use women unless we have to."

"Why not?" I asked, thinking I would get the type of response I'd heard elsewhere—namely, that in Iran there is a chance that a woman will be considered "damaged goods" if she has donated a kidney. Less educated families sometimes worried that the scar left after donating a kidney might make a woman less attractive to a potential husband. Some even thought that donating a kidney might interfere with a woman's ability to do housework or have children. But the answer I heard wasn't related to any of these concerns.

"I just don't like women donors; their anatomy is harder to deal with." When Dr. Bastani sought clarification, the physician added, "You know, everything is smaller, making it harder to get in and out. Not worth the effort unless you need a kidney for a child."

Few Resources, Little Will, and No Impetus for Change

When we asked about cadaver organ procurement, we heard familiar responses. Even if they had the medical resources needed to harvest and store organs from deceased donors, they didn't have the manpower. They couldn't have surgeons drop whatever they were doing during the day or go to the emergency room in the middle of the night to harvest kidneys, let alone turn around and schedule transplant surgery within a few hours. This seemed to be truer in Kermanshah than in other cities we'd visited. We learned later that until that year, Kermanshah had never had more than two physicians qualified to surgically remove kidneys, and only one qualified to do transplants.

Later we spoke to Dr. Daryoush Reissi, who although recently retired, had been the only nephrologist (a physician who deals with the medical, not surgical, side of kidney transplants) in Kermanshah for over 20 years. He was kind enough to share his recently tabulated research data. Of the 1,300 transplant patients he had treated, about 10 percent had related donors, and the rest had unrelated, paid donors. He pointed out that not a single transplant he knew of involved a non-related, purely altruistic donor. He said it is probable that the donors were in part altruistic in their motives, but there wasn't a single one who wasn't also paid.

The part of town where the Kermanshah *Anjoman* was located was not only poor but also dingy and joyless. On the outside, the *Anjoman's* building reminded me slightly of the *Anjoman* in Shiraz, but unlike Shiraz, there weren't any trees, not even half-dead ones. The closest comparison I have is when my family visited Romania during the communist era. I remember noticing that there were no sidewalks along the streets, no flowerboxes in the windows, and no children playing anywhere. The roads looked like they hadn't been repaired after WWII bombings, and every door needed painting. The same was true in this part of Kermanshah. I wondered if some of the damage I saw was from the Iraq-Iran War that had ended 20 years earlier.

Mr. Amirali Biglary, head of the Kermanshah *Anjoman*, told us his city has some generous people, but as a whole the population is extremely poor. "We have a lot of war veterans here, there aren't any factories, and unemployment is very high." Funds are so tight, he remarked, that the *Anjoman* frequently goes months at a time without arranging a single transplant: They simply don't bring in enough charitable contributions to make up the difference between what recipients can afford and what most donors are willing to accept. (Perhaps Dr. Zargooshi did his dialysis-center interviews during one of these financial droughts.)

This was the only city in Iran where an *Anjoman* ever spoke of running out of money. Mr. Biglary said that, out of sheer desperation, his staff had at times circumvented the national rules against forum shopping and convinced an *Anjoman* from another district to help a Kermanshah resident get a kidney with financial assistance, and occasionally even a donor, from outside Kermanshah.

An Evolving Approach

At first all the interviews we did in Kermanshah were as expected: donors in debt, needing money to get their heads above water. Foad was paying all he could on a loan he had taken out more than a year ago, but despite his best efforts he had not managed to pay down any of the principal. Foad was 35 and married with two children. He didn't tell us what he did for a living—the implication was that he did odd jobs, whatever he could get. He looked uncomfortable at first, absentmindedly shifting his weight back and forth from one foot to the other as he stood in the doorway hesitating to come in. But once he settled into the interview, he answered with refreshing precision.

Foad didn't have any distinguishing physical features; he was a handsome, dark-haired, rugged-looking man with a full mustache and the usual five-o'-clock shadow. He wore a cream-colored turtleneck, a button-down shirt open at the neck with stripes in three shades of blue, and a gray windbreaker. But what did distinguish Foad was that once he felt at ease, he spoke with unexpected eloquence. We didn't note his level of education, but his handwriting on his interview consent form was controlled, well formed, and neat. He was definitely educated; my guess is he had attended at least some college.

Foad had twice been paired with a recipient, but the donations fell through at the cross-matching stage of testing, a test that checks if antibodies in the recipient's blood will attack the donor's kidney. The immune system of the first two recipients would have had an extreme reaction to Foad's kidney, so Foad had come to the *Anjoman* that day to discuss potential recipient number three. The *Anjoman* had promised him that one way or another, he would get the four million tomans he needed to pay off his loan.

When Dr. Bastani asked what would happen if Iran outlawed kidney selling, as is the case in all other countries, Foad exhibited a much deeper understanding of the kidney shortage than most donors we had interviewed. "Well, if there are enough corpses to meet the need, then that is OK, but there are a lot of patients on dialysis in need of kidneys, and with just that one method it wouldn't work."

Pleasantly surprised, Dr. Bastani clarified his question. "What problems would there be for donors? What would you do if there was no way you could donate a kidney for the four million?"

"Well, if I couldn't do this [sell my kidney], I would still be OK. I don't have the financial ability to pay off my loan now, but I might in the near future. I might have to sell my house, which wouldn't be ideal, but at least that's an option."

We were glad to hear from a donor who was not at the brink of financial ruin, bankruptcy, or debtors' prison. Foad went on to show an acute awareness of the underlying issues when he continued woefully, realizing his own good fortune, "Some people don't have houses. There are people I met when I went to do tests and their problems were definitely much worse. They didn't even have enough money to pay their rent!"

In the follow-up interview we had with Foad three years later, he told us he intentionally hadn't kept in touch with his recipient. "I did my part, and she did hers, and now it's over." In hindsight, he felt he had made the right decision. He said, "Overall my experience was fine. I just wish that I didn't have to donate, but since that was my fate in life, I am OK with it and don't regret it." He told us he had received three million from the *Anjoman* and one million from Tehran, but nothing from the recipient because her family was too poor.

Foad's life was "a thousand times better," partly because he was able to pay off his loan, but also because he finally had a job where he could earn a decent income. "Overall my life is much better than it was before, and I'm grateful for that."

I'm pleased we were able to reach Foad; he had been so articulate three years earlier and was so again. He ended the follow-up interview with his observations on the social costs of donation:

> Doctors and nurses treated me with respect, but it feels like society doesn't care. There is a lot of stigma against kidney donation: I haven't told my family, and I don't want my community to know. The stigma makes it feel like you've done something wrong when in fact it's something very good, and society needs to recognize that.

What Foad said was remarkably insightful and reflected the very thoughts I had after interviewing donors at the government-run Center for Special Diseases in Tehran. The only person to come close to verbalizing the same concern as articulately was Larry, Steve's donor back in the United States. Larry had told people about his donation expecting them to be impressed but found instead that they assumed Steve was his lover or that he donated his kidney to make up for some unfathomable wrong he had committed. When asked if anyone ever acknowledged that he had done an honorable thing, Larry dolefully said, "Never.... I don't talk about it anymore."

Several other donors we met at the *Anjoman* and Imam Reza hospital told stories about being in debt and how the donation, in conjunction with help from the *Anjoman*, saved them, at least temporarily. For example, Kiarash had a touching story about donating his kidney because his brother, who was too young to donate, had a *diye* against him that the family couldn't pay. But in the end, it was our conversation with Masoumeh that brought up some issues we hadn't considered, not even after hearing more than 200 donor stories. But that interview wouldn't come until our last day in Kermanshah.

Escape to Mt. Kooh-e-Sefid

On December 28, it was Ashura, the 10th day of the month of Muharram on the Arabic/Islamic calendar, the day that the Prophet Mohammad's grandson Husain (the third holy imam for Shi'ites) and his 72 faithful companions were martyred during the Battle of Karbala in 680 A.D. The whole month is a holy month, but Ashura, because it is the actual date of Husain and his companions' martyrdom, takes on special significance. Black flags were hanging in every city roundabout. Tents displayed books and pamphlets ranging from anti-West propaganda to Persian poetry. Loudspeakers broadcast recorded prayers. Posters with the faces of individuals martyred in the Iraq-Iran War were plastered on walls all over town.

This celebration, if it can be called such, made an already somber and depressing city even more so. Most people, including our driver and Dr. Bastani, took it all in stride, but for a Westerner like myself, who equates flags at half staff with death and black flags with anarchy, the sight was unsettling. The seemingly random people breaking down in tears, genuflecting on the street, repeating "*Allahu Akbar, Allahu Akbar*" ("God is great, God is great"), didn't help much. *Do I stop and wait until he is finished, or do I go around?* Most of the time we crossed the street or made a wide berth around mourners.

That evening, however, the mood lightened. We took a winding mountain road up the side of Mt. Kooh-e-Sefid. We stopped at an overlook to admire the view while we enjoyed corn dipped in salt water and grilled in the husk over a charcoal fire. The night was chilly but calm, no sand whipping down the street as we'd experienced earlier that day. I looked out at the city lights in the valley below and felt for the first time that Kermanshah had some charm after all.

An Unworthy Donor?

The next day, December 29, I could see the end in sight. It was our last day to interview donors and recipients and our last day in Kermanshah. We headed out to Imam Reza Hospital, not expecting anything out of the ordinary. We interviewed several donors and recipients, but most touching were the interviews we did with Arda and her donor Masoumeh.

We started with Arda. She was a 56-year-old Kurdish farmer, illiterate, with eight children—six sons and two daughters. She didn't speak Farsi, but rather a Turkic dialect, so one of the nurses translated for us. Arda wore a pink hospital gown and was wrapped in a blue hospital blanket. Her headdress was not the usual hijab, but aqua flaps of cloth that hung loosely over her ears and the back of her neck, held in place with a white stocking cap. Her leathery skin and yellow, cracked nails gave away that she habitually toiled in soil and sun. She was jovial and spoke freely, particularly when telling us about her children. She winced with pain when she shifted in bed, but that was to be expected three days after surgery. Her transplant must have gone well because she had color: the red, wind-burned cheeks of a countrywoman, not the sallow complexion of a dialysis patient. She told Dr. Bastani that her children wanted to donate a kidney for her, but she wouldn't hear of it. Instead her sons sold some of the family's land to cover the 3.5 million tomans they needed to pay her donor. Arda told us the family had enough land left to farm, so it wasn't as great a hardship as it may seem.

Then we interviewed Arda's donor, Masoumeh—what a stark contrast. Masoumeh said she didn't mind being interviewed but wanted the camera off. Immediately I thought Masoumeh looked out of place in Kermanshah. I could tell before she said anything that she had never planted a furrow or tended a goat in her life. She was a stunning young woman of 27 with piercing eyes, straight teeth, sculpted eyebrows, manicured nails, and just a touch of make-up (even sitting in a hospital bed). She wore the same pink hospital gown as Arda, but her headscarf was silk, subtly patterned in shades of brown and beige; she sat erect perhaps because of lingering pain from the operation, or perhaps because erect posture was part of her proud deportment. She told us she was married with two children. As it turned out, she was raised in Tehran, not Kermanshah.

Dr. Bastani sat close to her bed, clipboard in hand, and I sat a little farther back and to his right, camera equipment on my lap—viewfinder closed, but sound recorder on. Dr. Bastani explained the purpose of our research, and Masoumeh started to tell us about herself. Suddenly she turned to me and with a beseeching look asked me something in Farsi.

Dr. Bastani translated, "She asks you, 'Am I a bad person?'"

I stared at her, wide-eyed with disbelief. "Why would she think that?" *Maybe she is thinking that selling her kidney is bad in the sense we have heard before, in that it is akin to prostitution—that people will think, "What will she sell next?"* "No. Tell her, 'No, of course not.' She has done a good deed. She has saved a life."

Dr. Bastani told her what I'd said, but she never took her eyes off me, searching my face for a clue to see if Dr. Bastani's translation had accurately reflected what she'd asked and what I'd said in response.

I insisted, "How can saving a life possibly be bad?!"

She gently swept the edge of her hand across her face, smudging the makeup below her left eye.

I searched her face and saw a weary heaviness, emotional pain and sorrow. I asked Dr. Bastani, "Did I say something wrong?"

Dr. Bastani repeated, "Why would *you* think you are a bad person?"

She shifted her gaze to Dr. Bastani, then launched into a long explanation, looking back and forth between the two of us. She waved her hand at me, encouraging Dr. Bastani to translate as she spoke. She clearly wanted me in on the conversation.

"Her husband runs a video arcade that also sells games."

Go on, she motioned to Dr. Bastani.

"She says he is a good man, but he has a herniated disk in his back, and while they have managed to keep up with the medical bills, every time he goes to the hospital or is in too much pain to work, there is no income." Dr. Bastani inquired about her extended family and reported back, "They have gone to both his family and hers for help, but it is humiliating to continuously have to ask for money."

Their plan, Masoumeh confided, was to build an addition on their house and take in a boarder. That way if her husband were laid up because of his back, they would still have the monthly rent to help make ends meet until he could work again. They had saved up the amount they thought the project would cost and started construction, but now there were overruns that kept them from finishing the addition. They decided her husband would donate a kidney to make up the shortfall, but when he was disqualified because of health issues, they agreed that she should donate instead.

When it seemed she was finished, I persisted, "So why does she think she's a bad person?"

Dr. Bastani repeated the question; Masoumeh once again addressed me directly and continued to look me in the eye even once Dr. Bastani started translating. I leaned forward in anticipation of her response. Tears started to flow down her cheeks. "I don't need the money." She continued to watch me, but I looked over at Dr. Bastani, wondering if he had mistranslated. He saw what I was asking without my saying anything. "That is what she said—she doesn't need the money."

Her relentless gaze started to make me uncomfortable. Neither Dr. Bastani nor I knew what to say next, but she did. "Sure, we can use the money, but we don't really need it. Life is hard, but we aren't desperate." She straightened her headscarf. "People might think I'm greedy."

Dr. Bastani answered for the both of us, telling her, "How could caring for the future of your family be greedy? You and your husband are being responsible parents; you are saving someone's life in exchange for making your financial future more secure. There is nothing wrong with that!"

She nodded, wiping her eyes with the edge of her sheet. "Yes, the *Anjoman* has also arranged for healthcare vouchers for me and my family. I can renew them each year as long as I need them. Yes," she added, more to herself than to us, "yes, I did the right thing."

No doubt Masoumeh had expected something different when she married. But I don't think it is easy anywhere in the world to deal with health insurance issues as a small business owner. I could imagine what had gone through her mind at one point or another. *My husband is so young; how can he have back problems? To be a good wife I must stand by him and make sure my children have bread on the table even when he can't work. Is he ever going to get well enough to make a decent living? Will we end up trying to survive on boarders' rent? That would be a poor existence. Will I have sold my kidney to finish an addition on the house that some people might see as extravagant, only to go bankrupt in the end anyway? Is it fair that I have this safety net when so many people can't find a way out of their financial predicaments? My recipient's family sold part of the family farm—their safety net—so I could have mine.*

I wondered how long she had been keeping all these worries bottled up inside. I could see how it might be hard to complain when almost everyone around her, donors and recipients alike, faced more dire circumstances. Maybe she was experiencing something akin to survivor's guilt. By the time we left her room, she had dried her tears, and most of the dark smudges created by running makeup were gone. She seemed in better spirits. We thanked her for her time and wished her well. I suggested that Dr. Bastani tell her something we first heard from a donor in Shiraz: "The Qur'an says it is a good thing to help yourself by helping others."

Masoumeh's story made me realize that, despite the recurring themes we'd been hearing, ultimately each story was as unique as the donor or recipient who told it, and ultimately there were going to be as many different justifications for compensated kidney donation as there were legitimate reasons for why people need money.

Hope for Kermanshah

Organ procurement in Kermanshah left much to be desired. The city needed infrastructure to make cadaver organ donation possible (something which many Iranian cities lacked) but also needed someone like Dr. Alizadeh, the female physician who had us over for dinner in Shiraz, to teach the Kermanshah medical staff some lessons in patient-care ethics. But I must give the Kermanshah *Anjoman* some credit. Its staff was trying to do its best to meet the needs of both recipients and donors, and management had made a conscious decision not to arrange transplants unless the fee (and other benefits) provided were enough to solve individual donors' problems. Unfortunately, this meant that in some years there were several months where there were no paid donor transplants at all and that donors whose needs were too great were left without any assistance from the *Anjoman*. This dilemma is something all the *Anjomans* faced, but the needs of both donors and recipients in Kermanshah were exceptionally acute.

Mr. Rajab Ghasemi, chairman of the board of the Tehran *Anjoman*, told us he was lobbying the *Majilis* to create a special subsidy to help pay for kidneys for war veterans. Such a subsidy would be of considerable help in Kermanshah, particularly if it were also available to the families of war veterans. But we haven't heard any news from Iran that indicates movement on this proposal.

Kermanshah was disappointing as a city, and my main reason for going there, to get a taped interview with Dr. Zargooshi, never materialized. In retrospect, however, my visit provided a contextual perspective for the whole debate over organ selling in Iran. I learned it wasn't possible to use one region's program to generalize about the Iranian experience. If all I knew of the Iranian system were based on Kermanshah, or Tehran for that matter, I would have come away with a very different understanding of what was happening in Iran. Once again, I'd learned the answers weren't as simple as many people made them out to be.

۱۰ (10)

Making My Way Home

Once we left Kermanshah, we had a few days in Tehran to make our final preparations for returning to the United States. We copied all our taped interviews, notes, and consent forms and left them with Dr. Bastani's family and friends. Dr. Bastani's mother-in-law helped him pick out a Persian carpet for his son, and I roamed bookstores looking for something on Iranian medicine or ethics in English but couldn't find anything. I did, however, find a couple of nice tourist-oriented coffee table books, although I couldn't help but wonder if there was much of a market for such books, given the government's attitude toward foreigners, particularly Americans. One of the books I purchased was in German and another in French. My guess is the books in English weren't so much for British or American tourists as for tourists from other parts of the Middle East or Europe who don't speak Farsi, French, or German. I also brought back volumes of poetry by Hafez and Sadi and some discs of traditional Persian music.

Freedom from What?

My major concern thus far had been protecting my research materials from the Iranian government, but reentry into the United States could also put my data at risk. What if my laptop and portable hard drives were confiscated? Just a year earlier Dr. Bastani and his family had traveled to South America, and when they arrived back in the United States, customs held them for hours. U.S. officials thoroughly searched all their luggage, took his laptop, and demanded to know where he and his family had been on "vacation," clearly doubting whether it had been a vacation at all. I'm not an Iranian citizen like Dr. Bastani, so I wasn't sure what to expect, but I had been warned by others that customs coming home could be just as hair-raising as the customs of unwelcoming countries. In my case, I would be pleased if U.S. customs agents were as polite as the officials at Khomeini International had been two months earlier.

On New Year's Eve, just before midnight when my visa would expire, Dr. Bastani and I boarded a plane in Tehran for the first leg of our flight back to the States. Nothing unusual happened—no questioning, no searches, nothing. Once in the air, we both let out a sigh of relief. I wanted to tear off my hijab and start talking to Dr. Bastani about everything we had experienced, but a sense that we weren't completely out of the woods made me hold back.

It was after clearing the gate at Frankfurt International Airport that I finally felt comfortable enough to take off my hijab. A quick trip to the restroom and I had changed into jeans and a T-shirt, the official garb of the West. I came out tossing my long blond hair, appreciating my Western freedoms in a new light.

Dr. Bastani laughed and winked. "It's a bit late if you're trying to seduce me."

I winked back as I flung my bag over my shoulder and headed for my gate. "You're a good man, Bahar. We'll talk soon."

The most disconcerting thing about Iran was the sense that something could go wrong and there would be no one to help. Securely in Europe, I felt the weight of oppression, the uneasiness, and the fear that at any moment the government might take issue with something I was doing lifted from my shoulders. I could breathe easy again knowing that if I were falsely accused of something, at the very least, my access to help could not be denied. Once again, I had some rights I was sure of.

American Customs

I was exhausted by the time I got to New York City's JFK airport. I had spent half the flight from Frankfurt to New York trying to figure out what, if anything, I could tell customs agents to dissuade them from searching or keeping my laptop and hard drives. While the contrast between the oppressive government presence in Iran and the freedoms I usually enjoy as an American was never far from my mind, I knew customs was a no man's land where I couldn't count on my constitutional rights being respected.

First stop, passport check. "Are you bringing in any agricultural products?"

"Yes, roasted pistachio nuts."

"Go that way." The agent pointed me in one direction while using his other hand to wave forward the next person in line. People from other passport stations rushed past me in typical New York fashion. They made a beeline for the baggage scanners as I struggled with my luggage. I let them pass and waited my turn, giving a little shrug and half jump every few seconds to keep my suitcase strap from falling off my shoulder.

Suddenly, a burly woman in uniform standing by the conveyor belt called out, "Hey you!"

I looked around and pointed to myself, wondering if I was being singled out for an in-depth luggage search or perhaps questioning.

She nodded her head, smiled, and gave me a drawn out, "Yyyeesss."

I started to move apprehensively in her direction, ready for the worst. But then her smile broadened, showing perfectly aligned, recently-whitened teeth — the kind of smile no one had given me in months, the kind of smile so many Americans don't hesitate to share with even a total stranger but Iranians, particularly Iranian women, generally reserve for family and the closest of friends.

"Love your hair!" she exclaimed, showing me her long braid and motioning me to bypass the line altogether.

I could hardly believe my good fortune, and I quickly headed for the doors separating the restricted area from the rest of the airport. *I'd better get out before she changes her mind!*

I flashed her the biggest smile I could muster and passed through the doors marked "No Return Entry," calling out over my shoulder, "And a Happy New Year to you, too!"

I was back, I was safe, and now the real work would begin. *How will I get 100 hours of video translated? Is there anyone who might help turn my video footage into a documentary? What about a book? Should I write one? How could my findings help the United States solve its own organ shortage?*

A Painful Reality

After spending a few weeks catching up with family and friends, I focused on getting my video interviews translated and on reconnecting with Steve Lessin.

Had he found a donor during the two months I was gone? He wanted to hear about Iran, and I wanted to see how he was doing. Steve listened intently to my stories about Iran but then shared with me the type of bad news so many dialysis patients face after a few years of treatment.

"My heart... well, it's a bitch. I probably couldn't survive a transplant. I say, 'Go for it anyway,' but the doctors patronize. They say, 'First get a kidney, and then we'll talk about it.' "

"Have they taken you off the list?"

"No one says it, but ..."

I was both angry and dejected. I knew something was wrong the moment I walked in. Steve's demeanor had changed. He seemed to move more slowly, and he avoided eye contact as if he felt guilty about something—as if he had failed by not getting a kidney instead of the system having failed him. I was at a loss for words. My eyes welled up with tears. I ran to the bathroom to splash water on my face and regain my composure. Steve was different when I returned. He seemed to have some of that old drive back, but he had shifted gears: Now his strength was no longer for himself, but for my project. He wanted to help others like himself even if it was too late for him.

"Go ahead and roll your tape. I want to tell the world what life on dialysis is really like." He kept speaking while I set up the camera. "This week, I'm kind of optimistic. I'm not going to die this week. But there are a lot of weeks where I'm ready.... To use the word engineers and physicists love to use, 'entropy.' I'm fighting entropy."

"What do you mean?"

"The major problem is that dialysis really doesn't work. It gets rid of only about 10 percent of the toxins in your blood. You're poisoning your body, and your body cannot take poisoning itself forever. Dialysis is a half-assed fix, you might say. It barely gets you by."

Steve exhaled. "Let's be honest: I wish nephrologists would be more open about what patients are really up against—that this progression I'm experiencing is 95 percent normal—and just make it very clear.... Basically it sucks."

Steve saw me adjusting my camera angle and waited, then continued. "I mean, the impact on my quality of life is just fantastically negative. I used to love my work, but now I can't do more than a few hours a day, if that. I can't play guitar anymore because my fingers are too stiff. I really can't go out at night. I can't ski anymore. I don't see my friends much. My libido's gone. There's really not much of a life at all; between the uremia and the heart disease, I can't do jack. Dialysis is not just a nuisance; it's a living death sentence."

"So how long have you been on dialysis now?"

"Almost four years.... And believe me, sometimes I worried I wouldn't make it to my 54th birthday. I've had like eight months where every month I was in the hospital four or five days. It's a sense of constant, ongoing exhaustion and planning your life to fit the exhaustion."

Steve and I spoke either in person or on the phone almost every week, then almost every day. He was energized, excited about my documentary project, and eager to get as much on tape as he could. I didn't fail to notice how quickly he weakened. Often I would just sit with him and watch TV or talk about inane things. Then, when I would get up and say I should go, or that he needed his rest, he would object.

"Stay, let's do another taped session. There is so much more I need to say."

So I would.

One day, I arrived at Steve's apartment and no one answered the door. I had visited the day before, so I knew he was expecting me. I called his cell phone. I knocked. Steve's car was in the parking lot—could something have happened? I tried to find a neighbor to ask if an ambulance had been there, but no one was home. I just kept knocking, wondering whom I should call.

A deliveryman came by and waited with me for a while but gave up and left boxes of dialysis supplies outside the door. He told me that every other time he had come by, Steve had been there and had told him to put the supplies directly into a back room. I sat on the steps, trying to figure out what to do next—knocking seemed futile. I was in the process of calling Steve's cousin, the only relative I knew, when the door finally opened, more than 30 minutes after I first arrived.

Steve was half-dressed; his shirt was open and his pants were zipped, but unbuttoned. He was barefoot. His hair was flat on one side of his head and sticking up at odd angles on the other, and he needed a shave. Worst of all, his skin was a slightly damp, translucent grey, and his eyes were so puffy I could hardly tell if they were open.

"Hello," I smiled, hoping to hide my shock at seeing the state he was in. "Sorry. I didn't mean to surprise you."

"No," he answered slowly as if each syllable took effort, "It's been a weird night."

He took his hand off the door and steadied himself on my shoulder. I held him up from behind, and we started back toward the bedroom.

"The damn power shut off last night."

"Sit down." I guided him to the bed, trying to get him comfortable. "Here are some pillows."

"My cycler stopped. I turned that thing off and clamped off things … but my insulin pump ran out." His words were coming out in sporadic spurts; I was worried that something was seriously wrong.

"You don't look well. What can I get you?"

I leaned him back, propped up by a few pillows, but one leg dangled over the edge of the bed. He looked uncomfortable, but when I tried to move his second leg onto the bed, he told me not to and tilted his head back as if he were dizzy or in pain.

"Should I call 911?"

"I don't know. Let's just see if I …"

He fumbled to try to take his blood pressure with the machine by his bed but then seemed to give up.

"Can I help?"

"Yeah. The problem is that …"

"Did you check your blood pressure? Do you want to?"

"They tell … look, just …"

Steve gave up on the blood pressure cuff and reached for the phone. He dropped it.

"Here!" I picked it up and gave it to him, but he could barely hold on to it.

"I'm going to call hospice," he said. "They always say that if you feel like you're really out of it, call them first, not …"

"Not 911?!" After all the conversations we'd had, including ones about going on hospice, I didn't know he had followed through and contacted them.

"Christ, God, … I've got it here in my wallet—here," he pointed.

I fumbled to get his wallet out of his pants. He winced as I tugged at his pocket. I opened the wallet with trembling fingers, trying not to let Steve see just how distressed I was. I dialed the number and put the phone to his ear.

"Yeah, this is Steve Lessin. I'm a patient of you people. I feel like I'm totally out of it. Can you send an ambulance or something?"

I felt relieved that Steve wanted an ambulance. He lay on the bed in a half-stupor, still with one leg dangling off the edge, fading in and out of consciousness. *Hurry! Hurry!* I kept thinking. *What should I do? Should I keep him awake?* "Do you need to drink something? Is there some medicine you should take?"

He shook his head no. Then—at a moment like this!—he thought of me and said, "I know you got appointments today, so …"

"No, that's OK. I'm not moving. I'm not leaving. I'm staying. … I'm staying. I'll call someone to pick up my daughter." I took his hand. "Your hands are cold."

"That doesn't worry me." Then after a long pause and without looking at me, he said, "I'm old."

Hospice called back and told me a nurse was on the way. I panicked, "No ambulance?"

The person on the other end of the line said, "Mr. Lessin is on hospice. A nurse will be right there."

Why won't they send an ambulance? "Steve, I want to call 911."

"Are they coming?"

"Hospice is sending a nurse."

He reached over and took the phone from me. "I'm fine, but ... can you send someone?" He said in a stronger voice than I'd heard since I arrived. "How long will they be?" Then he whispered, "Yes, please."

"Steve!" I grabbed the phone and told the person on the other end of the line to please send someone as soon as possible. "I don't know what's going on. Maybe he's in diabetic shock."

She was so composed. She told me to be calm and that they would send someone as soon as they could, that things were under control. *How could she say that? How could she know? She wasn't here.*

The next hour and a half was torture. I kept wanting to call 911, and Steve kept begging me to wait. "Hospice will be here any minute." A couple of times I stepped out of the room, telephone in hand, ready to dial for help against his wishes, struggling with myself: *What if he dies? What if he's delusional and does-n't know what he's saying?* Then, I would hear a groan from the next room and Steve, as if he knew what was running through my mind would sit up a little straighter and say, "I'm getting better.... You can call and cancel hospice."

"Absolutely not," I would say, but the urgency of the situation would fade just a bit—at least, until a few moments later, when he would ask me to call hospice and check when the nurse would arrive.

But then he genuinely started to improve. He pulled his leg up onto the bed and sat up, adjusting his pillows. He asked for a soda. His skin tone improved from stone grey to pasty, and he began to talk, answering questions that had been silently running through my mind.

"Do you know that feeling of just being too tired to fight? That's why I brought in hospice. I mean, my wife said, 'Well, why do you keep lopping off things and all the surgery and this and that? Then you're miserable in the hos-pital. The rehab doesn't work.'"

Steve shook his head. "I'm thinking I don't have it in me anymore, Sigrid. When I tell you I don't know how much time I have left, I'm not just making this up. This is really unnerving now, with what happened here.... I feel like I'm getting near the end—that's the problem. And I don't have the strength. I'm just not sure what to do. Look, Sigrid, I don't think I've made this clear. Maybe I have or haven't, but I don't really know how much time I have left."

Then after glancing at my face, which I'm sure looked pretty ashen, he tried to make light of the situation, "Maybe I just had an anxiety attack."

"Steve, no! This is serious. Probably your sugar dropped way too low, and maybe your blood pressure too."

Then, returning to his previous remark, as if he were trying to convince himself and not me that all he had was a panic attack, he said, "I've got all kinds of things that I could take for anxiety, but I'm better off doing nothing. You know what I mean? I mean in this case when you don't know what's going on, and I better not do anything until the nurse takes a look."

I nodded my head in agreement and, making sure Steve could see me smirk, added, "Where's your stash? I could use some Valium." We both laughed, and I knew the worst had been averted.

But that day I saw another change in Steve. I was pretty sure the taped interviews were over. Steve had shifted his focus to planning a different type of project. He started meeting more and more with hospice counselors, and when he called to chat, he no longer wanted to talk about his illness. I thought he wanted to discuss philosophy, current events, and the meaning of life because he was getting better, but it was the calm before the storm.

Just a few weeks later, Steve surprised me by asking if I wanted to film his next visit to the nephrologist.

"Is Dr. Mahoney OK with my tagging along?"

"Yup. I asked him, and he said it's fine." Steve was in a great mood that morning, joking with Abe, the van driver who transported him—wheelchair and all—to the doctor's office. He teased me about my wheelchair-driving skills and joked about tripping passersby with his cane, but once we were in with Dr. Mahoney, his tone changed.

After five minutes or so of jovial banter, Dr. Mahoney asked Steve what was on his mind. "Well, I've spoken to hospice." I had trouble holding up the camera. I knew what was coming and had to muster all my strength not to cry. "I'm stopping dialysis. Not totally sure when, but this is probably my last visit."

Dr. Mahoney put his hand on Steve's shoulder. "That's a huge decision."

"It was a … it was a tough call, but it got so mentally exhausting, I thought, I've fought long enough."

Dr. Mahoney's voice was calm, measured, and practiced, "Did anybody talk with you about what to expect?"

"Well, it's kind of a slow sleep. They give you things so you don't feel bad."

The last meaningful thing Dr. Mahoney said before the awkward goodbyes was, "I really admire how you are at peace with all this. And I think that you are making an extremely brave, but appropriate decision. And I think to sort of take control and say, 'No, I've decided this is the time,' rather than to go through amputations and such, I think there's a lot of wisdom in that. I really do."

I wondered how often Dr. Mahoney had said essentially those same words to other dialysis patients.

Two weeks later, on July 3, 2009, Steve stopped dialysis. I tried to talk him out of it; I'd been trying ever since I learned his plans during our visit to Dr. Mahoney. Steve, I think, was tired of hearing people telling him he shouldn't give up. He stopped seeing anyone, even his wife, and six days later he died in his apartment with only a hospice nurse at his side. I wondered if I had been a good friend. Maybe I should have been more supportive of his decision to end treatment, but I just couldn't bring myself to condone his giving up. I know life wasn't easy for him. It was horrible, and I know only he could make that call. Maybe I was being selfish. I wanted our talks to go on. I wanted to see him smile and laugh at my jokes—and most of all, I wanted to keep laughing at his.

Motivated to Help

In part because I was grieving over Steve's death and in part because of what I'd experienced in Iran, I called someone I'd befriended in Ann Arbor, Michigan when I went there to do dialysis-patient interviews before my research trip. Maurie had been one of the optimistic ones. At the time he'd been on dialysis barely a year, and he was hopeful that he might get lucky moving his way up the deceased donor list, or that one of his friends might offer him a kidney. His first replacement kidney had come from his mother, and his second, which had lasted 20 years, came from a deceased donor. When I spoke to him after Steve died, he wasn't as optimistic anymore. I didn't have to think long. I offered to be his third donor.

We got the process rolling right away. It took a few months to get all the tests done, but as I was going through the final psychological testing, my sister, who had been battling cancer for years, told me she needed me. I flew down to Texas to be with Ingrid as she died. Then, all of a sudden, the one person I could always share childhood memories with was gone. It was as if my childhood had died with her. Four months later, when I was ready to continue with the donation, Maurie had taken a turn for the worse. His heart, like Steve's, and like so many dialysis patients', had grown too weak, and he no longer qualified for a transplant. At this point, I too was growing emotionally exhausted.

I felt like I was failing everyone. The documentary project was stalled, and I hadn't worked on the book in almost a year. I pooled my efforts and a friend,

Michele Battle-Fisher, put me in touch with Mary Anne Benner, who put to-gether a YouTube video for me, honoring Steve's desire to inform the world about what life was like on dialysis.* I then turned my attention to this book. It had taken almost two years to get the video footage from Iran translated, and I needed to go through nine binders of transcripts, several notebooks, and boxes of notes to tabulate the data. The best I could do for Steve and Maurie at this point was finish my book. That would be my testimony to their lives and all the lives that had touched me in Iran.

My pilgrimage is not over: I'm still searching for solutions to the organ short-age. My hope is that the stories in this book will help people think realistically about helping the more than 100,000 Americans actively waiting for a kidney before, like Steve and Maurie, they die needlessly after languishing on dialysis.

---

* www.ethical-solutions.org/projects/steve_lessin/

Conclusion:
Can the U.S. Organ Shortage
Be Solved?

The Current State of the U.S.
Kidney Shortage

These are the facts:

- Approximately four hundred thousand people in the United States are on dialysis.
- A quarter of these people—over one hundred thousand as of the end of 2013—are listed as actively waiting for a kidney. Most of the rest are either too old, too sick, or too weak for a transplant, but many could have benefited from a transplant before years of dialysis took its toll.
- Most will die waiting. Every year only about 15% of those on the active waiting list get transplants. Another 7–8% die or drop off the list without getting a kidney. This translates to approximately 20-25 American dialysis patients dying needlessly every day.
- "Survival" is the most honest word for existence on dialysis, because for most it is a life hardly worth living.

I only came to fully realize this last point when I got to know Steve and personally witnessed his suffering. Yes, he survived for a time, but he didn't really live. And as I got to know him, I came to understand his final, tragic choice. I learned similar lessons from the other dialysis patients I met. Until we find a solution to the organ shortage, we sentence kidney disease patients to a great deal of suffering, and most to an earlier death than necessary.

The other unfortunate fact is this: We can *never* overcome the organ shortage with cadaver organs or with stop-gap policies that reduce the pool of patients eligible for a transplant. Just do the math. In the 1980s, Congress gambled with trying to solve the kidney shortage through a combination of cadaver and altruistic living donations without resorting to a system that allowed remuneration. Since then it has become evident that even if we had mandatory deceased organ donation or presumed consent—that is, a system where everyone is an organ donor unless they have clearly indicated otherwise—there would still be a serious kidney shortage. There has been some movement toward compensating donors for expenses, but those efforts are meager and have done little, if anything, to increase kidney donations.

There has also been a slight increase in one kind of living donation called chain, or domino, transplants. These are cases where a linchpin donor says, "I am a match for your loved one, but you are not. I will donate to your loved one as long as you donate to someone else." The linchpin donor is an altruistic donor who sets a chain of transplants in motion by providing the kidney necessary to guarantee that others will indirectly help their loved ones by donating to someone else. It is touching to hear of chains of up to 20 or more people helping each other in this way, but, to put it bluntly, this is only a drop in the bucket. Such arrangements often receive significant press coverage, and I'm glad they do; a recent front-page story in *The New York Times* showcased a record-breaking domino donation chain connecting 30 kidneys and the children, spouses, siblings, and friends who donated to save their loved ones.

However, stories like this can create a false impression that such innovative approaches could honestly solve the organ shortage. They can't. In 2012, living kidney donations in the United States from all sources, including chain donation, amounted to 5,622 cases. This is admirable, and such donations should be encouraged, but they amount to not even 6 percent of the people currently waiting for a kidney. Without some drastic change, altruistic living donations will never close the ever-growing gap between the number of people on dialysis who could benefit from a transplant and the number of kidneys available from cadaveric sources (only 10,868 in 2012).* It is also worth noting that for some reason living kidney donations in the United States have dropped in the last few years. The United States Renal Data System (USRDS) reports that in 2004 there were 6,647 living donor transplants but in 2012 there were only 5,619. The decline in living donors is probably caused by a variety of factors not the least of which is an ailing economy—it takes time and money to be a living kidney donor.

---

* A living donor has only one kidney to offer, but a cadaver usually has two. Note, however, that more kidneys are lost in the cadaver harvesting process than when procuring a kidneys from live donors. See Notes section for more details.

Unintended Consequences

The United States banned the sale of organs in order to prevent exploitation. This was an understandable reaction to the ghoulish proposal to import impoverished people from developing countries so Americans could buy their kidneys. But a blanket ban may have been too broad a solution to deal with one narrow and fatally flawed proposal, to say nothing of the numerous, unintended consequences that have flowed from the embargo. We have not prevented exploitation; we have merely hidden it.

Americans with financial resources who are unwilling to brave the waiting list sometimes avail themselves of the black market. The black market exploits vulnerable populations (usually poor donors from developing nations), not by paying them, but by buying into a system where there are no legal protections for either donors or recipients. Donors are lied to, cheated, and left without sufficient post-operative care. Recipients risk contracting diseases such as HIV, hepatitis, or even cancer from improperly screened donors. Both donors and recipients risk infection and other surgical complications from sub-par operating facilities. And neither donors nor recipients have legal recourse to remedies if they are cheated or mistreated. It is believed that a thousand or more Americans purchase illegal organs (mostly abroad) every year.*

But there is another tragic consequence inherent in the American system of altruistic organ donation that many people are not aware of, an insidious injustice so profound one might question whether our current policy is any less barbaric than the exploitation it sought to eliminate. By mandating altruistic living kidney donations, the United States has inadvertently relegated some very specific groups of Americans to die on dialysis while creating opportunities for others to get kidneys for free. Someone well-to-do or well-connected, or even someone who is a middle-class, white-collar worker is far more likely to have friends or relatives who qualify to donate than someone who is poor, unemployed, or a blue-collar worker.

Listed here are some of the qualifications for being a living kidney donor:

○ Donors must be healthy and insured. They can't have diabetes, hypertension, or heart problems; can't be more than a little overweight; and preferably don't have a history of diabetes or heart disease in their immediate families. These are prevalent illnesses among Americans—an estimated 8.3 percent of Americans suffer from diabetes, and heart disease caused nearly 25 percent of American deaths in 2008—but the problem

---

* See Notes section for Introduction for more on the black market in kidneys.

is especially acute among the poor and minorities. A growing body of evidence points to strong links between socioeconomic status and the prevalence of diabetes, hypertension (a risk factor for heart disease), and end-stage renal disease. On top of this, donors need health insurance, which practically speaking means that donors or their spouses must be full-time employees in a business large enough to provide insurance, must be making enough to purchase their own insurance, or must be under 26 and covered by their parents' health insurance.

- Donors must have time to spare. First, they need to make 3 to 10 weekday trips to a hospital, clinic, or lab for pre-op meetings and testing with lab technicians, doctors, social workers, and psychologists. Then after the operation, they need two to seven days to recover in the hospital and at least two weeks to recover at home. Even after three weeks, however, it remains unwise to do any heavy lifting. The period to limit heavy lifting might last anywhere from 2 to 6 months or longer depending on the age and general health of the donor, whether there were any complications during surgery or afterwards, and how quickly the donor is healing. This means taking a good deal of time away from work or other responsibilities, particularly if the donor has to do more than is generally required of someone with a desk job.

- Donors must have a support group with time to spare. They need help during the donation and recovery period. Donors can't drive themselves home from the hospital after the operation. They need people who can take care of them for at least the first week or two after surgery. And of course, someone must take on the responsibilities donors are unable to fulfill during recovery: any job-related duties as well as home responsibilities, such as caring for children, older relatives, the household, pets, and the yard.

- Donors must have money. The actual nephrectomy is covered through the recipient's insurance or federal and state health programs like Medicare and Medicaid, but there are donation related costs that are not covered. Donors may have travel-related expenses like gas, flights, hotels, and food while getting pre-operative testing done and before and after surgery. If a donor's friends and family can't take off time to help the donor (or can't take off weeks or months), the donor might have to hire someone to help with non-work related obligations: for example, a babysitter, a pet sitter, and someone to clean the house and/or mow the lawn. It is also quite possible that donors may need to take off more time from work than they have paid leave. (Recipients are legally permitted to reimburse donors for lost wages, but not all recipients, and particularly not impoverished ones, have the financial means to cover lost wages. Furthermore reimbursing the self-employed is prohibited because there is no clear measure, such as a salary, to value their work. State and federal programs provide some financial assistance for donors, but most of those programs only provide need-based support for travel expenses or only compensate donors a small percentage of their costs after the fact.*)

The up-front costs associated with kidney donation are simply too great for many potential donors, particularly if they are members of an underprivileged socioeconomic class. The costs of donating are not limited to the out-of-pocket expenses that might not be reimbursed. Taking too many days off work can jeopardize a donor's job status: A donor may lose his or her position altogether, fall behind in work responsibilities, or lose seniority when it comes to promotions or other benefits. There are also secondary costs such as the financial and emotional strain donation puts on family members and friends when they contribute financially or take time off work to help the donor during recovery.

Given these restrictions, how many people do you know who would qualify to be kidney donors? White-collar workers might be able to "afford" to donate if they have enough vacation time, enough money saved to pay for donation-related expenses up front, friends and family who can take time off work to help with everyday responsibilities, and a job to return to that doesn't require heavy lifting.

Blue-collar workers are far less likely to have the resources needed to be living donors. They might not have sufficient, if any, paid leave, may not have friends and family who have enough free time to help with children and household responsibilities, and are more likely than white-collar workers to have jobs that require heavy lifting.

Now consider the self-employed, people like family farmers and small business owners. How can they find the time or money to donate? And even if the self-employed qualify to donate, who would run their businesses in their absence, and how many of them have jobs that won't require at least some heavy lifting?

---

* There have been some successful efforts to lessen the financial burdens of being a living donor, such as a federal fund that covers travel and other incidental costs on a proof of need basis, and some efforts to provide extra (paid or unpaid) leave for government employees and even in some cases private employees. Some states have implemented tax deduction options for donation related expenses. But, while a step in the right direction, these efforts do not go far enough. For more detail see the Notes section for this chapter.

And what about homemakers or people who care for children or elderly relatives? Who would take on their responsibilities while they arrange for and recover from a kidney donation, let alone the risks of heavy lifting too soon after surgery?

Finally, poor and minority communities are harder hit with problems of obesity, diabetes, and hypertension, making it less likely that a potential recipient's friends and family will even qualify medically as donors, let alone have the financial resources necessary to donate. And what about the unemployed? They don't qualify because they don't have insurance. So the unemployed, or even friends or relatives who work part-time, might not qualify to donate because they don't have adequate insurance coverage.

As a result, the United States has a kidney donation system that, in the name of altruism, makes it possible for the well-to-do, leisure class, and upper-middle-class to get living donor kidneys for free, while the average working class laborer, the poor, and the unemployed have to watch their friends and family die on dialysis, waiting for second-best cadaver organs that rarely come.

Lessons from Iran

The kidney shortage can be solved. We know because Iran has done it. Some people may disagree with the Iranian approach, but to say a system that has a waiting list *for donors* hasn't solved the kidney supply side of the organ shortage is willful ignorance. Iran's legalized system of compensated kidney donation is far from perfect, but it has come a long way. It would be a mistake to dismiss what Iran has learned over its 25-year history of experimentation with regulated kidney sales simply because of political differences between our countries.

Many will say such a solution is a bridge too far. They will argue that the United States and other countries took a stand against exploiting the poor and that it would be a mistake to change course now. Whatever strides a country such as Iran has made toward alleviating its organ shortage, these critics will claim, we should not abandon important principles. But, we must ask, has sticking to principles achieved what we thought it would? Also, some Westerners have suggested that Iran's system isn't working, but those critics haven't witnessed the Iranian system firsthand, and other than arguably in Kermanshah, their assertion is false.

On one level, the options we face are pretty straightforward: The United States can either continue its current policies and face a growing crisis with its attendant suffering and needless deaths, or we can make fundamental changes to address the problem. On the ethical level our choices are more complicated.

It is not simply a question of whether we are willing to learn from a country like Iran or that we must simply *overcome* our natural objections to exploiting the unfortunate because we need their organs. We need to *recognize* the full ethical dimensions of the choices we have already made. Is the system we have developed actually morally superior to what Iran has done? We may not have offered poor people choices we find unsavory, but we have instead sacrificed justice on the altar of altruism. The current policies of the West, and particularly the United States, feed a black market and covertly discriminate against poor prospective donors and recipients alike.

The United States should be ashamed to be outdone by a country like Iran. This is not to suggest that what Iran has done is flawless. The Iranians should be more proactive about informed consent and provide life-long health insurance for donors, and a city like Kermanshah is clearly lacking in the financial and medical resources necessary to make any form of organ procurement system work. It would also improve the Iranian system if they could find a way to take the bargaining out of living kidney donation, perhaps by raising the government contribution to the going rate of four or five million tomans so fewer donors will haggle for more, and fewer will feel cheated or undervalued. The United States, on the other hand, could introduce compensated living kidney donation without facing most of the problems Iran has faced. For one, informed consent is already part of the U.S. medical and social ethos. Also, from an administrative perspective, paying donors instead of paying for dialysis should be a relatively easy transition.

Such a system would not be just another government boondoggle; it could actually cut government healthcare costs. The federal government already pays for kidney disease treatment for those without private insurance, so some or even most of the money saved by providing transplants in lieu of dialysis treatment could be used to provide health insurance and other forms of compensation for kidney donors. Medicare costs for dialysis for a single patient on average in 2010 was $77,156—but that doesn't include coverage for treating common complications not directly related to dialysis, such as diabetes and heart disease—when these treatment costs are factored in, estimates are that the average Medicare cost of treating a dialysis patient may be closer to $375,000. The average Medicare cost for a transplant patient (cost of the transplant operation, post-operative care, maintenance medications, and surgical removal if the transplant failed) in 2010 was only $32,914.* This also doesn't include the cost of treating comorbidities, but if a patient received a preemptive transplant

---

* The initial cost of a transplant operation can vary from about $50,000 to $200,000, but the average cost of maintaining a transplant is only about $15,000 a year. See Notes section for more detail.

or a transplant within the first six months of going on dialysis, such costs are likely to be very low compared to those of patients who spend longer on dialysis. Statistically, medical costs rise exponentially the longer a patient is on dialysis because of a high rate of general system deterioration.

These data suggest that the federal government could save on average over $200,000 a year per patient if we find a way to provide preemptive transplants, or at least provide transplants before a patient is on dialysis longer than six months. The longer the patient remains on dialysis, the higher the overall treatment costs become, and the lower the chance that the transplant will succeed. Some would even argue that my estimates are conservative, because they don't take into consideration the fact that most dialysis patients don't work and thus receive disability payments or other government support. Preemptive transplants allow patients who are working to continue their employment, contributing to society as workers and taxpayers.

The United States already has an extensive, well-developed infrastructure for dealing with living donation: Almost half of all current kidney donors are living donors, meaning currently about a third of all kidneys transplanted in the United States come from living donors.* There wouldn't be a need to set up NGOs like in Iran; existing avenues for vetting and testing potential altruistic donors could simply be expanded, and the system in place for paying donation-related expenses could be increased to give donors more substantial compensation. Determining how much to pay donors requires further study, but the basic principles of supply and demand could guide the way. A price could be set, and the government could see how many people step forward. The more potential donors are needed, the higher the incentive should be. There would be nothing wrong with implementing a payment scheme that takes into consideration a recipient's ability to pay. For example, a sliding scale could be used so wealthier kidney recipients, or those who have insurance to cover transplant-related costs, contribute more to a government-set price than those who don't have the money. That way, money that might otherwise be spent purchasing a kidney on the black market would go toward helping defray kidney transplant costs for less wealthy Americans.

Despite objections to the contrary, there is little chance that such a plan would be a free-for-all with donors from developing nations coming to the United States to sell their kidneys. An important lesson from the Iranian experience is that both donor and recipient rights can best be protected if the program is closed to noncitizens (or at least to anyone who is not a legal resident). In the United States such

---

* Each living donor can donate only one kidney, while potentially two kidneys can be retrieved from each qualifying cadaver.

restrictions would be necessary to ensure: 1) that citizens' tax dollars in this situation are only used to help other Americans, 2) that promised long-term benefits such as health insurance can be guaranteed, and 3) that the well-being and health of both recipients and donors can be tracked. Ocassionally non-citizens get transplants in Iran, but it is hard to believe the United States couldn't do at least as well as Iran in limiting its living donor program to its own citizens (or its own citizens and long-term resident aliens).

Finally, the issue of organ shortage versus kidney shortage needs to be addressed. Up until now I've intentionally focused on the kidney shortage, instead of the organ shortage as a whole. Kidneys comprise at least 84 percent of the U.S. transplant waiting list, so solving the kidney shortage would go a long way toward solving our organ shortage. But what about the 16 percent who need other organs? Iran may not have a kidney shortage, but it certainly has a shortage in other organs that is just as acute or worse than the shortages experienced in other parts of the world. Because of its lack of medical resources and infrastructure, Iran concentrated on the largest part of the organ shortage, and in some ways, easiest to deal with, namely kidneys. But if you are an Iranian who needs a heart, liver, pancreas, or another vital organ, the chances that you can be helped in Iran are much lower than in many other countries, particularly if that country, like the United States, has a well-developed deceased donor organ program.

Iran's cadaver transplant network is under-developed. It is easy to assume this is because Iran has focused its efforts on its living donor program, but there are many other reasons for the shortcomings of its cadaver donor program. As is the case in most developing countries, scarce resources and inadequate medical infrastructure have slowed down the development of a cadaver transplant program. But religious and cultural issues, such as the Qur'an's apparent prohibition against the dismemberment of dead bodies and the psychological taboo of receiving organs from the dead, have also delayed the development of a system for recovering organs from the deceased.

As far as the United States is concerned, we already have a well-developed cadaver organ procurement program, arguably the best in the world, and there is no evidence that encouraging living donation impacts negatively on the rate of deceased donations. On the contrary, we saw in Iran how raising awareness with respect to either living or cadaver donation sometimes made people more willing to consider both forms of donation. Individuals who made inquiries about living donation were usually willing to also sign deceased donor cards. Also, one person we interviewed became a living donor after he learned about the kidney shortage during an educational event where people were signing cadaver donor cards.

The Next Step

It's not logical to ignore Iran's more than 25 years of experience with living kidney donation simply because we have negative feelings about that country's regime. It is also a huge mistake to confuse a regulated, government-sanctioned and subsidized, living donation program with illegal trafficking in human organs. One of the main advantages of a legalized market is that it prevents the horrors of the black market. It is time U.S. lawmakers take a hard look at the lessons that can be learned from Iran's incentivized kidney donation program and try an experiment of their own. Start small. Begin by allowing a few regional, or even single-institution-based, pilot projects where donors receive healthcare benefits and are compensated for more than their transplant-related expenses. For example, a pilot project could offer donors healthcare for life and pay them $50,000, thus allowing Americans—those out of work, those behind on their mortgages, those who need help paying for an education, or those who want to start a business—to get a leg up in life.

Would it really be so bad if Americans, along with all the wonderful opportunities they may or may not already have, also had the option of getting paid to save someone from the indignities of dying on dialysis? If you've read this book, you know how Iranians who donate their kidneys for money would answer. The poor often face difficult choices that we wish no one had to face. But selling a kidney to help one's family and save a life at the same time should be one of the easier decisions to make.

Acknowledgments

Without Bob's love and understanding, the adventure that led to this book could never have taken place. I am also grateful to my children, Nathan, Ian, Jackson, and Lauren, who showed a remarkable acceptance of my need to travel to Iran and the years I spent preoccupied with researching and writing this book.

I also owe endless gratitude to Dr. Bahar Bastani, who handled every step of our research trip once inside Iran. He arranged all our meetings, conducted interviews in Farsi, and explained to me the cultural context for what I experienced.

I can't thank Deborah Chen enough for her steadfast support. She is the only person, other than Bob, who stood by this project from beginning to end. Before I left for Iran, she helped prepare me for my trip with research on organ procurement in Iran and other countries. Upon my return she double-checked all my data entries and tabulations and helped me with background research. Finally, she commented and made editorial suggestions on several versions of this book.

Simin Golestani was my center's most productive translation intern, translating almost half of all my taped interviews from Farsi to English. She also did follow-up interviews for me when she went to visit relatives in Iran in August 2011. Other translation interns included Jennifer Kiel, Farhoud Faraji, Farshid Faraji, Zahra Siahi, my friend Bozy Bahary, Parivash Biglarbeigi, Aurelia Tunru, Jason McZara, Asal Baragchizadeh, Ehsan Mansouri, and Nahzy Buck.

Along with Deborah Chen, Cathy Dutchak helped research organ procurement in Iran. Other interns such as Golanna Ashtari and Sardar Hosseini translated documents I brought back and helped research the aliases I used to protect the privacy of Iranian kidney sellers and recipients. Alex Lynch helped transcribe Dr. Bastani's taped notes, and Huan Zhu helped confirm the proper English spelling of notable Iranian people and places.

Without the initial contacts supplied by my friend Allison Griffin, the project would never have gotten off the ground. She called her father, Michael Griffin, who helped me contact Professor Assefi. It was Dr. Assefi's daughter Nassim who put requests out in the American-Iranian community for people who might be interested in helping me with my research. This was how I met Dr. Bastani.

David Donadio, Karen Cantor, Robert Veatch, Benjamin Hippen, Diane Tober, and Theresa Gheen were an inspiration early on in the project, and my center co-board members Rod Carveth, Michele Battle-Fisher, and Shane Steinfeld have shared in the excitement of my successes and helped me weather my setbacks.

There are far too many people to thank whom I met while traveling in Iran. All were gracious with their time, and many took me in, fed me, and showed me around. Most importantly, many introduced me to hospital and *Anjoman* administrators who in turn allowed me to interview kidney sellers and recipients. A few people who absolutely need mentioning include: Dr. Ahad Ghods, Dr. Behrooz Broumand, Dr. Ali Nobakht, Dr. Reza Malekzadeh, Dr. Seyed Ziaoddin Tabei, Dr. Alireza Bagheri, Dr. Kavoos Basmanji, and Ayatollah Mohaghegh Damad.

Also hospitable and generous with their time were Dr. Seyed Ali Malekhosseini, Dr. Mahvash Alizadeh and her family, Dr. Tahereh Malakoutian, Dr. Mohsen Nafar, Dr. Sharifkazemi, Dr. Ai Nobakht Haghighi, Dr. Shiva Seyrafian, Dr. Abdol Amir Atapour, Dr. Farshid Saghila, Dr. Shahrzad Shahidi, Dr. Dr. Shiva Seyrafian, Dr. Hamid Tayebi Khosroshahi, Dr. Mohammad Reza Khatami and his wife, Dr. Ali Hamedanchi, Dr. Hekmat, Mr. Khaki, Mr. Fallah, Dr. Masih Naghibi, Dr. K. Raisee, Dr. Jamshid Roozbeh, Dr. Reissi Daryoush, Dr. Maryam Moeini, Dr. Mohammad Mehdi Sagheb, Dr. Jawad Afzali, Dr. Farzaneh Sharifi Pour, Dr. Ebrahim Khadegi, Dr. Nuzemian, Dr. Nooshin Mirkheshti, Dr. Mohammad Reza Ardalan and his family, and Dr. Fatemeh Zaemian and her family. Without their willingness to take a chance on me and open up to an American, none of what this book has to offer could have come to fruition.

I also must thank Dr. Bastani's relatives for their kind hospitality. This includes his most gracious parents, Mrs. Pary Rokh and Mr. Noorollah Bastani, and other genial relatives such as Mrs. Zahrabibi Dehdashti, Mr. Mehdi Bastani, Messrs. Mansoor and Masoud Alikhani, and all their families.

But no one inspired me more than Steve Lessin and Maurie Ferriter. I shared in their frustrations as they fought a losing battle against kidney disease. Both saw their beloved country fail them, and both saw a critical need for someone to tell the story of how Iran solved its kidney shortage.

Notes

This book is based on years of research. The video transcripts alone fill nine three-ring binders. I have file boxes full of Dr. Bastani's and my notes as well as pamphlets and copies of laws and policies I brought back from Iran and have collected since. Hundreds of people in Iran, and many in the United States and elsewhere, helped gather the background information for this book. Unfortunately, I'm not able to formally acknowledge everyone, but those who provided the greatest assistance are listed in the acknowledgments.

The most significant resources for this book were the Iranian kidney donors and recipients Dr. Bastani and I interviewed, but the U.S. dialysis patients, the kidney donors and recipients whom I interviewed in the United States were also valuable resources. Finally, our interviews with Iranian transplant staff, medical administrators, and *Anjoman* staff were invaluable because they explained how the Iranian system evolved and helped me distinguish historical from current practices.

Listed below by chapter are some commentary and noteworthy resources relevant to this book.

To see photos I took in Iran, please go to www.TheKidneySellers.com. For a discussion of the Center's SOS (Solving the Organ Shortage) project and other related issues, please visit www.ethical-solutions.org.

Mark Twain famously said, "There are three kinds of lies: lies, damned lies, and statistics." I hope the preliminary notes below help readers understand how to interpret the data presented in this book and other potentially relevant data referenced in the notes that follow.

Notes

- Context is everything.

When were the data collected and where? How large was the sample size? What conclusions can be reasonably drawn from the data? Don't assume the date an article was published reflects how recently the data were collected. The most recent data, even in government reports, are often at least a few years old. That is why in this book, I often cite U.S. renal disease and treatment statistics from between 2009 and 2012. I always cite the most recent data I had access to at the time this book was written, but readers are encouraged to check the resources listed in the chapter notes for more recent data.

- Organ procurement in Iran is **not** one static system.

Iranian laws, regulations, guidelines, and practices governing transplantation have evolved over time. Their implementation also varies considerably from region to region and even sometimes from one institution to the next. Regional and institutional differences also exist in the U.S. organ procurement system, but it is my impression that United Network for Organ Sharing (UNOS) guidelines are applied more uniformly in the United States than Ministry of Health guidelines are applied in Iran. Also Iran has no equivalent to the U.S. Organ Procurement and Transplantation Network (OPTN) or the U.S. Renal Data System (USRDS), so the collection of national data on renal disease, organ procurement, dialysis, and transplant outcomes is less systematic in Iran than in the United States.

- How much do Iranian kidney sellers get paid?

This is not an easy question to answer. During the time I was in Iran, donors on average were paid five million toman. At the time I was in Iran, the exchange rate was approximately one thousand toman for one dollar so five million toman would exchange for approximately five thousand dollars. But that is an incomplete answer because an average Iranian can do much more with five million toman than an average American can do with five thousand dollars. Once average incomes, standard of living, and purchasing power are considered, the correct answer for how much kidney sellers are paid comes closer to something between $15,000 and $30,000. But there is yet another caveat: Living kidney donors in Iran always receive goods and services in addition to monetary payment. So when those additional benefits are included, the average purchasing power of a kidney seller's compensation in 2013 U.S. dollars is closer to $45,000. For more on this issue, please see the notes for Chapter Two.

◦ Some important kidney shortage facts to keep straight.

- Living donors can safely donate only one kidney, while usually two kidneys can be harvested from each deceased donor. For the past ten years approximately half of all donors were living donors. (Between 2000 and 2004 living donors outnumbered deceased donors, but since 2004 the number of living donors has declined.) That makes it seem like two out of three transplants should involve cadaver organs, but while every deceased donor can potentially provide two kidneys, in reality, not every cadaver donation translates into two useable kidneys. In 2012, for example, 5,622 live donors provided a total of 5,619 transplantable kidneys, while 7,420 deceased donors provided a total of only 10,868 kidneys.

- In 2008, 80% of people on the U.S. organ waiting list needed kidneys. In the summer of 2013 the percentage was closer to 90%. Please take note of the following when evaluating numbers on the UNOS waiting list:

    Factors that reduce the actual number of people actively waiting for a kidney in any given year:

    1) Patients who are listed multiple times because they are on the list in several regions should only be counted once.

    2) People who have become too sick to get a transplant should not be counted. But sometimes it is fair to keep patients on the list as "inactive" if their condition could improve to the point where they would once again qualify for a transplant. In 2011, 5,139 patients were removed from the list because they died, and 1,903 were removed because they were too sick for a transplant. See the Organ Procurement Transplantation Network (OPTN) and Scientific Registry of Transplant Recipients (SRTR)'s *2011 Annual Data Report: Kidney*, KI 1.8.

    3) Sometimes people get well enough not to need a transplant. In 2011 that number was 135. See the OPTN/SRTR's *2011 Annual Data Report: Kidney*, KI 1.8.

    4) Sometimes people refuse a transplant for reasons other than that they are too sick: For example, they are hoping for a better quality kidney, say from a younger deceased donor or a donor that didn't have cancer. In 2011, 406 patients refused kidneys when they were offered. See the OPTN/SRTR's *2011 Annual Data Report: Kidney*, KI 1.8.

Factors that increase the number of people actively waiting for a kidney in any given year:

1) People who are waiting for a kidney/pancreas combination are listed separately, but should be included in the total number of people who need kidneys (in July 2013 there were 96,735 listed with UNOS as waiting for kidneys and 2,059 listed as waiting for a kidney/pancreas combination).

2) Some preemptive living donor transplants take place without the patient ever being listed with UNOS. I could not find a reliable estimate for how often this occurs.

3) Technically the total number of people needing kidneys should also include people who could be listed but don't ask to be listed because they realize their chances of getting a kidney is slim. There were 400,000 Americans on dialysis in 2012, but despite my best efforts, I couldn't come up with a reliable measure for estimating how many of those people could have potentially benefited from a transplant but were never listed.

• The U.S. cadaver organ procurement system is already incredibly efficient. Increasing its efficiency further might increase the supply of kidneys slightly but never alleviate the shortage. Don't forget that fewer than 1% of all deaths result in potentially harvestable organs. Most people who die are too old or too sick, or their bodies are too damaged or arrive at the hospital too late for useable organs to be retrieved.

◦ Evaluating transplant and dialysis related costs.

• The real cost of a kidney transplant depends on many factors. For example, preemptive transplants are generally less expensive than transplants after a patient has been on dialysis. The longer patients are seriously ill, or the longer a patient is on dialysis, the more expensive that patient's total treatment becomes because of costs accrued before the transplant and because of the increased risk of complications and transplant failure. This means the most expensive route possible for the treatment of end-stage renal disease (ESRD) is the one commonly followed in the United States, namely to give patients transplants after they've already been on dialysis for four or five years. The cheapest option would be to do preemptive transplants or at least to do transplants as soon as possible after a patient starts dialysis.

• In the United States caring for ESRD patients cost $42.50 billion dollars in 2009 ($29.03 billion paid by Medicare and $13.47 billion by private funds). In 2010 caring for ESRD patients comprised 6.3% of the total Medicare budget. This is why so much discussion regarding treatment options for kidney disease patients focuses on potential cost savings for the federal government.

- Hard to measure, but not insignificant, are the costs of pain and suffering associated with life on dialysis which, in general, are estimated to be much higher than the costs associated with having a transplant. Also, nearly impossible to calculate are costs to society when dialysis patients stop working, such as disability payments, lost tax revenue, and the financial and emotional stress on family and friends. Note that patients who go on disability when they start dialysis rarely return to work, even if they get a transplant. People who get a preemptive transplant usually return to work after taking medical leave.

Notes for Individual Chapters

Prologue: A Personal Journey

Some academics argue that it is a contradiction to call a kidney seller "a donor." Some of the sellers/donors we interviewed in Iran spoke of selling their kidneys, but *all* spoke of what they did as a donation or gift. They *all* thought of what they did as at least partially, if not primarily, altruistic.

In this book I use "seller" and "donor" interchangeably and variations on the term "compensated donation" throughout. In each case I make it clear whether the donor received money or not, but, in general, I am persuaded by the learned Mohaghegh Damad's argument (presented at the end of Chapter Five) that saving a life by giving up part of one's body is so valuable that it is futile to try to put a price on it. According to the Ayatollah Damad, and I agree, giving up a kidney is such a profound sacrifice that it must be at least partially altruistic. Thus selling a kidney is always, at least in part, an altruistic donation. And all kidney sellers are practically speaking, if not by logical necessity, also always kidney donors.

It is worth noting that the Iranian government's violations of human rights are not limited to women. The government is also guilty of mistreating Baha'is, journalists, and young people (adolescents can face the death penalty in Iran).

Introduction: A Critical Need

The McGraw Hill Medical Text *Living Donor Organ Transplantation*, 2008, is an excellent resource for a thorough overview of the history of transplantation, particularly the use of living donors. This textbook also includes articles that cover a number of different countries in addition to the United States; an article by Dr. Ghods on Iran begins on p. 75. Another slightly more recent but not as comprehensive resource is G. Danovitch's *Handbook of Kidney Transplantation* (5th Ed. 2009). Also, see G. Danovitch, et al.'s article "Living Donor Kidney Transplantation In The United States—Looking Back, Looking Forward" in the *American Journal of Kidney Diseases* (2011) Vol. 58, no. 3, pp. 343–48. Two good sources for information on kidney disease and transplantation in Iran are the *Iranian Journal of Kidney Diseases* (available at www.ijkd.org) and *The International Journal of Transplant Medicine* (available at www.home.sums.ac.ir). The best resources for up-to-date information on the extent of the U.S. organ crisis are the United Network for Organ Sharing (UNOS)'s website at www.unos.org, the Organ Procurement and Transplantation Network (OPTN)'s website at www.optn.transplant.hrsa.gov, the United States Renal Data System (USRDS)'s website at www.usrds.org, and the National Kidney and Urologic Diseases Information Clearinghouse (NKUDIC)'s website at www.Kidney.niddk.nih.gov.

The number of kidney transplants for the United States mentioned in this book (fewer than 16,500 in 2012) comes from the most current data available from OPTN. See www.optn.transplant.hrsa.gov. (Note this is a page where a report based on preliminary data can be generated. The most recent published OPTN annual data report was for 2011. The official 2012 annual data report is due out by the end of 2013). The 2011 OPTN annual report states that the number of transplants is not expected to either increase or decrease dramatically over the next few years (averaging fewer than 17,000 annually over the last five years). On the other hand, the number of people needing transplants is expected to continue to rise. The number of end-stage renal disease (ESRD) patients has grown from 60,000 patients in 1980 to nearly 600,000 in 2010. That is a 1,000% increase in 30 years.

While it seems as if everyone testifying before Congress in 1983 uniformly argued that the United States could solve its organ shortage through creating an efficient infrastructure for the harvesting of cadaver organs, one man disagreed. Roger W. Evans, Ph.D., testified, "I think the conclusion that must be reached is clear: The supply of [deceased] donor organs will never be sufficient to meet the need." His testimony can be found in Hearings before the Subcommittee on Health and the Environment of the Committee on Energy and Commerce, House of Representatives, 98th Congress, 1st session, on H.R. bill 4080. Serial no. 98-70, 1984, 50-72:59.

Later, documented on pp. 238–56 of the hearings, the committee discussed Dr. Barry Jacobs' business plan. The following exchange occurred between Rep. Al Gore and Dr. Jacobs:

> Mr. GORE. I will be brief because Dr. Jacobs and I have had an opportunity to discuss this together before, and we will have another opportunity next month with a series or group of bioethicists who are going to come to discuss this in some more detail.
>
> But, just for the record, Dr. Jacobs, what I have heard you propose in the past is not inconsistent with this. But just so we will have more of the details on the table, I have heard you talk about going to South America and Africa, to Third World countries, and paying poor people overseas to take trips to the United States to undergo surgery and have a kidney removed for use in this country. That is part of your plan, isn't it?
>
> Dr. JACOBS. Well, it is one of the proposals.

In fairness to Dr. Jacobs, the main thrust of his proposal at the hearing was to have the government pay consenting adult Americans as an incentive to donate their kidneys. However, his name has since become synonymous with the proposal to import kidney donors from developing countries.

It is hard to estimate the size of the black market in kidneys because it is hard to collect data on people who are getting away with something illegal. Nancy Scheper-Hughes suggests a conservative estimate of 15,000 kidneys sold worldwide every year. See N. Schepter-Hughes' article "15,000 Kidneys Trafficked Each Year: Organ Watch" in *MSN News India*. Another source for information on the black market in kidneys is S. Calandrillo's article "Cash for Kidneys? Using Incentives to End America's Organ Shortage" in the *George Mason Law Review* (2004) Vol. 13, no. 1, p. 87 and J. Berr's article "Buying A $100,000 Kid-

ney: A Story of Supply and Demand" in *24/7 Wall St.* (April 12, 2011). Also, see
N. Scheper-Hughes' article "Organs Without Borders" in *Foreign Policy* (2005).
The exact share of this market by U.S. buyers is hard to estimate. If 5–10%
of all kidney transplants are illegal transplants as estimated in the United Nations report cited below, then in 2012 the number of kidneys purchased illegally by Americans, mostly abroad, could be as high as 1,000 or more. Also,
see A. Caplan, et al.'s, *Trafficking in Organs, Tissues and Cells and Trafficking in
Human Beings for the Purpose of the Removal of Organs*, a Council of Eu-
rope/United Nations Study, 2009. Global Financial Integrity estimates in a
2011 report that the global trade in organs is between $600 million and $1.2
billion a year. J. Haken, *Transnational Crime in The Developing World*, a Global
Financial Integrity Report, Feb. 2011.

Until recently, all studies I'm aware of showed that kidney donors have no
greater risk of kidney disease or any other long-term complications from having donated a kidney than what exists in the general population. I found some
evidence to the contrary in a British study which indicates that more than half
of donors will have some chronic kidney disease (CKD) a year after donating
but the study also concluded that the small decline in renal function remains
stable for at least five years **and** patients rarely suffer adverse cardiovascular
events and cardiac mortality. See J. Charnow's article "CKD Develops in Many
Living Kidney Donors" in *Renal & Urology News* (2011). On the other hand a
more recent study found no significant difference in the rate of acute dialysis
between living kidney donors and the normal population. Wolters, et al.'s article "Risks in life after living kidney donation," in *Nephrol Dial Transplant*
(2012) Vol. 27, no. 8, pp. 3021–23. (Note that the findings in these two articles are not necessarily contradictory.)

For more on the debate over legalizing kidney sales see F. Delmonico, and M.
Dew's article "Living donor kidney transplantation in a global environment"
in *Kidney International Journal* (2007) no. 7, pp. 608–14; M. Cherry's book *Kid-
ney for Sale by Owner: Human Organs, Transplantation, and the Market* (2005);
B. Hippen and A Matas's article "Incentives for organ donation in the United
States: Feasible alternative or forthcoming apocalypse?" in *Wolters Kluwer
Health* (2009) no. 14, pp. 140–46; A. Caplan and D. Coelho's book *The Ethics*

of Organ Transplantation: The Current Debate (1998), and T. Beard, et al.'s book *The Global Organ Shortage: Economic Causes, Human Consequences, Policy Responses* (2013). Also see the book edited by S. Satel titled *When Altruism Isn't Enough: The Case for Compensated Kidney Donation* (2008), and for a more comprehensive list of books and articles, both pro and con incentivized organ donation, see www.stoporgantraffickingnow.org.

Chapter 1: No Turning Back

The New York Times reported that in 2011 there were over 400,000 people on dialysis who at one point or another in their treatment might have benefited from a transplant. K. Sack, "Lives Forever Linked Through Kidney Transplant Chain 124" *The New York Times* (2012) sec. Health.

Chapter 2: Getting There

I conferred with my friend David Robinson at the International Monetary Fund to help me determine how best to give my readers a sense of the value of money and services being exchanged on the Iranian kidney market. With his help I came to understand that currency exchange rates are almost irrelevant for the type of comparison I wanted to make. I needed to find a way to show how selling a kidney affected a donor's standard of living. Someone in a very poor country may earn only a dollar a day, but in that country a dollar might be enough to feed a family. Context is everything! Ultimately what makes a difference is how much of certain goods kidney sellers can purchase with what they earn where they live.

It was hard to decide which measure would provide the clearest comparison. I didn't want to use adjusted values such as PPP or per capita income based on a country's GDP, because, while those figures are good for making overall country comparisons, they were too removed from what real individuals experience. I used statistics from 2008 or 2009 whenever I could because that is when I was in Iran, but I couldn't find income data for those years for all the countries I was interested in comparing. Also, Iran's per capita income jumped considerably between 2008 and 2010, so using data from 2010 or later would be misleading when most of the discussion of compensation for kidneys and living costs in this book date from 2008 or earlier.

Perhaps the best way to understand how much kidney sellers are paid in Iran is to use the type of comparison Dr. Ghods used when I spoke with him in New Haven, Connecticut in April 2008. He told me the going rate for a kidney at the time we spoke was equivalent to six months' salary for a registered nurse. In the United States the median salary for six months for a registered nurse in 2008 was

$32,565. See the Bureau of Labor Statistics website at www.bls.gov. To expand on this type of analysis, the going rate for a kidney when I was in Iran at the end of 2008 was almost twice what the average Iranian made that year or enough to feed a rural family of four for several years. (It takes more than twice as much to stay above the poverty line in Tehran than in outlying areas.) Yet, even this type of analysis is incomplete because almost all kidney sellers received more than just monetary payment: They also received goods and services, such as health insurance vouchers, dental care, job placement services, and donations of household goods, clothing, and food. I estimate that a more realistic U.S. equivalent in purchasing power for the overall fees and services received on average by kidney sellers in Iran is closer to $45,000.

Two good sources for information on the risks of living donation are the U.S. Organ Procurement and Transplantation Network (OPTN)'s website at www. optn.gov and A. Hartmann's article "The risk of living kidney donation" in *Nephrology Dialysis Transplantation* Vol. 18, no. 5, pp. 871–73. Also, see notes above for the Introduction and notes below for the Conclusion.

The penalties for being involved in providing "valuable consideration"—that is, any kind of payment—for organs for transplantation are set forth in the National Organ Transplant Act, 42 USC 201, PL 98-507, 1984.

Two helpful resources for a description of the inefficiencies of dialysis and its debilitating side effects are the websites of the Centers for Disease Control and Prevention (CDC) (available at www.cdc.gov) and the National Kidney Foundation (available at www.kidney.org). Also, see the sources listed in the notes for the Conclusion section below.

In an article published by Dr. Ghods, he provides a citation for the news story about how a transplant unit in Tehran suspected of providing illegal transplants to foreigners was shut down. The news article is entitled "Renal transplantation for foreign nationals: Modarres hospital scandal" and is cited in Dr. Ghods' article entitled "Ethical Issues and Living Unrelated Donor Kidney Transplantation" in the *Iran Journal of Kidney Disease* (2009) Vol. 3, no. 4, pp. 183–91.

Chapter 3: Transplanting Ideas and Organs

It was pointed out to me by Nassim Assefi that Iranian planes are old and badly maintained in part due to the U.S. embargo that doesn't allow for the export of Boeing parts or Boeing engineers to travel to Iran to fix the planes.

Chapter 4: Law, Hypocrisy, and the Black Market

A description of the fate of the Iranian chocolate thief can be found in the article "Iranian Chocolate Thief Faces Hand Amputation" in the BBC, *Middle East Section Report* (2010). R. Spencer comments on the ruling on the *Jihad Watch* blog in an entry entitled "Iranian Chocolate Thief to Have His Hand Chopped Off."

Dr. Broumand told me that the Iranian community was galvanized into action when a donor, who had been invited into his recipient's home, stabbed two of the recipient's children to death. The transplant community doubled its lobbying efforts, and the national government was primed to help. I see no reason for Dr. Broumand to misrepresent what happened, but I could not independently verify his story.

Dr. Ghods reviews the history of Iranian organ-procurement in his article "Renal Transplantation in Iran" in *Nephrology Dialysis Transplantation* (2002) Vol. 17, no. 2, pp. 222–28. Another good summary of the history of organ procurement in Iran is A. Nobakht Haghigh, et al.'s "Organ Transplantation in Iran before and after Istanbul Declaration, 2008" in the *International Journal of Organ Transplantation Medicine* (2011) Vol. 2, no. 1, pp. 1–3. Discussions of the Iranian system by U.S. authors can be found in B. Hippen's article "Organ Sales and Moral Travails: Lessons from the Living Kidney Vendor Program in

Iran" published as a *Cato Policy Analysis Report* (2008) no. 614 (This is the policy report I commissioned and helped edit), and D. Tober's article "Kidneys and Controversies in the Islamic Republic of Iran: The Case of Organ Sale" in *Sage Publications* (2007) Vol. 13, no. 3, pp. 151–70. (This article is based primarily on data collected from one nurse at one hospital in Tehran. There were no personal interviews of kidney sellers. Diane Tober was the medical anthropologist whom I asked to join me on my research trip to Iran, but her visa was denied.)

For a recent summary of the different regional living donor research projects conducted by Iranians over the years see M. Mahdavi-Mazdeh's article "The Iranian Model of Living Renal Transplantation" in *Kidney International* (2012) no. 82, pp. 627–34. (The studies summarized in this article were by different investigators in different regions and over a span of more than 20 years during which the laws, regulations, and practices governing kidney donation in Iran changed. I caution against accepting any generalized conclusions drawn from combining the data from such disparate studies.)

Chapter 5: Bargaining for Body Parts

In Tehran and throughout Iran, I interviewed many healthcare professionals who were instrumental in developing and implementing the Iranian organ-procurement system. Most of what they said was similar to what Drs. Ghods and Broumand told us. Please see the acknowledgments for a list of people who were kind enough to contribute their time and expertise in providing us background on the Iranian system, its history, and its current internal workings.

Note that it is possible to perform liver, lung, and even intestinal transplants using living donors, but these extractions are much riskier for donors than nephrectomies; thus, cadaver organs are generally used. Both the United States and Iran now have over 20 years of experience with safely performing living donor kidney transplants. See the R. Gruessner and E. Benedetti's (eds.) textbook *Living Donor Organ Transplantation* (2008), p. 21, Table 3.1-1 and pp. 43–44, and in general Dr. Ghods article on Iran in the same volume at pp. 75–80. Also, see N. Simforoosh, et al.'s article "Comparison of Laparoscopic and Open Donor Nephrectomy: A Randomized Controlled Trial" in *BJU International* (2004) no. 95, pp. 851–55. And in general see articles in the *Iranian Journal of Kidney Diseases,* index available at www.ijkd.org. Lung, heart, and small bowel transplants using cadaver organs have been performed at Tehran University, but these transplants do not occur on a regular basis anywhere in Iran, nor do they occur anywhere else in the world at nearly the same rate as kidney transplants.

In an interview with the *Vanderbilt Lawyer* Justice O'Connor attributes what I heard her say about wise men and wise women to Ruth Bader Ginsburg. See the Vanderbilt interview at www.law.vanderbilt.edu.

Chapter 6: The Poor and the "Lucky"

The composition of the Iranian parliament described in this chapter reflects the *Majilis* makeup in 2008, before the 2009 elections.

Chapter 7: The Rich and the Holy

Recently in Iran there has been a backlash against women being educated, at least in certain traditionally male-dominated fields, such as physics and engineering. See the article "Male-order Education: Iran Bars Women from 77 University Courses" in *RT.com* (August 21, 2012).

OPTN data for U.S. kidney transplant survival rate based on donor type as of July 5, 2013 are available at www.optn.transplant.hrsa.gov:

For grafts:

Donor Type	Years Post Transplant	Number Functioning	Survival Rate	95% Confidence Interval
Cadaveric	*1*	*23072*	*89.0*	*(88.6, 89.4)*
Living	1	17899	95.1	(94.8, 95.4)
Cadaveric	*3*	*23570*	*77.8*	*(77.3, 78.3)*
Living	3	17981	87.8	(87.4, 88.3)
Cadaveric	*5*	*18166*	*66.5*	*(66.0, 67.1)*
Living	5	12532	79.7	(79.2, 80.4)

For Patients:

Donor Type	Years Post Transplant	Number Alive	Survival Rate	95% Confidence Interval
Cadaveric	*1*	*24134*	*94.4*	*(94.2, 94.7)*
Living	1	18304	97.9	(97.7, 98.1)
Cadaveric	*3*	*25145*	*88.2*	*(87.9, 88.6)*
Living	3	18742	94.2	(93.9, 94.5)
Cadaveric	*5*	*19871*	*81.8*	*(81.3, 82.3)*
Living	5	13272	90.1	(89.6, 90.6)

Chapter 8: Organs for Opium

A brief summary of the inequality of women and men according to Iranian law can be found in M. Celizic's article "Beyond the Veil: Lives of Women in Iran" in *Today.com* (2007).

Adverse effects of time on dialysis on the success of renal transplants are documented in H. Meier-Kriesche, et al.'s article "Effect of Waiting Time on Renal Transplant Outcome" in *Kidney International* (2000) Vol. 58, no. 3, pp. 1311–17. Also, see F. Cosio, et al.'s article "Patient Survival After Renal Transplantation: I. The Impact of Dialysis Pre-transplant" in *Kidney International* (1998) Vol. 53, no. 3, pp. 767–72.

Chapter 9: Too Poor to Pay

Dr. Zargooshi's work on kidney donors includes the articles "Quality of Life of Iranian Kidney 'Donors'" in *The Journal of Urology* (2001) Vol. 166, no. 5, pp. 1790–99 and "Iranian Kidney Donors: Motivations and Relations with Recipients" in *The Journal of Urology* (2001) Vol. 165, no. 2, pp. 386–92. Zargooshi also authored "Commercial Renal Transplantation in Iran: The Recipients' Perspective" and "Iran's Commercial Renal Transplantation Program: Results and Complications" in W. Weimar, et al's (eds) book *Organ Transplantation: Ethical, Legal and Psychosocial Aspects. Towards a Common European Policy* (2008).

Chapter 10: Making My Way Home

The Center for Ethical Solutions has a short documentary film about Steve Lessin. That video, fact sheets about kidney disease, and more can be found on the Center's SOS (Solving the Organ Shortage) project page: www.ethical-solutions.org.

Please also see Notes section for this book's Introduction for more sources on kidney disease, the organ shortage, and the black market in kidney sales.

Conclusion: Can the U.S. Organ Shortage Be Solved?

Most of the figures and statistics cited in this chapter come from three sources: The United Network for Organ Sharing (UNOS) website, available at www.unos.org; the Organ Procurement and Transplant Network (OPTN) website, available at www.optn.transplant.hrsa.gov; and the United States Renal Data System (USRDS) website, available at www.usrds.org. Also, of special interest are C. Suddath, and A. Altman's article "How Does Kidney-Trafficking Work?" in *Time* (2009); G. Cohen's book *Global Health and the Law* (2013); and G. Cohen's article "Transplant Tourism: The Ethics and Regulation of International Markets for Organs" in *Journal of Law, Medicine and Ethics* (2013) Vol. 41, p. 1.

A good background article about kidney chains is K. Sack's article "Lives Forever Linked Through Kidney Transplant Chain 124" in *The New York Times* (2012) sec. Health.

Under the most optimistic of predictions, which include considering all potential cadaver donations as actual donations, the number of potentially available kidney donors under the current system would be less than 1% of deaths each year. E. Sheehy, et al.'s article "Estimating the Number of Potential Organ Donors in the United States" in the *New England Journal of Medicine* (2003) Vol. 349, no. 7, pp. 667–74.

Assuming 1% to facilitate our calculation and 2,513,171 deaths in 2011 (see CDC data available at www.cdc.gov), that makes a total of approximately 50,000 potentially viable kidneys for transplant if every potentially harvestable kidney were in fact used. Note that the conversion rate for kidneys harvested to kidneys actually transplanted in the United States for 2011 was 82%. See OPTN Annual report for 2011. UNOS data for 2012 up through September is 81%, but my personal experience at the Washington Regional Transplant Community (WRTC) is that the conversion rate drops as efforts are made to retrieve more organs from more borderline donors. By "borderline," I mean cadaver kidneys retrieved from older donors and donors who suffered considerable system deterioration from trauma or prolonged illnesses before death. The average conversion rate at WRTC for the first seven months of 2013 was only 70%. As a result the real number of available transplantable kidneys under a system where every potentially harvestable kidney is recovered is probably fewer than 30,000 — a number clearly not anywhere large enough to satisfy the current need for kidneys given the over 100,000 people actively waiting on the UNOS list, not to mention the unknown number of additional Americans among the 400,000 on dialysis who could potentially benefit from a transplant or could have benefited from one earlier in their treatment.

Note that some patients never qualify for a transplant, not even when they first go on dialysis. Some have underlying illnesses that would attack and destroy a newly transplanted kidney; others are too old or too sick when their end-stage renal disease is discovered to survive a transplant operation.

Facts about diabetes and other causes of renal failure can be found at the American Diabetes Association's website at www.diabetes.org; the Centers for Disease Control and Prevention website at www.cdc.gov; in M. Hossain, et al.'s article "CKD and Poverty: A Growing Global Challenge" in the *American Journal of Kidney Diseases* (20 09) Vol. 53, no. 1, pp. 166–74; in J. Robbins, et al.'s article (2001) "Socioeconomic Status and Type 2 Diabetes in African American and non-Hispanic White Women and Men: Evidence from the Third National Health and Nutrition Examination Survey" in the *American Journal of Public Health* (2001) Vol. 91, no. 1, pp. 76–83; in C. Vargas, et al.'s article "Incidence of Hypertension and Educational Attainment: The NHANES I Epidemiologic Followup Study" in the *American Journal of Epidemiology* (2000) Vol. 152, no. 3, pp. 272–78; and in G. Lee and M. Carrington's article "Tackling Heart Disease and Poverty" in *Nursing & Health Sciences* (2007) Vol. 9, no. 4, pp. 290–94.

Health insurance requirements for organ donors are listed on the National Conference of State Legislation's website at www.ncsl.org.

For some of the specific qualifications for being a kidney donor and what can be expected before and after surgery see, the University of Maryland Medical Center website at www.umm.edu and the Hennepin County Medical Center website at www.hcmc.org.

As of this writing, the following government-sanctioned benefits exist for kidney donors:

- The federal government has a $2 billion annual fund to cover travel and other incidental expenses for living donors. This is a needs based program. See the Organ Donation and Recovery Improvement Act (ODRIA) (Public Law 108-216) (2004), available at www.livingdonorassistance.org.
- Federal employees can receive up to 30 days additional paid leave for organ donation. See Organ Donor Leave Act (ODLA) (Public Law 106-56) (1999), available at www.gpo.gov.
- In 26 states at least some categories of government employees are afforded anywhere from 2–30 days extra paid or unpaid leave for the purpose of organ donation depending on the state. In three states similar provisions apply to private employers. See www.transplantliving.org.
- In 16 states organ donors have the option of claiming a state income tax deduction or credit for donation-related expenses. In most states that deduction or credit is limited to $10,000. See www.transplantliving.org.

For a calculation of the cost-effectiveness of living donor transplants over dialysis see A. Matas and M. Schnitzler's article "Payment for Living Donor (Vendor) Kidneys: A Cost-Effectiveness Analysis" in the *American Journal of Transplantation* (2004) Vol. 4, no. 2, pp. 216–21. For analysis done using different parameters see M. Abecassis, et al.'s article "Kidney Transplantation as

Primary Therapy for End-Stage Renal Disease: A National Kidney Founda-
tion/Kidney Disease Outcomes Quality Initiative (NKF/KDOQITM) Conference" in the *Clinical Journal of the American Society of Nephrology* (2008) Vol.
3, no. 2, 471, and the University of Maryland Medical Center's article "The
'Break Even' Cost of Kidney Transplants Is Shrinking" in *Current News Releases*
(1999).

The dollar amounts for the calculations made in the above cited sources
change rapidly. The National Kidney Foundation states that the average cost
of a living donor kidney transplant for an adult in 2011 was $262,900. This
figure includes a pre-transplant work-up, 180 days of postoperative care for
both donor and recipient, and a yearly average of $36,400 for immunosup-
pressant drugs. See www.transplantliving.org. Dialysis on the other hand in
2009 cost per person on average $82,285 for hemodialysis and $61,588 for peritoneal dialysis. See the United States Renal Data System. (USRD)'s article "Costs
of ESRD." In the *2011 USRDS Annual Data Report*. (2011) Vol. 2, pp. 281–90.

Index

Pages marked with *n* refer to footnotes.